THE COMPLETE IDIOT'S GUIDE® TO

Bartending

by Amy Zavatto

ALPHA

A Member of Penguin Group (USA) Inc.

ALPHA BOOKS

Published by the Penguin Group

Penguin Group (USA) Inc., 375 Hudson Street, New York, New York 10014, U.S.A.

Penguin Group (Canada), 10 Alcorn Avenue, Toronto, Ontario, Canada M4V 3B2 (a division of Pearson Penguin Canada Inc.)

Penguin Books Ltd, 80 Strand, London WC2R 0RL, England

Penguin Ireland, 25 St Stephen's Green, Dublin 2, Ireland (a division of Penguin Books Ltd)

Penguin Group (Australia), 250 Camberwell Road, Camberwell, Victoria 3124, Australia (a division of Pearson Australia Group Pty Ltd)

Penguin Books India Pvt Ltd, 11 Community Centre, Panchsheel Park, New Delhi—10 017, India

Penguin Group (NZ), cnr Airborne and Rosedale Roads, Albany, Auckland 1310, New Zealand (a division of Pearson New Zealand Ltd)

Penguin Books (South Africa) (Pty) Ltd, 24 Sturdee Avenue, Rosebank, Johannesburg 2196, South Africa

Penguin Books Ltd, Registered Offices: 80 Strand, London WC2R 0RL, England

Copyright © 2005 by Amy Zavatto

International Standard Book Number: 1-59257-412-2
Library of Congress Catalog Card Number: 2005928083

07   06   05   8   7   6   5   4   3   2   1

Interpretation of the printing code: The rightmost number of the first series of numbers is the year of the book's printing; the rightmost number of the second series of numbers is the number of the book's printing. For example, a printing code of 05-1 shows that the first printing occurred in 2005.

Printed in the United States of America

Note: This publication contains the opinions and ideas of its author. It is intended to provide helpful and informative material on the subject matter covered. It is sold with the understanding that the author and publisher are not engaged in rendering professional services in the book. If the reader requires personal assistance or advice, a competent professional should be consulted.

The author and publisher specifically disclaim any responsibility for any liability, loss, or risk, personal or otherwise, which is incurred as a consequence, directly or indirectly, of the use and application of any of the contents of this book.

Most Alpha books are available at special quantity discounts for bulk purchases for sales promotions, premiums, fund-raising, or educational use. Special books, or book excerpts, can also be created to fit specific needs.

For details, write: Special Markets, Alpha Books, 375 Hudson Street, New York, NY 10014.

Publisher: *Marie Butler-Knight*
Editorial Director: *Mike Sanders*
Senior Managing Editor: *Jennifer Bowles*
Senior Acquisitions Editor: *Renee Wilmeth*
Development Editor: *Christy Wagner*
Senior Production Editor: *Billy Fields*
Copy Editor: *Janet K. Zoya*

Cartoonist: *Shannon Wheeler*
Cover Designer: *Trina Wurst*
Book Designers: *Bill Thomas and Trina Wurst*
Indexer: *Angie Bess*
Senior Layout Tech: *Angela Calvert*
Proofreading: *Donna Martin*

To my in-laws—Aurora and Felix Marotta, Carlos, Josephine, Christian, and Sabrina Gueits. I realize this career I have seems a little kooky sometimes. Thanks for always understanding and giving me the room I need to get this stuff done.

Contents at a Glance

Contents

Introduction

When my husband Dan and I started house-hunting in the tepid last-grasping month of late winter 2002, we had a list of things we desperately wanted as new homeowners. After 10 years in a one-bedroom brownstone apartment in Carroll Gardens, Brooklyn, we grew weary of hauling our laundry to the Laundromat, driving around and around the block to jockey for a coveted parking space within some kind of non–marathon walking distance from our front door, and listening to the F train subway rattle by our kitchen window (although, I admit, I found that a little romantic).

More than anything, though, we wanted space. Not just for clothes or furniture and all other forms of random stuff, but for entertaining. There's nothing we both like better than throwing a big ol' party to get friends and family together.

When we walked through the door of the house we would eventually call home, we, like a lot of other first-time home buyers, got that feeling. We knew this was The One. But the thing that confirmed it? The full-on, brass-railed, lights-mirror-taps-whole-shebang old-fashioned chestnut wood bar in the basement. Neither of us had ever seen anything like this outside of an actual, real bar. We looked at each other, smiled, and said, "We'll take it."

Since we moved in two-plus years ago, we've thrown many a party. Being a food and spirits writer by trade, it's something I take great interest in keeping up with. What did we run out of quickly? What didn't go? What mixer or liqueur would have really been great to have on hand? What's the latest cocktail making the scene we could replicate for our own guests? And on and on.

How to Use This Book

When I started thinking about what would make a cocktail book most useful to me, two things came to mind. One, I would want a lot of useful how-to information without a lot of clutter and gabbiness—some fun facts, a little history, and a lot of practical, useful, easy-to-understand information.

That's what you find in **Part 1, "Stepping Up to the Brass Rail."** This is where you learn to discern your resposado from your añejo; your Scotch from your bourbon. What's the difference between brandy and cognac? Look no further! Want to know if sake is supposed to be hot or cold? Here's where you'll find your answer. You also get great "grocery lists" for when it comes time to stock your own bar (from minimum to all-out maximum home-bar potential), what glasses to use, measurements and equivalents, and a shaker full of great advice on all things mixing.

And then there's **Part 2, "The Recipes"**—1,500 of them! I arranged this massive assortment of mixables by liquor. Why? Because when I want to make a cocktail, 9 times out of 10 I know what liquor I want to use. I bet you do, too. If you're in the mood for gin, turn to the gin chapter (Chapter 6). Want to find a new way with whisky? There's a whole Scotch and Canadian world to discover there (Chapter 10). And if you want to peruse all the drinks in this book alphabetically, simply turn to the handy-dandy Index of Drinks in the back for a full-on listing of each and every concoction compiled.

Extras

Along the way I wanted to share a few bits and pieces of information with you. This info has been neatly placed into three different sidebar categories:

Cocktail Conversation _____

These are full of useful tips and fun facts, all of which are sure to be useful at your next sipping soirée—even if only to liven up the conversation.

Liquor Lingo _____

Never heard of Strega? Don't know much about crème de menthe? Liquor Lingos define all that befuddles you.

Spills _____

It's much better to avoid a mess than to worry about spilled sake. Here you get advanced notice on possible pratfalls and how to avert them.

Acknowledgments

The biggest thank you of all must go to my husband, Dan Marotta, who tolerated various cocktail experiments gone awry, much wasted, precious liquor, and several bouts of typical writerly grumpiness. I wouldn't be doing this without you. You believe when I don't, thank goodness.

Thanks must also go to Joy Tutela of David Black Inc., my amazing agent whom I think must have a degree in psychology stashed away somewhere—I owe her a big, fat martini; Renee Wilmeth for giving me the green light, her constant epicurean enthusiasm, and her patience toward the end when I couldn't seem to stop writing; the ever-wonderful and suspiciously cheerful Christy Wagner—it's always a pleasure; Jan Zoya, for her keen copyediting skills and for laughing at my jokes; Magdalena Spirydowicz; Mary-Catherine Deibel and Deborah Hughes of UpStairs on the Square; Brigid Finley, Nadia Al-Amir, Rachel Mays, Geraldine Grzywna, and Victoria Stein at Wagstaff Worldwide, Inc.; Andria Chin and Laura Lehrman of Lehrman and Chin Public Relations; Aurura Kessler and Chloe Mata of Baltz and Company; Maud Noirot of Sel de la Terre; Kenneth McClure, food and beverages director at The World Bar in The Trump World Tower, Talia Rosen at Rubenstein Public Relations, the folks at Peristyle restaurant in New Orleans; Tocqueville, Riingo, Paul Muszynski at Bistro 110, Koi, Cuba restaurant, Arterra, Nolita, Joseph's Citarella, Rosa Mexicana, Devi, Montage Resort and Spa, SushiSamba Rio, Roppingi, the dear and lovely and inexhaustible Sylva Popaz of Vida restaurant in Staten Island; Julia Helton of the Family Wash in East Nashville; Paul Grosz of the innovative and ever-lovely Cuisine in Detroit; Tony DiDio for waiting; my sisters for being … my sisters; and my dad, Mike Zavatto, for teaching me how to make a Brandy Alexander. And if I forgot anyone, oh heavens, I am so very sorry.

Of course, I wouldn't have happily consumed half the cocktails I have without the help of some really great people I'm lucky enough to call my friends. You know who you are.

Special Thanks to the Technical Reviewer

The Complete Idiot's Guide to Bartending was reviewed by an expert who double-checked the accuracy of what you'll learn here, to help us ensure that this book gives you everything you need to know about bartending. Special thanks are extended to John James.

Trademarks

All terms mentioned in this book that are known to be or are suspected of being trademarks or service marks have been appropriately capitalized. Alpha Books and Penguin Group (USA) Inc. cannot attest to the accuracy of this information. Use of a term in this book should not be regarded as affecting the validity of any trademark or service mark.

Part 1

Stepping Up to the Brass Rail

You might have the urge to go right to the recipes chapters in Part 2 and start mixing away, but hold on just a second. Before you do, wouldn't it be better to get the skinny on the sleek techniques that will crown you the Sir or Madam Mix-a-Lot of your friends and family? That's just what you'll learn in Part 1: how to shake, stir, blend, purée, muddle, mix, chill, pour, and prep. You'll also get a down-and-dirty, fast-fact lowdown on the major liquors that make up a basic bar—and a little history, too!

Top Shelf: The Lowdown on Liquor

In This Chapter

- The basic makeup of spirits
- A short spirited history lesson
- Average prices from affordable to bank breakers

So you want to be the mixologist with the most, eh? Or if your ambitions are slightly less lofty, you at least want to be able to hold your own when hosting a party. Not a problem. You can do it, and I'm here to help. But the very, very first thing you need to do is this: learn your way around a liquor shelf. You can't mix up delectable drinks if you're unfamiliar with what, exactly, you're working with. It's all about the tools. In this chapter, study the main ingredients for your quaffing creations, a little history on their origins, and, because in the end it all comes down to your wallet, how much they cost.

Bourbon

Bourbon is an unblended American corn-based whiskey made from one or two different kinds of mash, which is the crushed, ground corn and other grain(s) used in the fermentation process. The mash is either sour or sweet. Sour mash is new sweet mash combined with some of the residue from the previous batch's fermentation. Sweet mash is made from scratch with fresh yeast.

Bourbon's rich, golden-tinged, dark-brown hue and distinctive ever-so-slightly sweet, woody flavor come from the minimum 2-year aging process in brand-new charred American oak casks, although many bourbons age as much as twice that long. (After the aging in the new oak casks is finished, the casks are never used again to age bourbon. Instead, they are often used to age Scotch whisky.) By law, to be considered bourbon, the liquor must be made from a minimum of 51 percent but no more than 79 percent corn and the rest wheat, rye, or other grains. The alcohol content can be no more than 160 *proof*, which is usually taken down to between 80 and 100 proof after the distilling

> **Liquor Lingo** _____
>
> The amount of alcohol in a spirit is measured by its **proof.** In the United States, proof translates into twice the percentage of alcohol, e.g., 100 proof bourbon contains 50 percent alcohol. In other countries, the measurements are slightly different.

process.

Bourbon takes its name from Bourbon County, Kentucky, where it was first produced and shipped down river to the original sin city, New Orleans. Before shipping, barrels were stamped with the corn whiskey's place of origin, and the name just stuck. Although today many bourbon distilleries exist outside Bourbon County, 90 percent of all bourbon still comes from the bluegrass state in Anderson, Franklin, Nelson, Woodford, and Jefferson counties.

Although the legal stipulations have to do with what's in it, as outlined above, some feel strongly that if it's not from Kentucky, it just ain't bourbon. It's something else, like Tennessee whiskey, for instance. Many people make the mistake of calling Tennessee whiskey, like Jack Daniel's or George Dickel, bourbon. For one, the procedure used is different: part of the distilling process for Tennessee whiskey requires steeping the whiskey in charcoal vats, which gives it a much different flavor. Second, it's made in … Tennessee! Not Kentucky. And if that's not enough proof for you, then maybe you'll take the federal government's word for it—they put Tennessee whiskey in its own, regulated category.

Thank Heaven for the Reverend

As with any story about the origins of a cocktail, the origins of liquor are at times equally as debated. In the tradition of the American tall tale, bourbon is no different. Here's the story I'm told: the first person to distill bourbon—or at least be recorded as the first person to distill

 Cocktail Conversation

Heaven Hill Distilleries in Bardstown, Kentucky, makes a rare single barrel, 18 year aged bourbon named after the lovely liquor's founder-apparent, Elijah Craig.

bourbon because he was, in all likelihood, in the company of folks who could read and write—was the Reverend Elijah Craig.

Born in Virginia, Craig was a Baptist minister who gave his sermons all around the southland until he finally settled in Bourbon County, Kentucky, in the mid-1780s. Craig was an enterprising businessman, but it wasn't until he decided to store his corn-based whiskey in charred white-oak barrels that he became known as the inventor of that magical amber liquid, bourbon. Storing whiskey, which is clear after it's distilled, in the charred oak turned the local white lightening into a dark, rich, superior-tasting tipple.

Naming Names

Many fine bourbons are on the market. Some are reasonably priced and good for mixing cocktails. Others are sipping bourbons to be savored and consumed neat (without ice) or on the rocks (with ice). Here are some names to know and their general price at press time.

Affordable	Mid-Range	Bank Breaker
Old Forester, $15	Woodford Reserve, $30	Elijah Craig Single Barrel, $45
Wild Turkey, $15	Knob Creek, $32	Booker's 8 year, $55
Elijah Craig Small Batch 12 Year, $18	Maker's Mark, $25	Jefferson Kentucky Bourbon, $50

Gin

The original martini maker, this juniper berry–based spirit has a distinctive, herbal taste that seems to draw very clear-cut reactions from imbibers: they either love it or hate it.

The name is derivative of its main ingredient, from the Dutch word *jenever*. In fact, gin seems to have originated in Holland as well, although some argue that it was first made in Italy. Wherever you believe its origins are rooted, the creation process is the same. Gin is made when juniper berries are distilled with a grain mash usually made up of some or all of the following—corn, barley, rye, and wheat—and other flavors such as cassis, coriander, fennel, ginger, lemon peel, and a host of other special (and almost always unnamed for reasons of holding onto secret recipes) botanical flavorings.

For our purposes, I'm dividing gin into two main types/categories:

◆ **Dry gin.** Dry or London dry gin is generally around 80 to 90 proof and is the most common gin used in cocktail mixing and general bar requests. Ordering a gin and soda? The barkeep will use dry gin. Old Tom is a version of London dry that is given a little sweetness with simple syrup. Plymouth gin is a London dry that's not sweetened at all.

◆ **Dutch gin.** Dutch gin (a.k.a. Holland gin, genever, genievre, or Schiedam) is generally around 70 to 80 proof and is really more of a sipping gin with a malted grain flavor and aroma along with the juniper influence.

The Way It Was

The person responsible for putting the G in your G&T was Dr. Franciscus Sylvius, a seventeenth-century Dutch chemist at the University of Leyden. It was for medicinal purposes, not martinis, that Doc Sylvius concocted the elixir and added juniper berries to make it more palatable (sort of like cherry cough syrup and such). This so-called medicine became pretty darned popular with British soldiers embroiled in the Thirty Years War, who dubbed it "Dutch Courage."

England's taste for gin soared ever higher when King William III banned the import of French wine and other spirits (which wouldn't be the last grumbling between France and England) and gin production soared. It became extraordinarily popular with the poor and working class; maybe a little too popular. In 1739, England enforced the Gin Act, which raised the cost of the spirit so much that the poor couldn't afford it. But the will of the common man was too fierce for the social experiments of the educated—riots broke out and chaos ensued. Three short years later, the Gin Act was repealed and the millions of gallons of mother's milk (a.k.a. gin) being produced flowed into the glasses of the common folk.

A Bin of Gin

For those who love the botanical beauty of gin, there are many lovely examples from which to choose in all price ranges and for mixing or sipping purposes. Here are some names to know and their general price at press time.

Affordable	Mid-Range	Bank Breaker
Beefeater, $20	Plymouth, $22	Old Raj, $50
Gordon's, $13	Junìpero, $30	Boodles, $44
Seagram's Extra Dry, $14	Tanqueray, $24	Tanqueray No. Ten, $35
	Bombay Sapphire, $30	

Rum

Rum. The word conjures up dreamy images of palm trees and sandy beaches and bluer-than-blue skies. You can almost hear the steel drums and the waves lapping against the shores. And with good reason, as much of it is produced in the gentle lands of the West Indies and the Caribbean.

Rum is made from boiled-down sugarcane, which eventually goes through a few processes before it becomes molasses. The thick, pungent-sweet molasses is heated and combined with water and yeast during the distillation process, and the rum is then aged in oak barrels from 6 months to 7 years, depending on what the desired final product is. For instance, light and gold rums are aged from the minimum amount—6 months—up to 4 years. Dark rum gets a taste and color boost from the addition of caramel and an aging minimum of 3 years, although the process can go on as long as 12 years.

Rum comes in three general types—light bodied (white or silver), medium bodied (gold or amber), and heavy bodied (my favorite: dark!)—from several balmy and beautiful places, such as the following:

- **Jakarta.** Medium bodied. Known for the gorgeous elixir Batavia arak, which uses red rice from Java in the fermentation process along with the molasses and is aged for several years.

- **Guyana.** Medium bodied. Known for dark-hued rum with a high alcohol content called Demeraran rum.

- **Haiti.** Medium bodied. Haitian rum has a slightly different distillation technique, whereby the juice of the sugarcane is concentrated and distilled but not made into molasses.

- **Jamaica.** Heavy bodied. Dark, rich, and aged, this gorgeous, spicy rum gets a little extra coloring from its long aging process and extra added molasses.

- **Martinique.** Medium bodied. Like Haitian rum, light rum from Martinique is made from the juice of sugarcane.

- **Puerto Rico.** Light to medium bodied. Known for light and gold rums, and one of the most famous producers of it: Bacardi.

- **South America.** Light to medium bodied. Although South American countries produce several fine rums, often referred to as *aguardiente de caña*, the most popular here is cachaca, distilled from the juice of sugarcane and the rum to use in the delicious Brazilian delight, the Caipirinha.

◆ **The Virgin Islands.** Light-bodied. Known for light rums similar in style to Puerto Rican rums.

There are, of course, flavored rums, too, such as coconut, lemon, spiced, and lime. These are fine for mixing purposes (although, I prefer to use real, basic ingredients).

The Dark Side

Although rum might be the most visually projecting, feel-good spirit of them all (remember those palm trees from before?), it's also a liquor with a sad, sordid past. Think back to your history books, kids. Remember the lesson on the triangle trade? Well, rum was part of that triangle, which also consisted of slaves and sugarcane. Or specifically, rum was traded for slaves for labor; slaves were traded for molasses, which was made into rum state-side; the rum was sold at a high price for a good profit.

The creation of rum, though, is also as much a part of West Indian, South American, and Caribbean culture as winemaking is in Europe. And it may have been the first new-to-them liquor (they brought Madeira and such with them) introduced into the New World during the days of Columbus's exploration of the Americas and the West Indies.

Captain Morgan Drove Me Home Last Night

Okay, that's not really very funny—and, no, you shouldn't ever drive under the influence. Period. It's just plain dumb, dangerous, and dopey. Quite frankly, you know better (and you knew that lecture was coming, so stop acting so shocked).

After your keys are safely in the hands of a sober friend, or if you know you're heading home on foot, try one of the following rums depending on what price point you're willing to shell out.

Affordable	Mid-Range	Bank Breaker
Bacardi Gold, $16	Montecristo 12 year, $30	Angostura 1824, $60
Barbancourt 3 Star, $18	Pusser's British Navy, $25	Zaya 12 year, $44
Gosling's Black Seal, $19	Mount Gay Extra Old Rum, $29	Sea Wynde, Pot Still Rum, $44
Mount Gay Vanilla Rum, $15		

Tequila

It's got a song. It's got romance. It's sometimes even got a mascot (that scary occasional worm). But what you need to know about tequila is this: it comes in two overarching categories: mixto (average stuff) and 100 percent blue agave (the good stuff!). Mixto must contain a minimum of 51 percent blue agave (the beautiful, spiky plant that grows in abundance in Mexico). The rest of the mix can come from other sources. To be 100 percent blue agave, well, it's got to be made from 100 percent blue agave. Period.

Within blue agave and mixto categories are four classifications of tequila:

- ◆ **Blanco.** Also called silver or white tequila, blanco must be wood-aged less than 60 days.
- ◆ **Joven abocado.** Gold tequila (probably the one you are most familiar with). It gets its appearance and taste from the addition of caramel.
- ◆ **Reposado.** Reposado (which in English means "rested") must be wood-aged 60 days to a year. Caramel may be added for coloring and taste as well.
- ◆ **Añejo.** The good stuff. Añejo is wood-aged for at least a year.

Cocktail Conversation

Tequila gets its name from the eponymous town it is named for in the Jalisco province of Mexico. Just about all tequila is made there. In fact, by law, to be able to call it tequila, it must be made in or around Tequila.

The Birth of Tequila

Back in the Aztec days, a beverage called *pulque*, fermented maguey tree sap, was the drink of choice. Sounds kind of strange? The Spanish conquistadors thought so, too. They turned the Aztecs on to the technique of distilling, which became *mezcal*. Eventually they began experimenting with the blue agave plant, and tequila was born.

Silver and Gold

If you like tequila but you haven't ventured out of the *mixto* yet, I can't begin to stress how great it is the first time you taste a super-duper 100 percent blue agave tequila. It's a whole different flavor sensation. It's clear, elegant, and smooth. If you don't want to plunk down the money for a bottle, head to a reliable watering hole and do a sampling.

For all your tequila needs, here are some basic prices of everything from your run-o'-the-mill perfectly acceptable affordable tequila to the auspicious añejos.

Affordable	Mid-Range	Bank Breaker
San Matias Blanco, $18	Herradura Silver, $39	Tonala Anejo, $60
Jose Cuervo Silver, $18	Sauza Conmemorativo Anejo, $25	Cabo Wabo Anejo, $70
Sauza Gold, $19	San Matia Anejo Gran Reserva, $30	Del Maguey Patron Anejo, $60

Vodka

It's crystal clear. It's easy on the palate. From coast to coast, it's one of the most popular spirits for mixing. Every freezer really ought to have a nice, chilly bottle of it inside. It's vodka—and no bar should be without it.

Sometimes folks get confused with how vodka is made and have a notion that it's all about potatoes. Although, yes, there is potato vodka, most vodkas are made with corn or wheat grain. Vodka is a *rectified spirit*, or goes through at least three rounds of the distilling process. During the final round, it is filtered through charcoal. Because of their abundance of grain, Eastern Europe and Russia is where vodka was born.

Liquor Lingo

A **rectified spirit** is an alcoholic beverage that goes through a minimum of three rounds of distilling.

Back in the Old Country

When the name given a spirit is a derivative of the Russian word for "water" (*voda*), you know the creators of it take it very, very seriously.

Both Poles and Russians claim to have distilled the first batch of vodka, but Russia documented it at the end of the eighth century, so they get the honors here. By the mid-sixteenth century, it was the national drink of both Russia and Poland. But it wasn't until the eighteenth century, when a Russian professor in St. Petersburg discovered the process of charcoal filtering, that vodka became the spirit we know and happily drink today.

The Bolshevik nabbing of private distilleries during the Russian Revolution and the altogether ban on private distilleries after World War I proved problematic for vodka-making devotees, and many left the Mother Land. One such family, the Smirnoffs, decided to bring their distilling talents to America and set up the first vodka distillery in the United States in 1934, just after the end of Prohibition.

La Vida Vodka

Don't know your Absolut from your Olifant? Here's a rundown by price of who's who on your liquor store shelves.

Affordable	Mid-Range	Bank Breaker
Absolut, $19	Charbay, $32	Ultimat, $50
Smirnoff United States Grain, $18	Ketel One Triple Distilled, $26	Jewel of Russia, $40
Skyy United States Grain, $16	Stoli Ohranj, $25	Level Single Batch, $60
Olifant Citron, $15		Hangar One, $35

Whisky

Whisky lovers and connoisseurs may well be the most opinionated tipplers of the lot. Sure, tequila devotees and gin gurus and wine lovers have their very, very strong opinions, but whisky drinkers? Just see what happens when you make a declaration statement around one. It's begging for trouble—or, at least, an hours-long conversation about everything whisky.

In general, whisky is made from grain. However, which grains, how much, where from, and the process used determines what kind of whisky you're drinking. In Ireland and Scotland, whisky is made from barley, oats, rye, or wheat. The grain (or grains) is malted (after it has sprouted, it is dried in a kiln and ground into a powder), which causes it to turn starch into sugar and then to alcohol. Scotch whisky, however, takes on a smoky flavor because the drying part of the process occurs over burning peat. Irish whiskey grains are dried in a kiln, and the whiskey has a gentler, sweeter flavor and aroma than Scotch whisky. Canadian whisky undergoes a similar process to Scotch but is always designated as blended (more on that in a minute). American whiskey is made from corn and grains.

Now, as to the business of blended or straight whiskies, here's a quick cheat sheet for you:

- **Straight whisky.** The American classification for straight whisky. It must have 51 percent of one particular grain and must not be blended with any other whiskey or grain neutral spirit. It must be aged in oak barrels for a minimum of 2 years.
- **Blended whisky.** A blended whisky is exactly what it sounds like. A minimum of 20 percent must be from one particular grain. But the rest? That can be an amalgam of other whiskies, grain neutral spirits, grain spirits, fortified wine, or even fruit juices. By law, all whiskies in North America must be labeled blended or straight.
- **Blended straight.** When two or more straight whiskies are blended.
- **Light whiskey.** Often used for blending, light whiskies are distilled at an above-the-average alcohol level (e.g., more than 160 proof) with water added later to dilute the alcohol content. Light whisky is stored in uncharred oak casks.
- **Single malt whisky.** Unblended Scotch whisky.

Cocktail Conversation

The spelling of this spirit may leave you a bit befuddled at times. Is it *whisky* or *whiskey?* And what's the difference? In Scotland and Canada, it's *whisky.* In Ireland and America, it's *whiskey.* There now. That wasn't so hard, was it?

The Gaelic Water of Life

Whisky originated in the misty green lands of Ireland and Scotland, where it was called *uisge beatha, or* "water of life." It's not exactly clear which country gets the distinction of being the first, although evidence of early whisky production has been found going back as far as the fifteenth century. Not surprisingly, once whisky caught on and became a popular beverage, the English government (true to their tax-happy form) placed a malt tax on whisky production. This tax, which went into effect in 1624, only increased over the years with whisky's popularity. In fact, by the early 1900s, the tax was doubled to discourage whisky consumption.

Dropping Names

Be it Canadian, Irish, or Scotch, there are plenty of fine whiskies from which to choose. Check out the following sampling of variously priced whiskies to help you familiarize yourself with what's available.

Affordable	Mid-Range	Bank Breaker
Forty Creek Canadian Whisky, $19	Dewar's White Label Scotch Whisky, $30	Connemara Single Malt Irish Whiskey, $40
Kilbeggan Irish Whiskey, $19	Tullamore Dew Irish Whiskey, $27	Johnnie Walker Gold Scotch Whisky, $80
	Ballantine's Scotch Whisky, $21	

Brandy

Regardless of which brandy's your pleasure, the basics are still the same. Brandy is distilled from wine and/or fermented juices (peach, apple, pear, or cherry, for instance). Like French wine, French brandy is known for its high quality and strict regional demarcation.

There are many types of brandy, including …

- ◆ **Armagnac.** From the vineyards in Armagnac in the Gascony region of southwestern France near Bordeaux. It is distilled only once, and no sugar is added. It is aged for up to 40 years in black oak.

- **Calvados.** From Calvados in Normandy of northern France, this is a dry apple brandy that is distilled twice and aged for a minimum of a year.

- **Cognac.** The big mac daddy of brandies, cognac—from the town of Cognac in western France—is double distilled after the fermenting process and must age at least 3 years in Limousin oak. You might notice that bottles of cognac have stars. These are to let you know how long the brandy has aged: 1 star is 3 years, 2 stars is 4 years, and 3 stars is 5 years. Anything older gets the slightly silly but descriptive *V.S.* (very superior), *V.S.O.P.* (very superior old pale), *V.V.S.O.P.* (very, very superior old pale), or X.O. (extra old) distinction.

- *Eau-de-vie.* Literally translated as "water of life" in French, this brandy is distilled from fermented fruit juice (other than grapes) and is colorless.

Liquor Lingo

Eau-de-vie is a clear, fruit-based French brandy; examples include kirschwasser and frambois.

- **Fruit brandy.** Unlike eau-de-vie, a fruit brandy (by U.S. law) must be made with a base of wine-brandy and be more than 70 proof.

- **Grappa.** An Italian eau-de-vie made from the residue of grape skins and seeds that are extracted during the winemaking process (how's that for being resourceful?).

- **Koniak.** Greek brandy that has a grape base and is given extra sweetness with the addition of caramel.

- **Spanish brandy.** From the Andalusian town of Jerez de la Frontera, Spanish brandy is often distilled from sherry and subjected to a complicated aging system.

Brandy: Getting Burned

Brandy came into being when a clever Dutch trader tried to condense his cargo by taking the water out of wine by heating it and putting it back in once he reached his final destination. The taste of it after this process earned it the name *brandewijn,* or "burned wine."

Which Brandy Is for You?

Not sure which brandy is the best for you? Here are some examples of what's available.

Affordable	Mid-Range	Bank Breaker
E&J Brandy, $12	Clear Creek Bartlett Pear Brandy, $35	Laird's 12-Year-Old Rare Apple Brandy, $50
Hiram Walker Blackberry Brandy, $12	Askalon Arack Extra Fine, $20	Frapin V.S.O.P. Cognac, $60
Laird's Applejack, $14	Menorval Calvados, $29	Courvoisier Napoleon Cognac, $70
		Jean Danflou Armagnac Exceptionnel Reserve, $90

Liqueurs and Cordials

Liqueurs and cordials are generally served as after-dinner drinks and range from 40 to 60 proof. What's the difference among them? Nowadays, nothing—at least in conversation. But technically, there is a distinction: liqueurs are herb-based, and cordials are fruit-based.

Cordials and liqueurs are made from one type of major spirit as the base and then punched up in flavor with fruit, nuts, flowers, herbs, seeds—you name it. These flavors become part of the final product through one of four methods:

- **Distillation.** The base liquor is blended with the additional botanical flavor prior to a second distilling process.
- **Infusion.** Just like tea leaves in hot water, the desired flavoring agent is steeped in the warmed base liquor, which takes on its aromatic and flavor qualities.
- **Percolation.** Remember that old coffee percolator your parents or grandparents used to have? The process is similar for a liqueur/ cordial product using this method, except instead of coffee, botanical flavor is used.
- **Maceration.** Like infusion, the main flavoring element is steeped in the base spirit and then mixed with a neutral spirit and the additional sugar (which they all must have 2½ percent of).

A Cordial Look Back

The first-known liqueur was most likely created by French or Italian monks, but the one we know about for sure is from Catalan chemist and theologian Arnau de Vilanova at the University of Montpellier in the latter part of the thirteenth century. Vilanova was intrigued by botanicals, and by using methods of infusion, he discovered that the resulting potable was quite tasty.

Cordially Yours

Cordials come in an incredible array of flavors and, depending on your personal taste, you can do a whole lot of sampling. Here are some main liqueurs that are readily available and their general price range.

Affordable	Mid-Range	Bank Breaker
Bonnie Doon Framboise liqueur, $13	Amaretto di Saronno, $20	White Cranberry Aquavit, $30
	Marie Brizard Crème de Menthe, $25	Chambord raspberry liqueur, $30
Hiram Walker Crème de Banana, $9	Frangelico, $21	Grand Marnier, $39
Midori Melon Liqueur, $18	Kahlúa, $22	

Wine

Ah, the fruit of the vine. So many people find this alluring alcohol intimidating when really there's no reason for it. This is salt-o-the-earth stuff (or more accurately, rootstock of the earth stuff). Fear not. Once you get a handle on a few terms of the trade and start experimenting with varying grapes, you'll get to know what you like and what you don't.

Red wine and white wine are exactly the same ... that is, until the fermentation process begins and then the big difference becomes clear. Grapes for white wine are stripped of their skin, stems, and seeds. With the latter discarded, they are then mashed and fermented so the clear juice from the fruit is what you end up seeing in the glass. Red wine, however, is fermented with its skins, et al., which is where it gets its color and tannic nature.

It's not just all about reds and whites, of course. There's champagne, too. Champagne—or sparkling wine when not produced in the Champagne region of France—has that wonderful effervescence we all know and adore for celebratory occasions. But here's something that may surprise you: champagne is made up of three grapes—and two of them are red. Yup, that's right: one white (chardonnay), two red (pinot noir and pinot meunier). The process of making bubbly is long, extraordinarily complicated, and filled with mathematical equations to make your head spin more than the bubbles will. Simply put, though, the bubbles come from a part of the process that occurs when carbon dioxide gas is trapped inside each bottle during a second fermentation process.

And then there's also *fortified wine*, better known to you as sherry, port, and Madeira. These, too, go through quite a complicated process before becoming the richly textured wines they are, but the most important thing to know is that these wines are fortified with another spirit, hence their name.

Liquor Lingo

Fortified wines are those that have been fortified with another spirit such as brandy. The best examples of this are sherry, Madeira, and port.

Tracing Back the Grapevine

Wine has such a long and complicated history that there's just no way to give you the whole shebang in a paragraph or two. So I'll give you the crib notes. Who "invented" wine? Nobody really knows for sure, but evidence shows wine was being produced in the ancient lands of Mesopotamia in the fertile Tigris-Euphrates valley. The Egyptians were the first to record any evidence of winemaking, around 3000 B.C.E. But it was during the era of the Roman Empire that wine became available to the masses (which was a good thing, because the water was undrinkable!). Techniques were refined, mostly in monasteries, and by the eighteenth century, European wine was widely lauded and celebrated.

Wine of the Times

Although it would be impossible to name every wine from every country (impossible to write and impossible to read), and even in giving suggestions I know I'm leaving out so very much. I offer the following suggestions to guide you at your local wine shop, but I highly encourage you to ask for help and guidance at your favorite wine merchant and to try lots of things.

Want more help? My dear friend Tony DiDio and I wrote a book on wine and food pairing: *Renaissance Guide to Wine and Food Pairing* (Alpha Books, 2003). Check it out for a short but good wine primer section in the front of the book.

Affordable	Mid-Range	Bank Breaker
Boony Doon Pacific Rim Riesling (California), $10	Trefethen Dry Riesling (California), $15	Hanzell Chardonnay (California), $55
Four Sisters Sauvignon Blanc (Australia), $10	Cable Bay Chardonnay (New Zealand), $22	Baron de Ladoucette Pouilly Fume (France), $55
Morro Bay Chardonnay, $10	Alois Lageder "Benefizium" (Italy), $21	Arrowood Cabernet Sauvignon Reserve, $54
Alamos Malbec, $10	Argyle Pinot Noir (Oregon), $17	Miner Family Pinot Noir, Gary's Vineyard (California), $60
Louis Jadot Beaujolais Village, $9	Pellegrini Coverdale Ranch Cabernet Sauvignon (California), $20	
Yalumba Oxford Landing Cabernet-Shiraz, $8	Raphael Estate Merlot (Long Island), $20	

Prices given for 750 milliliter bottles.

Beer

Although it's not usually the first thing that comes to a mixologist's mind, beer is always important to have on hand when you're expecting guests. But what is beer, exactly? Beer is made from barley that's soaked, sprouted, dried in a kiln (similar to the process for whisky), and crushed (not ground, like whisky). This is added to purified, heated water to break down the starch into sugar and then other starch from corn, wheat, or rice might be added, depending on what the desired final product is. It then goes through several other processes of straining, boiling, fermenting (with yeast), aging, and filtering. All that just so you can have a cold one!

Follow the Barley Trail

Like wine, it's difficult to pinpoint exactly when beer was first brewed, but ample evidence shows the ancient Egyptians were quite fond of it. In fact, some pharaohs even designated that beer be part of their burial booty to carry them into the next world. But although beer has been brewed and consumed for thousands of years, it was truly during the Christian era when monks perfected the technique. By the seventeenth century, it was a staple in most European diets.

 Cocktail Conversation

The oldest brewery in America is Pennsylvania's own Yuengling. You can still find Yuengling beer in most markets.

Beer Here and Now

Depending on your preferences (dark? light? amber?), you have so many beers from which to choose from many, many countries, each with its own style. Check out the following table for a smattering of great beers from all over the world to sample.

Affordable	Mid-Range	Bank Breaker
Yuengling, $5/6-pack	Corona Extra, $7.50/6-pack	Corsendonk, $10/750 ml bottle
McSorley's, $5/6-pack	Bass Ale, $8/6-pack	Young's Oatmeal Stout, $9/4-pack
Miller High-Life, $6/6-pack	Samuel Adams Cherry Wheat, $8/6-pack	Franziskaner Hefewiesse, $9/6-pack
Tecate, $6/6-pack	Boddington's, $7/4-pack	Anchor Steam, $9/6-pack

Sake

Although many people call sake "rice wine," it's not. Sake is actually a brewed beverage with rice as its main ingredient; therefore, it's much more akin to beer than to wine. However, its clear, sometimes earthy, sometimes bright taste is indeed reminiscent of wine. It can be consumed warmed or chilled, in small, earthenware sake cups, in cedar masu sake boxes, or even in a cocktail glass, as is common in stylish cocktail lounges across the country.

Sake comes in several different types, but they all have two things in common. The first is how much fat and protein is milled (i.e., polished) off the rice grain. The more you mill, the higher quality the sake. Most sake is simple table sake (*futuu-shu*), which is about 20 to 25 percent milled. Premium sakes, which are the best of the best, fall into three categories based on their milling (and, as a general rule, are more often than not consumed chilled):

◆ **Honjozo and junmai.** These have a minimum of 30 percent grain milled away.

◆ **Ginjo and junmai ginjo.** These have a minimum of 40 percent grain milled away.

◆ **Daiginjo and junmai daiginjo.** These super-premium sakes have a minimum of 50 percent grain milled away.

The second important factor in sake production is the water. Each city in Japan known for its stellar sake production also has a stellar water source.

The Drink of Dynasty

While evidence of sake production in China goes back thousands of years, it was Japan that refined the art. Sake's history in Japan goes all the way back to 300 B.C.E., when particular methods of rice planting and cultivation were introduced to the country. Although it was likely that sake production also began around that time, we don't see recorded evidence of sake until 300 C.E. Much sake was produced by and for individual families, but eventually the production became far more intricate and far-reaching. By the time the thirteenth century rolled around, sake was being mass-produced and consumed not just by peasants, but by the inhabitants of the Imperial Palace. Today, with changes and modernization of equipment, sake is produced in mass quantities all over Japan (and lately, it seems to be catching on here, too!).

Affordable	Mid-Range	Bank Breaker
Hakutsuru, $10	Tentaka Kuni, "Hawk of the Heavens" (Junmai), $30	Nanbu Bijin, "Ancient Pillars" (Junmai Daiginjo), $75
Fukunishiki, $18	Sato No Homare, "Pride the Village" (Junmai), $50	Otokoyama (Junmai of Daiginjo), $125
	Wakatake Onikoroshi (Ginjo), $30	
	Rihaku, "Wandering Poet" (Junmai Ginjo), $35	

Prices given for 750 milliliter bottles.

The Least You Need to Know

◆ When you understand how a beverage is made, it's easier to distinguish why—and which examples of it—you like best.

◆ From pioneers to pirates, every spirit has its own fascinating story. Behind each bottle are hundreds—sometimes thousands!—of years of history, travel, and travails before it gets to your shelf.

◆ Even though prices vary from reasonable to very expensive, price does not necessarily dictate quality. Discern what your price point is and go from there.

Chapter 2

Jigger Me This

In This Chapter

- ◆ The basics on barware
- ◆ Learn your glasses!
- ◆ Extra-extra: the stuff you don't know you need
- ◆ Standard measurements for mixing and mingling

Don't know a sherry glass from a sour glass? Can't point out a pilsner glass? Haven't the faintest what a Delmonico is? Grab a stool, friend. This chapter is going to school you on glasses, gadgets, measurements, and some extra cool stuff to have around that will, I promise, come in awfully handy.

Bartender's Toolbox

A shaker, a strainer, a lemon zest grater. You'll need to get your hands on several small but important gadgets to set up your bar properly. Be sure to have the following indispensables on hand:

All-purpose pitcher

Bar spoon

Bottle opener

Can opener

Channel knife

Liquor Lingo _____

A **channel knife** is a handy-dandy tool for making those adorable little twists you see in cocktails. (So that's how they do that!)

Cocktail shaker (metal)

Corkscrew (waiter's)

Corkscrew (winged)

Cutting board

Grater/zester

Ice bucket

Ice tongs

Manual citrus juicers

Martini pitcher

Jigger

Cocktail Conversation _____

When shaking a cocktail, you should, of course, find the most comfortable and least messy method for you. Some folks love a standard metal cocktail shaker. Some love using the metal bottom of the cocktail shaker paired with a mixing glass (when paired, sometimes called a Boston shaker). I prefer the latter. I find I never spill a drop with this method—and it looks impressive to my unsuspecting guests!

| Measuring cup | Measuring spoons | Mixing glass | Muddler (wooden) | Pairing knife | Strainer |

Spills

Always, always, always thoroughly wash your barware after using it. Also wash garnishes such as lemons, limes, apples, et al., before using them.

A Glass of ...

Do you know the difference between a highball and a Collins? You will after you get through with this section! You don't necessarily have to have each and every possible glass for each and every possible kind of cocktail, but it's certainly useful to know what they all are to better understand the nature of the mixing business (or at least, the drinking part of it). Here are the usual suspects behind any fully stocked bar:

| Beer mug (14 to 16 oz.) | Brandy snifter (6 to 10 oz.) | Champagne flute (6 oz.) | Cocktail (4 to 6 oz.) | Collins (12 to 14 oz.) |

| Delmonico or sour glass (5 to 8 oz.) | Highball (10 to 12 oz.) | Irish coffee (6 to 8 oz.) | Old-fashioned (6 to 8 oz.) | Pilsner (12 to 14 oz.) | Pint (16 oz.) |

Pousse-café
(3 oz.)

Punch bowl and cup
(6 oz. per cup)

Sherry/port
(6 oz.)

Shot (1½ oz.)

Wine
(6 to 8 oz.)

> **Liquor Lingo**
>
> A **Delmonico glass** holds about 5 to 6 ounces and is used for fizzes or Rickeys. It was named after the near-ancient restaurant responsible for many coiffing and edible originals: the once-glorious Delmonico's in New York City.

Ready for Action

You've got spirits; you've got bar tools; you've got glasses. Sounds like you're all ready to go, right? Well ... not exactly. Almost! You still need to know a few sundries that are the unsung heroes of a good cocktail—the swizzle stick, the toothpick, the coaster, etc. ... you get the picture. This section is all about those little bits and pieces that seem small, but have a big impact on a well-stocked bar.

Here's what you need:

- ❑ Bar towels
- ❑ Candles (because every bar needs ambience)
- ❑ Coasters
- ❑ Cocktail napkins
- ❑ Cut-resistant gloves
- ❑ First-aid kit
- ❑ Matches and/or a lighter
- ❑ Paper towels
- ❑ Saucers (for dipping glasses in salt and sugar)
- ❑ Straws
- ❑ Swizzle sticks
- ❑ Toothpicks

Spills _____

Why a first-aid kit? You might be working with several sharp objects in your bartender tool kit, so why not be safe rather than sorry?

Measure of a Mixologist

Ounces, pints, liters, fifths. A whole lot of weighty words are tossed around in the bartending world. Most of this book deals in ounces in cocktails, but it's good to have a quick reference for general measurements and equivalents. Don't say I never gave you anything: here's your Betty-Crocker-for-the-Bar handy-dandy measurement guide.

Measurement	Ounces	Metric
Dash	⅟₃₂ ounce	
Teaspoon	⅛ ounce	
Tablespoon	⅜ ounce	
Pony	1 ounce	
Jigger	1½ ounces	
Cup	8 ounces	200 milliliters
Half pint	8 ounces	200 milliliters
Pint	16 ounces	500 milliliters
Fifth	25½ ounces	750 milliliters
Quart	32 ounces	1 liter
Magnum	50½ ounces	1.5 liters
Half gallon	64 ounces	1.75 liters

The Least You Need to Know

◆ It's important to take stock of your barware to be sure you have the appropriate gear on hand.

◆ Not all glasses are created equal—and that's not just in shape. Different glasses hold different amounts of liquid and, therefore, are appropriate for different types of cocktails.

◆ Keeping your bar stocked with the "extras" is not a frivolous task— bar towels, coasters, toothpicks, and swizzle sticks might not be the first thing you think of when mixing a drink, but they're most certainly important items for the finished product.

3

Top It Off and Mix It Up: Garnishes and Mixers

In This Chapter

- Garnishes and how to make them
- Some mixers basics
- Techniques for tipplers

A Manhattan without some bitters and a maraschino cherry is like ... Bella Abzug without a hat. Bono without sunglasses and a cause. Woody Allen without neuroses. It's just not the same. An original is the sum of all its many exciting parts. The garnish in a drink is no exception. And what about mixers? Is it enough to twist open a bottle of margarita mix and dump it in a blender? Heavens no! Why do that when, really, using fresh juices and fresh ingredients is so easy—and usually pretty inexpensive? Put it all together with a little mixing know-how, and you'll be ready to start mixing it up and throw a great cocktail party.

The Must-Have List

Plain and simple, this list of garnishes and other bar-related items is pretty much all you'll need to make just about any cocktail in this book—or any other, I'd imagine:

♦ **Cherries.** Red maraschinos are a must, but green are nice to keep on hand, too.

♦ **Cinnamon sticks.** For hot drinks or for grating.

♦ **Cucumbers.** A thin slice or strip of cucumber is gorgeous in any sake concoction, and it's also a must in one of my favorites, a Pimm's Cup (recipe in Chapter 12).

♦ **Granulated sugar.** For mixing and rimming.

♦ **Kosher or bar salt.** This thick-grained salt is the right touch for a fresh margarita and other drinks well-complemented by a little salty zing.

♦ **Lemons and limes.** You'll likely use these more often than any other fruit garnish.

♦ **Mint.** For muddling or visual and aromatic decoration.

♦ **Nutmeg.** Freshly grated, please.

♦ **Olives.** Green and pitted are the most popular, but other stuffed versions are fun, too, from pimento to jalapeño!

♦ **Onion.** A sophisticated touch on a sophisticated tipple.

♦ **Oranges.** Great for tropical drinks and fantastic flavor.

♦ **Pineapple.** Fresh is the best. (Later in this chapter I give instructions on how to wrangle one into garnishing perfection.)

♦ **Superfine sugar.** Just like granulated, important for mixing and rimming, but also a key ingredient in simple syrup.

♦ **Table salt.** For occasional flavoring.

 Cocktail Conversation

This might cause a little controversy with purists, but as far as olives go, I say … use what you like. Many mixologists would rather be dragged naked by a bus down Broadway than serve a pimento olive in their martinis. Actually, I kind of like them. Does this make me such a bad person? Well, no. I like 'em all. So do as you will. Be pure, be indiscriminate, but do garnish.

Lemony Slice-It

Don't know your twist from your wedge? No problem. Follow these instructions for perfect citrus sight and sampling adornments every time. I'll use a lemon as an example here, but the same applies to limes and oranges as well:

For twists:

1. Using a sharp kitchen knife and cutting board, cut off the nubby end on each side of the fruit. Place the fruit right side up, so one of the cut ends is flat on the cutting board.
2. Use a channel knife in a top-to-bottom swipe to slice off pieces of the fruit's skin. Or use a pairing knife to slice off ½-inch-thick peels of the skin and then cut those into ¼-inch twists.
3. Don't throw the rest away! Reserve the skinned fruit for juicing purposes.

For slices:

1. Using a sharp kitchen knife and cutting board, cut off the nubby end on each side of the fruit. Place the fruit right side up, so one of the cut ends is flat on the cutting board.
2. Next, cut the fruit in half lengthwise.
3. Place it fruit side down, skin side up on the cutting board.
4. Cut the fruit horizontally into ½-inch slices.

 Cocktail Conversation

When cutting oranges, you might have to slice off much more of the ends than you would for lemons or limes.

For wedges:

1. Using a sharp kitchen knife and cutting board, cut off the nubby end on each side of the fruit. Place the fruit right side up, so one of the cut ends is flat on the cutting board.
2. Next, cut the fruit in half lengthwise.

3. Cut the halves in half lengthwise once more, so you have cut the fruit into four lengthwise quarters.

4. Finally, slice the quartered pieces in half horizontally.

For wheels:

1. Using a sharp kitchen knife and cutting board, cut off the nubby end on each side of the fruit. Place the fruit right side up, so one of the cut ends is flat on the cutting board.

2. Turn the fruit on its side. Firmly hold it down with one hand and cut the fruit into nearly ½-inch slices.

3. Make a single slit from the center outward. (This is how you anchor it onto a glass when you are ready to garnish.)

Spills _____

Remember those cut-proof gloves I told you to buy in Chapter 2? This would be a good time to use them! However, if you don't have a pair, when you hold down the fruit, be sure you curl your fingertips in slightly, so if your knife slips you won't slice your fingertip.

A Word About Juice

Fresh juice can make an ordinary drink a truly extraordinary imbibing experience. For kicks one day, I would even recommend you make two margaritas—one with fresh lime juice and one with a bottled or canned mix. The difference is astounding. Once you go fresh, you'll never go back.

With that said, you should know a few things about juicing. For one—and this bears repeating—always rinse your citrus fruits before using them. This isn't always the first thing that comes to mind with citrus fruits because we don't eat the skin; however, bacteria can live on the outside of a lemon, lime, or orange, and you really don't want to be messing around with that. Your stomach will thank you for the courtesy.

Next, believe it or not, room-temperature citrus fruits are easier to juice than super-cold refrigerated ones. Store your citrus fruits in the fridge, but remove them an hour or two prior to prepping for your desired cocktail.

Finally, unless you're making ceviche, trying to store juice overnight or long-term doesn't work. It gets ... yucky. Acidic. Pungent. It's not going to yield the same effect as when it's freshly squeezed.

The Pine-Apple of My Eye

You might be inclined to pick up a can of sliced pineapple and call it a garnish. Certainly, that's fine. But if you plan on making tropical drinks for your cocktail cohorts, why not buy the real, fresh thing? There's nothing in the world quite like the aroma of fresh pineapple—and it's really good for you, too. Lots of vitamin C in there. But don't be intimidated by the often-heard conundrum with pineapples: how do you cut it open and make garnish-worthy wedges? That's easy:

1. Using a sharp kitchen knife and a cutting board, turn the pineapple on its side and cut about 1½ inches off each end.

2. Next, you can do one of the following:

    a. Leaving the outside skin on, slice the pineapple horizontally into 1-inch rounds. Then, cut each round into 6 or 8 wedges (3 or 4 side to side cuts around the circular slice).

    b. Cut the pineapple in half lengthwise. Then, cut the halves in half lengthwise. Make 1-inch horizontal slices from each quarter section.

Spills

While I'm on the topic of tropical drinks, let's talk for a second about blended concoctions and the fruit that goes into them. When using berries, just like with any other fruit, *wash them first*. But just like with citrus juice, you really don't want to preprep your fruit and let it sit overnight. Washed berries, no matter how well drained, will get mushy and kind of gross. Bananas turn brown; mango does okay overnight. But the best rule of thumb with fruit is the fresher the better.

Oh, Brandy, You're a Fine Fruit

If your recipe calls for brandied fruit, this will take a little time. It's very, very simple to make, but it requires at least a month storage time before it'll be ready. You can brandy berries, peaches, cherries, pineapples, and melon. However, apples and pears do not fair well—they get mushy.

To brandy fruit:

1. Add 2 cups sugar to 2 cups fruit in a large, sealable jar.
2. Add 1½ pints (24 ounces) brandy (or rum or bourbon, which technically doesn't make the fruit "brandied" anymore, but the results are just as tasty).
3. Allow the mixture to sit unrefrigerated for at least 3 weeks and up to 1 month prior to using.

In a Muddle

From cobblers to caipirinhas and other fruity concoctions, muddling is *the* technique to know. First, you need the obvious tool: a muddler. This is simply a wooden pestle with a nubbed, rounded end to get the job done (see the muddler pictures in Chapter 2). Muddling releases the precious oils in a mint leaf or citrus skin and melds flavors to create new flavors. In short, it's a must-learn technique. And hey, lucky you, it's easy! Simply drop your to-be-muddled fruit or botanical in the bottom of a mixing glass, grab your muddler, and grind away. That's it. Obviously, a lemon wedge will take more muddling than, say, a delicate mint leaf; use common sense.

Cocktail Conversation

I can't discuss muddling without bringing up the name Nick Mautone, a double-decade mixologist veteran of some of New York's most respected bars. His book, *Raising the Bar: Better Drinks, Better Entertaining* (Artisan, 2004), not only has some incredible, original drink recipes that will wow your guests, but he also is the king of the muddle. From rosemary to ginger, Mautone will teach you how to add extraordinary flavors to any cocktail.

Sir Mix-a-Lot

I'll say it yet again: fresh mixes are the way to go. Here are a few basic recipes for staple mixers that will make your cocktails go from ho-hum to yum!

Bloody Mary Mix

Makes about 12 drinks.

46 oz. tomato juice
10 oz. beef bouillon
1 TB. celery salt
2 tsp. fresh black pepper
3 TB. Worcestershire sauce
2 tsp. Tabasco sauce
2 oz. lemon juice

In a large, sealable jar, combine tomato juice, beef bouillon, celery salt, pepper, Worcestershire sauce, and Tabasco sauce. Give it a good stir. Add fresh lemon juice to the mix when you're ready to serve. Lemon juice–less mix can be stored in the refrigerator for 1 week.

Simple Syrup

4 cups sugar
2 cups water

In a large saucepan, pour in water and add sugar. Heat over low heat until sugar is completely dissolved. Allow to cool and then store in a quart-size sealable jar in the refrigerator for up to a year.

Sour Mix

6 oz. lemon juice
6 oz. lime juice
18 oz. water
¼ cup sugar

Combine lemon juice, lime juice, water, and sugar in a sealable quart-size bottle or jar. Give it a good shake. Store for up to a week.

Variation: For a frothier sour mix, add an egg white to the mix.

It's All in the Wrist and the Twist

Of course, you'd never admit to any of your friends that you've watched that cinematic crime on humanity, *Cocktail*. And you most definitely wouldn't admit to having watched it more than once. But all that shaking and pouring and fancy under-the-leg, over-the-shoulder bartending work was downright exciting, wasn't it? Okay, okay. I've watched it, too. More than once (heaven help me). But you've probably also seen fantastic bartending at your favorite watering hole. To see a skilled, practiced bartender in action is a beautiful thing. A ballet of booze, if you will.

Although I'm not going to turn you into the next Baryshnikov of the bartending world, I can give you a few easy instructions to get you mixing, stirring, shaking, and pouring. Grab an apron (because the first few times might be messy), a bar towel, and let's get mixing.

> **Cocktail Conversation**
>
> Some drinks call for lighting things on fire. I haven't included those in this book, because that's a technique best left to the pros. But I highly recommend checking out super-master-mixologist Dale Degroff's *The Craft of the Cocktail* (Clarkson Potter, 2002). It'll teach you all about fiery garnishes, for which he is famous, and it's a beautiful book to have on your bar. You can also check out his website, www.kingcocktail.com, for great cocktail news and tips.

Shaking

To shake a drink:

1. Fill a mixing glass ½ full with ice (filling it all the way cuts down on your shaking action and, thus, lessens the desired result of the whole effort).

2. Take main shaker part of a metal cocktail shaker set and snugly place it over the top of the glass.

3. Using *two hands* (yes, I know, Tom Cruise used one—but don't do that), pick up the shakers and shake about 10 times. (This is what I mean when I say "give it a good shake" in the recipes.)

4. When mixing cocktails that require egg whites, egg yolks, or whole eggs, increase the amount of shakes. You want to make absolutely certain the egg has been properly mixed into the cocktail.

Spills _____

You might be thinking, *Eggs? Raw eggs? Is that safe?* Well, here's how it is: no, I can't guarantee the safety of your local supermarket's consumer health practices. Generally, if an egg is used within the appropriate time period, as stamped on the expiration date label of the carton, heaven hoping, you should be A-OK. But ... eggs are perishable items. You don't know if, or how long, that egg carton in your refrigerator sat out somewhere, unrefrigerated.

Stirring

To stir a drink:

1. Fill a mixing glass or drink glass ½ to ¾ full with ice.
2. Pour in your ingredients.
3. Using a bar spoon (see Chapter 2), give the drink 5 to 8 stirs. If the drink has champagne or another alcoholic or nonalcoholic sparkling beverage, stir less so as not to diminish the effervescence.

Pouring

To pour a drink:

1. Place a strainer (see Chapter 2) firmly atop your mixing glass.
2. Pick up the mixing glass, and use your index finger to hold the strainer in place.
3. Tilt and pour.

Cocktail Conversation _____

Before I got the hang of it, I used to spill some of each and every cocktail I made when I poured it. My tilting and pouring just weren't up to snuff. I discovered a little cheating technique I'm happy to share with you: assuming you're making at least two cocktails, place the glasses next to each other. Pour one, positioning the shaker so the back of it is over the mouth of the second glass. That way, any dripping runoff goes into the other glass—not all over your bar or countertop.

Blending

To blend a drink:

1. Fill a blender ¼ full with ice. (Any more will make it hard to crush and blend it all and, potentially, burn out your blender's motor.)
2. If using fresh fruit or other whole ingredients, add those first.
3. Next add juices, creams, simple syrup, or sour mix.
4. Add alcohol, if using any, last.
5. Blend on medium speed for about 15 seconds.

Popping

Champagne or sparkling wine is a lovely way to start out an evening or, of course, celebrate a special occasion. But those corks! Some people find the whole process of popping a cork, no matter how fun the sound, a bit intimidating. Really, it's no big deal. Here's all you need to do:

To open a champagne bottle:

1. First and foremost, *always* point the bottle away from people, animals, glass, or any potentially breakable or hurtable object.
2. Gently remove the foil wrapping and metal twisty and cap, keeping one hand palm side down over the top, just in case the bottle has been improperly corked and can potentially shoot out before you actually loosen it.
3. Grab the neck of the bottle with one hand and place your other hand, palm side down, over the cork. If you like, you can use a towel to do this, as it will doubly ensure the cork will not fly out and will also absorb some of the requisite spillage.
4. Slowly twist the cork until it pops.

Spills _____

Although the look of a popping cork shooting into the air and champagne overflowing is certainly the romantic ideal of celebratory behavior, it's kind of wasteful. And more important, it's potentially dangerous. Follow the instructions here, and you'll still get that great, popping sound—safely—and you won't waste any precious bubbly.

To open a wine bottle:

1. Remove the bottle seal by running a knife around it and peeling it off.
2. Center the corkscrew in the middle of the cork.
3. Twist down until the corkscrew is completely submerged in the cork. Use the arms of the winged corkscrew or leverage handle of the waiter's corkscrew to slowly pull out the cork.

Unfortunately, some corks, due to improper storage or sealing, are so dry they either crumble or break in half when opening, leaving you stuck with half a cork in your bottle. What do you do? Well, there's no guaranteed trick for this. I don't think pushing the cork into the bottle is ever acceptable. It's a mess, and the cork can have sediment or mold on it, which you don't really want bobbling around in your *vino*. I try to *gently* re-insert and twist in the corkscrew into the left-over, stuck cork and *slowly* pull it out. Usually, it works.

Chillin'

You have a few options when it comes to chilling or frosting a cocktail glass:

- ◆ Fill the glass ¾ with ice and a little cold water, and let it sit to chill while you prepare whatever cocktail you're making. When you're ready to pour, dump out the ice and water.
- ◆ Simply put the glass in the freezer ½ hour prior to mixing your desired drink.
- ◆ If you want the glass frosty, run it under water first and place in the freezer for ½ hour.

 Cocktail Conversation

There's nothing like a frosty beer mug or pint glass. Always keep a few in your freezer for a chilly mug of ale whenever you feel the need for a cold one.

You probably started out this chapter less than comfortable with at least a couple techniques. But see? That wasn't so hard. Whether you are muddling mint or popping champagne, it just takes a little instruction and a little practice before you're lookin' like a pro!

The Least You Need to Know

◆ Garnishes aren't just extras—they are key components to a drink. Take stock of your bar to be sure you have the proper components for your favorite cocktails.

◆ When juice is involved, fresh is always best.

◆ To get the hang of mixing and stirring techniques, try using non-alcoholic (i.e., inexpensive!) substitutes to get comfortable with the tools and moves.

◆ When opening champagne or sparkling wine, always be sure to point the bottle away from people, animals, light fixtures, glass—anything that could potentially be hurt or broken.

Chapter 4

The Best Bar in Town—Yours

In This Chapter

- ◆ Stocking your bar
- ◆ A word about responsible pouring

You've got the skills. You've got the tools. What's left? The liquor, of course. You know what you like to drink, but for entertaining, what exactly is a good, basic stock of liquor? That all depends on your purposes and how serious you want to be about your home bar. I give you several bar situations in this chapter and a shopping list of liquors and mixers to stock it with. Then, so you'll know what to do with all your new liquor, I give you some tips on hosting an A-1 shindig.

Stocking Up: The Minimum to Maximum Bar

Everyone's got a different style of entertaining. Some of us like to have the all-out bash, while others prefer small, intimate gatherings. And then there are those of us who just want to be prepared for … anything! Whatever your penchant or personal style, I've got some handy-dandy shopping lists for you in this chapter for the minimum, medium, and maxed-out bar. Pick your preferred party style, photocopy the appropriate list, and head out to stock up.

Always Have ...

For your average home bar, you want to be able to offer the basics. For this, keep 1 full bottle of each of the following:

- ❑ Bourbon
- ❑ Brandy
- ❑ Gin
- ❑ Rum
- ❑ Tequila
- ❑ Vodka
- ❑ Vermouth (dry and sweet)
- ❑ Whisky
- ❑ Red wine
- ❑ White wine
- ❑ Club soda
- ❑ Cola (regular and diet)
- ❑ Bitters
- ❑ Ginger ale
- ❑ Orange juice
- ❑ Tonic water

As well as:
- ❑ Lemons (for garnish and juicing)
- ❑ Limes (for garnish and juicing)
- ❑ Maraschino cherries
- ❑ Olives
- ❑ Salt (coarse)
- ❑ Sugar (granulated and superfine)

Spills

There's nothing more disastrous to a cocktail party than forgetting to buy ice. Oddly, it's the one thing many people always miscalculate or just completely forget to purchase. When you entertain, be sure you factor in about 2 pounds ice per person. Your freezer automatically makes ice? Great, but it won't make enough for your party, and it takes an awfully long time for it to refill. Plus, ice that's been sitting in the freezer takes on other odors, so be sure your ice is fresh and there's enough of it!

Gettin' Serious

A more serious bar takes the basic bar up a notch or two. If you're a little more serious about your home bar, have 1 full bottle of the following:

❑ Bourbon
❑ Brandy
❑ Beer (amber and dark)
❑ Coffee liqueur
❑ Gin
❑ Curaçao (orange)
❑ Crème de cacao
❑ Melon liqueur
❑ Schnapps (peppermint and peach)
❑ Pastis

❑ Rum
❑ Scotch (blended)
❑ Tequila
❑ Triple sec
❑ Vodka
❑ Vermouth (dry and sweet)
❑ Red wine (3 to 4 bottles)
❑ White wine (3 to 4 bottles)
❑ Sparkling wine (2 bottles)

For mixers:

❑ Bitters:
    ❑ Orange
    ❑ Angostura
❑ Club soda
❑ Cola (regular and diet)
❑ Cranberry juice
❑ Ginger ale
❑ Grapefruit juice
❑ Tomato juice
❑ Grenadine
❑ Lemon-lime soda
❑ Orange juice

❑ Tonic water
❑ Cream (light and heavy)
❑ Tabasco sauce
❑ Worcestershire sauce
❑ Cocktail olives
❑ Cocktail onions
❑ Lemons (for garnish and juicing)
❑ Limes (for garnish and juicing)
❑ Rose's lime juice
❑ Sugar (granulated and superfine)
❑ Salt (coarse)
❑ Maraschino cherries

Cocktail Conversation

You probably have heard at one time or another that maraschino cherries aren't so good for you. True, at one time, less-than-safe dyes were used for the standard bright-red hue, but no more. Today's maraschinos are soaked in a sulfur solution, which strips the cherry of its natural flavor and color, and the fruit's rinsed for several days to wash out most of the residual sulfites (although it does contain them in the finished product, so if you're allergic, forewarned is forearmed). Then comes the color: the cherries go through an up to 5-week process of soaking in corn syrup and food coloring to give them that super-sweet flavor and bright-red (or green, depending on the kind) color.

Super Stylie

If your desire is to have a your-wish-is-my-command kind of bar, 1 full bottle of each of the following ought to do it:

- ❑ Bourbon:
    - ❑ A medium grade for mixing
    - ❑ A higher grade for sipping
- ❑ Brandy:
    - ❑ Basic
    - ❑ Fruit (American and/or French)
    - ❑ Cognac
- ❑ Canadian whisky
- ❑ Gin
- ❑ Liqueurs:
    - ❑ Amaretto
    - ❑ Chambord
    - ❑ Chartreuse (green and/or yellow)
    - ❑ Cherry (maraschino) liqueur
    - ❑ Crème de bananes
    - ❑ Crème de cacao
    - ❑ Crème de cassis
    - ❑ Crème de menthe
    - ❑ Crème de noyaux
    - ❑ Coffee liqueur
    - ❑ Curaçao (orange, blue, green)
    - ❑ Frangelico
    - ❑ Irish cream
    - ❑ Kummel
    - ❑ Melon
    - ❑ Sambuca
    - ❑ Schnapps (your favorite flavors)
    - ❑ Southern Comfort
    - ❑ Pimm's

- ❑ Red wine (6 or more bottles of your favorite)
- ❑ Rum:
    - ❑ Dark
    - ❑ Light
    - ❑ Añejo
- ❑ Sake
- ❑ Scotch whisky
- ❑ Single malt whisky
- ❑ Blended whisky
- ❑ Sloe gin
- ❑ Tennessee whiskey
- ❑ Tequila:
    - ❑ Blanco or joven abocado
    - ❑ Reposado
    - ❑ Añejo
- ❑ Triple sec
- ❑ Vodka:
    - ❑ Russian or Polish
    - ❑ Fruit-flavored
    - ❑ Vanilla, pepper, et al.
- ❑ Vermouth:
    - ❑ Dry
    - ❑ Sweet
    - ❑ French
- ❑ White wine (6 or more bottles of your favorite)

🍸 **Cocktail Conversation** _____

For a party, a red zinfandel is a great full-bodied, fruit-forward way to go. It's got enough personality to stand on its own, but it also pairs well with many hors d'oeuvres. Ravenswood makes an excellent, reasonably priced option. For white, a dry Riesling is an excellent hors d'oeuvres option. Trefethen estate dry Riesling is also a favorite and is usually less than $20 a bottle. Remember, 1 bottle of wine will provide about 4 to 5 wine glasses worth per person, so plan accordingly for how many guests you will have.

For mixers:
- Bitters:
  - Orange
  - Angostura
  - Peychaud
- Club soda
- Cream of coconut
- Cola (regular and diet)
- Cranberry juice
- Ginger ale
- Grapefruit juice
- Lemon-lime soda
- Orange juice
- Passion fruit juice
- Pineapple juice
- Nectars:
  - Mango
  - Papaya
  - Peach
- Tomato juice
- Tonic water
- Cream (light and heavy)
- Tabasco sauce
- Worcestershire sauce

For garnishes and extras:
- Cocktail olives (an assortment of your favorite stuffed varieties)
- Cocktail onions
- Green cherries
- Lemons
- Limes
- Mint
- Sugar (granulated and superfine)
- Salt (coarse)
- Maraschino cherries

🍸 **Cocktail Conversation** _____

When setting up your bar, arrange it so the mixing's easy. Group your main liquors, liqueurs, mixers, and garnishes together for easy access. Always be sure you have ice nearby. Keep an appropriate stock of glassware and barware, too (remember the list in Chapter 2!), as well as bar towels or paper towels for quick cleanups. And of course, don't forget the music!

All's Well That Ends Well

You've made—and will continue to make—a million happy memories with your friends and family. This is what life's all about: the people we love and the experiences we have together. The fact of the matter is that alcohol can often be part of a celebration or gathering, and even in the smallest of quantities, gets us a little giddy. In large quantities it impairs judgment.

It's downright hilarious to allow your near and dear to reveal, after throwing back a few cocktails, that they know all the words to every single song on the soundtrack to *Grease;* it's quite another to let them get into a car and drive off half-crocked. Inner Olivia Newton John–ness can be laughed at; dangerous driving, incarceration, or worse cannot. None of us is a saint, or at least nobody I know. We all make mistakes; we all are guilty of errors in judgment. Drinking and driving is not a mistake any of us can afford. The cost can be quite dear: at best embarrassing, and at worst, life-taking. You know this. I know you know this. I'm not giving you a finger-wagging you haven't heard before. I've had friends take my keys from me, too—and boy, was I glad they did.

It's not always so easy to do the responsible thing. In fact, in those moments when you're a little high from the good times and good spirits, it's a downright drag to snap into caretaker, responsible-adult mode. But it's what you do—it's what you *must* do—for the people you love in your life and for those you don't know whose lives you may well affect by one bad decision that could have been averted.

Even when you're armed with the best intentions, though, sometimes it can be hard to know how much is too much. What follows are a few charts listing the *blood alcohol content* (BAC) for drinks consumed by men and women, plus how time factors into the equation to sober up. It's quite eye opening, isn't it?

I tell you what—I'll use myself as a guinea pig. Let's say I consume 2 drinks. That doesn't sound excessive, right? Two little drinks. No big deal. Well, actually, at my weight if I consume 2 drinks, I will have reached the limit at which I would be arrested for DWI if I chose to get in my car. Wow.

Metabolic Drinking Rates

Body Weight (lb.)	Number of Drinks									
	One	Two	Three	Four	Five	Six	Seven	Eight	Nine	Ten
For Males										
100	.043	.087	.130	.174	.217	.261	.304	.348	.391	.435
125	.034	.069	.103	.139	.173	.209	.242	.278	.312	.346
150	.029	.058	.087	.116	.145	.174	.203	.232	.261	.290
175	.025	.050	.075	.100	.125	.150	.175	.200	.225	.250
200	.022	.043	.065	.087	.108	.130	.152	.174	.195	.217
225	.019	.039	.058	.078	.097	.117	.136	.156	.175	.198
250	.017	.035	.052	.070	.087	.105	.122	.139	.156	.173
For Females										
100	.050	.101	.152	.203	.253	.234	.355	.406	.456	.507
125	.040	.080	.120	.162	.202	.244	.282	.324	.364	.404
150	.034	.068	.101	.135	.169	.203	.237	.271	.304	.338
175	.029	.058	.087	.117	.146	.175	.204	.233	.262	.292
200	.026	.050	.078	.101	.126	.152	.177	.203	.227	.253
225	.022	.045	.068	.091	.113	.136	.159	.182	.207	.227
250	.020	.041	.061	.082	.010	.122	.142	.162	.182	.202

The Time Factor

Hours Since First Drink	Subtract This from BAC
1	.015
2	.030
3	.045
4	.060
5	.075
6	.090

Source: Evans, Glen and Robert O'Brien, The Encyclopedia of Alcoholism, *1991.*

Okay, party people. You are now officially armed for any soirée you want to swan over as the host with the most. You can mix, garnish, sugar, and shake—and you even know when to tell your guests (and yourself) when it's time to call it quits. What's next? Recipes, of course! Read on for a multitude of mixables, from the classics to the new fantastics. I highly encourage you to experiment. If you think a recipe needs more of this or less of that, make notes. Take a pen to this puppy and scribble all over it with your own preferences. One person's perfect martini is another's imperfect use of vermouth. Just be sure you do one thing for me: have fun (safely!) and remember—good times are only as good as those with whom you share them.

The Least You Need to Know

◆ Think about how much you entertain and what kind of parties you tend to throw. Let that be your guideline for creating a home bar.

◆ If you're just starting out, start small—you can always add to it later.

◆ *Do NOT drink and drive; do NOT let your friends and family—or even people you don't like so much—drink and drive.* It is always a dangerous and foolish endeavor.

Part

The Recipes

From a Harvey Wallbanger to a Weep No More, this exhaustive listing of 1,500 recipes gives you the classics, the crazies, and some new hipper-than-thou favorites to shake up your next soirée. Find your favorite liquor, and peruse that chapter until you see something that whets your whistle. Or go right to that cocktail you've always wanted to learn how to put together. (A Mai Tai, maybe? Perhaps a Planter's Punch? Jonesing for a Julep?) Whatever poison you pick, it's here!

Chapter 5

Bourbon

How well I remember my first encounter with the Devil's Brew. I happened to stumble across a case of bourbon—and went right on stumbling for several days thereafter.

—W. C. Fields

All-American

1½ oz. bourbon
1½ oz. *Southern Comfort*
2 oz. cola

Fill an old-fashioned glass ½ full with ice. Pour in bourbon, Southern Comfort, and cola. Give it a good stir.

Liquor Lingo

Southern Comfort is a peach-flavored, bourbon-based liqueur with citrus hints. Many people frequently mistake SoCo (as it is sometimes referred to) for bourbon, but technically it falls in the liqueur category.

Allegheny

1 oz. bourbon
1 oz. dry vermouth
1½ tsp. blackberry brandy
1½ tsp. lemon juice
1 lemon twist

Fill a cocktail shaker ½ full with ice. Pour in bourbon, vermouth, brandy, and lemon juice. Give it a good shake, and strain into a cocktail glass. Garnish with lemon twist.

American Sweetheart

1 oz. bourbon
1 oz. peach liqueur
½ tsp. dry vermouth
1 oz. sour mix

Fill a cocktail shaker ½ full with ice. Pour in bourbon, peach liqueur, vermouth, and sour mix. Give it a good shake, and strain into a cocktail glass.

Anchors Aweigh

2 oz. bourbon
2 tsp. peach brandy
2 tsp. cherry brandy
2 tsp. *triple sec*
2 TB. heavy cream
1 maraschino cherry

Fill a cocktail shaker ½ full with ice. Pour in bourbon, peach brandy, cherry brandy, triple sec, and heavy cream. Give it a good shake, and strain straight up into an old-fashioned glass. Garnish with maraschino cherry.

Liquor Lingo

Triple sec is a strong orange-flavored liqueur made from the peel of curaçao oranges. It's most often used for mixing.

Back Street Banger

2 oz. bourbon
2 oz. Irish cream

Fill an old-fashioned glass ½ full with ice. Pour in bourbon and Irish cream. Give it a good stir.

Barbara East

2 oz. bourbon
1 oz. apricot brandy
1½ oz. grapefruit juice
½ tsp. sugar

Fill a cocktail shaker ½ full with ice. Pour in bourbon, apricot brandy, and grapefruit juice, and add sugar. Give it a good shake, and strain into a cocktail glass.

Barney French

1 orange slice
1 lemon slice
1 dash Peychaud bitters
3 oz. bourbon

Muddle orange and lemon slices with bitters in an old-fashioned glass. Fill with ice, and pour in bourbon.

Bluegrass Cocktail

2 oz. bourbon
¼ oz. cherry liqueur
1 oz. pineapple juice
1 oz. lemon juice

Fill a cocktail shaker ½ full with ice. Pour in bourbon, cherry liqueur, pineapple juice, and lemon juice. Give it a good shake, and strain straight up into an old-fashioned glass.

Bootleg

1 oz. bourbon
1 oz. anise liqueur
1 oz. Southern Comfort

Fill an old-fashioned glass ¾ full with ice. Pour in bourbon, anise liqueur, and Southern Comfort. Give it a good stir.

Bootlegger

1 oz. bourbon
1 oz. tequila
1 oz. Southern Comfort

Fill an old-fashioned glass ¾ full with ice. Pour in bourbon, tequila, and Southern Comfort. Give it a good stir.

Boston Sour

2 oz. bourbon
¾ oz. lemon juice
1 oz. simple syrup
1 egg white
1 lemon slice
1 maraschino cherry

Fill a cocktail shaker ½ full with ice. Pour in bourbon, lemon juice, simple syrup, and egg white. Give it a good, vigorous shake, and strain into a sour glass. Garnish with lemon wedge and maraschino cherry.

Bourbon Black Hawk

2½ oz. bourbon
1½ oz. sloe gin
1 maraschino cherry

Fill a cocktail shaker ½ full with ice. Pour in bourbon and sloe gin. Give it a few stirs, strain into a cocktail glass, and garnish with maraschino cherry.

Bourbon Cobbler

1 tsp. superfine sugar
3 oz. club soda
2½ oz. bourbon
1 lemon slice
1 orange slice
1 maraschino cherry

In an old-fashioned soda glass, add superfine sugar and pour in club soda. Fill the glass ¾ full with crushed ice. Pour in bourbon, and give it a good stir. Garnish with lemon slice, orange slice, and maraschino cherry.

 Cocktail Conversation

You can make a second, slightly tropical version of the Bourbon Cobbler by exchanging the garnishes for a wedge of pineapple, a strawberry, and a lime wedge.

Bourbon Collins

2 oz. bourbon
1 oz. lemon juice
1¼ oz. simple syrup
4 oz. club soda
1 orange slice
1 maraschino cherry

Fill a cocktail shaker ½ full with ice. Pour in bourbon, lemon juice, and simple syrup. Give it a good shake, and strain into a Collins glass ¾ full of ice. Pour in club soda, and garnish with orange slice and maraschino cherry.

Bourbon Cooler

2 oz. bourbon
4 oz. lemon-lime soda
1 lemon or lime wedge

Fill a highball glass with ice. Pour in bourbon and lemon-lime soda, and stir. Garnish with lemon or lime wedge.

Bourbon County

2½ oz. bourbon
½ oz. light cream

Fill a cocktail shaker ½ full with ice. Pour in bourbon and light cream. Give it a good shake, and strain into an old-fashioned glass ¾ full of ice.

Cocktail Conversation

The actual county in Kentucky known as Bourbon is, ironically, a dry (that is, liquorless by law) county. Go figure.

Bourbon Daisy

2 oz. bourbon
1 oz. lemon juice
½ tsp. *grenadine*
½ tsp. superfine sugar
1 orange slice
1 maraschino cherry

Fill a cocktail shaker ½ full with ice. Pour in bourbon, lemon juice, grenadine, and superfine sugar. Give it a good shake, and pour into an old-fashioned glass full of ice. Garnish with orange slice and maraschino cherry.

Variation: Make a slightly more kicked-up version of the Bourbon Daisy by floating 1 tablespoon Southern Comfort on top.

Liquor Lingo

Grenadine is a bright red, super-sweet syrup usually flavored with artificial pomegranate used in mixing alcoholic and nonalcoholic cocktails.

Bourbon Fix

2 oz. bourbon
¾ oz. lemon juice
1 oz. simple syrup
1 lemon slice
1 maraschino cherry

Fill a cocktail shaker with ice. Pour in bourbon, lemon juice, and simple syrup. Give it a good shake, and strain into a highball glass full of ice. Garnish with lemon slice and maraschino cherry.

Bourbon Flip

2 oz. bourbon
1 egg
1 tsp. superfine sugar
½ oz. light cream
½ tsp. grated nutmeg

Fill a cocktail shaker ½ full with ice. Add bourbon, egg, superfine sugar, and light cream. Give it a good, vigorous shake, and strain into a sour glass. Garnish with a little grated nutmeg.

Spills

Don't skip the nutmeg! Whole nutmeg is easy enough to find and is available in most grocery stores and gourmet food shops.

Bourbon Furnace

6 oz. apple cider
2 whole cloves
1 cinnamon stick
1½ oz. bourbon

In a saucepot, combine apple cider, cloves, and cinnamon stick, and heat over medium-low heat until nearly hot. Remove cloves and cinnamon stick. Pour bourbon in a mug, and pour in cider.

Bourbon Highball

2 oz. bourbon
4 oz. ginger ale
1 lime wedge

Fill a highball glass with ice. Pour in bourbon and ginger ale. Garnish with lime wedge.

Bourbon John Collins

2 oz. bourbon
¾ oz. lemon juice
1 oz. simple syrup
4 oz. club soda
1 orange slice
1 maraschino cherry

Fill a cocktail shaker ½ full with ice. Pour in bourbon, lemon juice, and simple syrup. Give it a good shake, and strain into a Collins glass ½ full of ice. Pour in club soda, and garnish with orange slice and maraschino cherry.

Bourbon Manhattan

2 oz. bourbon
1 oz. sweet vermouth
2 dashes *bitters*
1 maraschino cherry

Fill a cocktail shaker ½ full with ice. Pour in bourbon and vermouth, and add bitters. Give it a good stir, and strain into a cocktail glass (unless, of course, you'd prefer it on the rocks—this is perfectly acceptable Manhattan behavior). Garnish with maraschino cherry.

Liquor Lingo

Bitters is the result of distilling aromatic herbs, flowers, seeds, bark, roots, and other plant products. It's used to flavor cocktails or as a *digestif*. Bitters come in several varieties; among the most well known are Peychaud, Abbott's, Bonnecamp, Angostura, and orange.

Bourbon Milk Punch

2 oz. bourbon
½ oz. dark rum
1 TB. simple syrup
4 oz. milk
1 tsp. grated nutmeg

Fill a cocktail shaker ½ full with ice. Pour in bourbon, dark rum, simple syrup, and milk. Give it a good shake, and strain into a highball glass ½ full of ice. Garnish with nutmeg.

Bourbon Millionaire

1½ oz. bourbon
½ oz. orange *curaçao*
1 tsp. *pastis*
1 tsp. grenadine
1 egg white

Fill a cocktail shaker ½ full with ice. Pour in bourbon, curaçao, pastis, grenadine, and egg white. Give it a good, vigorous shake, and strain into a cocktail glass.

Liquor Lingo

Curaçao is an orange-flavored liquor made from curaçao oranges. Curaçao comes in several colors—orange, blue, green, and white (clear)—but all are orange flavored. **Pastis** is a generic French term for their slightly sweet version of anise-flavored liqueur.

Bourbon Old-Fashioned

1 tsp. sugar
2 dashes bitters
3 oz. club soda
2 orange slices
2 maraschino cherries
2 oz. bourbon

Muddle sugar, bitters, a splash of club soda, 1 orange slice, and 1 maraschino cherry in an old-fashioned glass. Remove orange rind. Fill the glass ¾ full with ice. Pour in bourbon and remaining club soda, and garnish with remaining orange slice and maraschino cherry.

Bourbon Sangaree

1 tsp. sugar
2 oz. club soda
2 oz. bourbon
½ oz. tawny port
1 lemon twist
½ tsp. grated nutmeg

Dissolve sugar in 1 teaspoon club soda in an old-fashioned glass. Fill glass ¾ full with ice, and pour in bourbon. Pour in remaining club soda, and float port on top. Garnish with lemon twist and nutmeg.

Bourbon Sling

1 tsp. superfine sugar
2 tsp. bottled water
1 oz. lemon juice
2 oz. bourbon
1 lemon twist

Fill a cocktail shaker ½ full with ice. Add superfine sugar, bottled water, lemon juice, and bourbon. Give it a good shake, and strain into a highball glass. Garnish with lemon twist.

Bourbon Smash

5 mint sprigs
1 tsp. superfine sugar
1 oz. club soda
2 oz. bourbon
1 lemon twist

Muddle 4 mint sprigs, superfine sugar, and club soda in an old-fashioned glass. Fill glass ¾ full with ice, and pour in bourbon. Give it a good stir, and garnish with remaining mint sprig and lemon twist.

Bourbon Sour

1½ oz. bourbon
3 oz. sour mix
1 maraschino cherry
1 orange slice

Fill a cocktail shaker ½ full with ice. Pour in bourbon and sour mix. Give it a good shake, and strain into a sour glass with ice. Garnish with maraschino cherry and orange slice.

Bourbon Stiletto

2 oz. bourbon
½ oz. amaretto
½ oz. lemon juice
1 tsp. lime juice

Fill a cocktail shaker ½ full with ice. Pour in bourbon, amaretto, lemon juice, and lime juice. Give it a good shake, and strain into an old-fashioned glass full of ice.

Bourbon Swizzle

2 oz. bourbon
½ oz. lime juice
1 tsp. simple syrup
1 dash bitters
3 oz. club soda

Fill a cocktail shaker ½ full with ice. Pour in bourbon, lime juice, and simple syrup, and add bitters. Give it a good shake, and strain into a highball glass ¾ full of ice. Pour in club soda, and serve with (of course) a swizzle stick.

Bouzo

2½ oz. bourbon
½ oz. ouzo

Fill an old-fashioned glass ½ full with ice. Pour in bourbon and ouzo. Give it a good stir.

Brighton Punch

1 oz. bourbon
1 oz. cognac
¾ oz. *Benedictine*
2 tsp. lemon juice
3 oz. club soda
1 orange slice

Fill a cocktail shaker ½ full with ice. Pour in bourbon, cognac, Benedictine, and lemon juice. Give it a good shake, and strain into a highball glass ½ full of ice. Top with club soda and garnish with orange slice.

Liquor Lingo

Benedictine is an herbal, cognac-based liqueur created in the sixteenth century by French monks. It can be consumed alone or in mixed drinks.

Brown

Similar to the Bourbon Trilby, the Brown instead uses dry vermouth in equal parts to bourbon.

1½ oz. dry vermouth
1½ oz. bourbon
2 dashes orange bitters

Fill a cocktail shaker ½ full with ice. Pour in dry vermouth, bourbon, and orange bitters. Give it a good stir, and strain into a cocktail glass.

Buddy's Favorite

1½ oz. bourbon
6 oz. water

Pour bourbon and water into a highball glass. Give it a good stir.

Bunny Hug

1 oz. bourbon
1 oz. gin
1 oz. pastis
1 lemon twist

Fill a cocktail shaker ½ full with ice. Pour in bourbon, gin, and pastis. Give it a good shake, and strain into a cocktail glass. Garnish with lemon twist.

Caterpillar

2½ oz. bourbon
1 oz. white grape juice
1 dash bitters

Fill a cocktail shaker ½ full with ice. Pour in bourbon and white grape juice, and add bitters. Give it a good shake, and strain into an old-fashioned glass filled with ice.

Chapel Hill

1½ oz. bourbon
½ oz. triple sec
1 TB. lemon juice
1 orange twist

Fill a cocktail shaker ½ full with ice. Pour in bourbon, triple sec, and lemon juice. Give it a good shake, and strain into a cocktail glass. Garnish with orange twist.

Comforting Coffee

1 oz. bourbon
1 oz. Southern Comfort
1 tsp. dark crème de cacao
4 oz. hot coffee
¼ cup whipped cream

In a large coffee mug, pour in bourbon, Southern Comfort, crème de cacao, and coffee. Give it a good stir, and dollop whipped cream on top.

Creole Lady

1½ oz. bourbon
1½ oz. *Madeira*
1 tsp. grenadine
1 maraschino cherry

Fill a cocktail shaker ½ full with ice. Pour in bourbon, Madeira, and grenadine. Give it a good stir, and strain into a cocktail glass. Garnish with maraschino cherry.

Liquor Lingo

Madeira is a fortified wine that comes from the eponymous island in Portugal. It was the drink of choice for Thomas Jefferson and the rest of the founding fathers. In fact, the colonies imported ¼ of all the Madeira produced during the eighteenth century.

Dallas Texan

2 oz. bourbon
1 oz. apricot brandy
½ oz. grenadine
¾ oz. lime juice
1 *green cherry*

Fill a cocktail shaker ½ full with ice. Pour in bourbon, apricot brandy, grenadine, and lime juice. Give it a good shake, and strain into a cocktail glass. Garnish with green cherry.

Liquor Lingo

Green cherries are green-dyed garnishing cherries preserved in sugar syrup.

Down the Hatch

2 oz. bourbon
1 oz. blackberry brandy
2 dashes orange bitters

Fill a cocktail shaker ½ full with ice. Pour in bourbon and blackberry brandy, and add orange bitters. Give it a good shake, and strain into a cocktail glass.

Fancy Bourbon

2 oz. bourbon
½ oz. orange curaçao
2 dashes bitters
1 lemon twist

Fill a cocktail shaker ½ full with ice. Pour in bourbon, curaçao, and bitters. Give it a good shake, and strain into a cocktail glass. Garnish with lemon twist.

Forester

2 oz. bourbon
½ oz. cherry juice
½ oz. lemon juice
1 maraschino cherry

Fill a cocktail shaker ½ full with ice. Pour in bourbon, cherry juice, and lemon juice. Give it a good shake, and strain into an old-fashioned glass full of ice. Garnish with maraschino cherry.

Fox and Hounds

1½ oz. bourbon
½ oz. pastis
½ oz. lemon juice
¾ oz. simple syrup
1 egg white

Fill a cocktail shaker ½ full with ice. Pour in bourbon, pastis, lemon juice, simple syrup, and egg white. Give it a good shake, and strain into a cocktail glass.

Fox River

2 oz. bourbon
½ oz. white crème de cacao
2 dashes orange bitters

Fill a cocktail shaker ½ full with ice. Pour in bourbon and white crème de cacao, and add orange bitters. Give it a good shake, and strain into a cocktail glass.

Geisha

2 oz. bourbon
1 oz. sake
2 tsp. simple syrup
1½ tsp. lemon juice

Fill a cocktail shaker ½ full with ice. Pour in bourbon, sake, simple syrup, and lemon juice. Give it a good shake, and strain into a sour glass.

Hot Bourbon Toddy

4 oz. water
2 tsp. honey
1 cinnamon stick
1 lemon slice
2 oz. bourbon

Boil water in a pot. Set aside. In a coffee mug, add honey, cinnamon stick, and lemon slice. Pour hot water in the mug, add bourbon, and give it a good stir.

Huntress

1½ oz. bourbon
1 oz. cherry liqueur
1 tsp. triple sec
½ oz. heavy cream

Fill a cocktail shaker ½ full with ice. Pour in bourbon, cherry liqueur, triple sec, and heavy cream. Give it a good shake, and strain into a cocktail glass.

Indian River

2 oz. bourbon
¼ oz. raspberry liqueur
¼ oz. sweet vermouth
1 oz. grapefruit juice

Fill a cocktail shaker ½ full with ice. Pour in bourbon, raspberry liqueur, sweet vermouth, and grapefruit juice. Give it a good shake, and strain into a cocktail glass.

Jillionaire

2 oz. bourbon
½ oz. triple sec
½ tsp. grenadine
1 egg white

Fill a cocktail shaker ½ full with ice. Pour in bourbon, triple sec, grenadine, and egg white. Give it a good, vigorous shake, and strain into a cocktail glass.

Jocose Julep

6 mint leaves
1 tsp. superfine sugar
2½ oz. bourbon
½ oz. green crème de menthe
½ oz. lime juice
3 oz. club soda

Muddle mint and superfine sugar in a Collins glass and then fill the glass ¾ full with crushed ice. Fill a cocktail shaker with ice, and pour in bourbon, green crème de menthe, and lime juice. Give it a good shake, and strain into the Collins glass. Top off with club soda, and give it a good stir.

Kentucky

2 oz. bourbon
2 oz. pineapple juice

Fill a cocktail shaker with ice. Pour in bourbon and pineapple juice. Give it a good shake, and strain into a cocktail glass.

Kentucky Cocktail

2 oz. bourbon
1 oz. pineapple juice

Fill a cocktail shaker ½ full with ice. Pour in bourbon and pineapple juice. Give it a good shake, and strain into a cocktail glass.

Kentucky Colonel

2 oz. bourbon
1 oz. Benedictine
1 lemon twist

Fill a cocktail shaker ½ full with ice. Pour in bourbon and Benedictine. Give it a good shake, and strain into a cocktail glass. Garnish with lemon twist.

 Cocktail Conversation

"Formulate a society to more closely band together this group into a great nonpolitical brotherhood for the advancement of Kentucky and Kentuckians," urged Kentucky governor Flem Sampson in 1930. Since then, the Honorable Order of Kentucky Colonels has grown as an organization whose members must demonstrate leadership, strong character, and a sincere dedication to the welfare of others. How do you become one? You are nominated by a present Kentucky Colonel and the governor of the Commonwealth of Kentucky approves—if you're lucky enough, that is.

Kentucky Mule

2 oz. bourbon
4 oz. ginger ale
1 tsp. Rose's lime juice

Fill a Collins glass ¾ full with ice. Pour in bourbon, ginger ale, and Rose's lime juice. Give it a good stir.

Kentucky Orange Blossom

1½ oz. bourbon
½ oz. triple sec
1 oz. orange juice
1 lemon twist

Fill a cocktail shaker ½ full with ice. Pour in bourbon, triple sec, and orange juice. Give it a good shake, and strain into an old-fashioned glass full of ice. Garnish with lemon twist.

Klondike Cooker

½ tsp. superfine sugar
6 oz. club soda
2 oz. bourbon
1 orange twist

Dissolve sugar with a little club soda in a Collins glass. Pour in bourbon and remaining club soda. Garnish with orange twist.

Long Hot Night

2 oz. bourbon
3 oz. pineapple juice
3 oz. cranberry juice

Fill a highball glass ½ full with ice. Pour in bourbon, and stir to chill. Add pineapple juice and cranberry juice, and give it a good stir.

Louisville Stinger

2 oz. bourbon
½ oz. white crème de menthe
1 dash bitters
1 lemon twist

Fill an old-fashioned glass ½ full with ice. Pour in bourbon and white crème de menthe, and add bitters. Give it a good stir, and garnish with lemon twist.

Lynchburg Lemonade

1 oz. bourbon
1 oz. triple sec
3 oz. sour mix
Splash of lemon-lime soda
1 lemon wedge

Fill a cocktail shaker ½ full with ice. Pour in bourbon, triple sec, sour mix, and lemon-lime soda. Give it a good shake, and strain into a highball glass full of ice. Garnish with lemon wedge.

Man o' War

1½ oz. bourbon
1 oz. orange curaçao
½ oz. sweet vermouth
½ oz. lime juice
1 maraschino cherry

Fill a cocktail shaker ½ full with ice. Pour in bourbon, orange curaçao, sweet vermouth, and lime juice. Give it a good shake, and strain into a cocktail glass. Garnish with maraschino cherry.

Manhattan Bella

3 oz. bourbon
¼ tsp. *Dubonnet* Rouge
¼ tsp. sweet *vermouth*
2 dashes bitters

Fill a cocktail shaker ½ full with ice. Pour in bourbon, Dubonnet Rouge, and sweet vermouth, and add bitters. Give it a good shake, and strain into a cocktail glass.

Liquor Lingo

Dubonnet is a *quinquina* (a sweetened aperitif wine), and comes in rouge (or red), which is the sweetest, and blonde, which is semi-sweet. **Vermouth** is a fortified wine that can be either sweet (usually brownish-red) or dry (clear).

Midnight Cowboy

2 oz. bourbon
1 oz. dark rum
½ oz. heavy cream

Fill a cocktail shaker ½ full with ice. Pour in bourbon, dark rum, and heavy cream. Give it a good shake, and strain into a cocktail glass.

Mint Julep

1 tsp. superfine sugar
6 fresh mint leaves, stems removed
2 tsp. water
3 oz. bourbon
1 mint sprig

In a Collins glass, muddle sugar, mint leaves, and water. Fill the glass with crushed ice, pour in bourbon, and give it a good stir. Garnish with mint sprig.

Cocktail Conversation

A feud regarding where the mint julep originated—Kentucky or Virginia—has raged since the eighteenth century, each state presenting convincing evidence that they possess the rights to the julep's roots. Regardless of what side of the state line you're on, you'd be remiss to let a Kentucky Derby Day go by without one.

Narragansett

2 oz. bourbon
¾ oz. sweet vermouth
¼ oz. *anisette*
1 lemon twist

Fill an old-fashioned glass ¾ full with ice. Pour in bourbon, sweet vermouth, and anisette. Give it a good stir. Garnish with lemon twist.

Liquor Lingo

Anisette is a clear, Italian, licorice-flavored liquor made from anise seeds.

Nevins

2 oz. bourbon
½ oz. apricot brandy
1 oz. orange juice
1 tsp. lemon juice
2 dashes bitters

Fill a cocktail shaker ½ full with ice. Pour in bourbon, apricot brandy, orange juice, and lemon juice, and add bitters. Give it a good shake, and strain into a highball glass full of ice.

New Orleans

1½ oz. bourbon
½ oz. pastis
1 dash orange bitters
3 dashes bitters

Fill a cocktail shaker ½ full with ice. Pour in bourbon and pastis, and add orange bitters and regular bitters. Give it a good shake, and strain into an old-fashioned glass.

Nocturnal

In some areas, a Nocturnal is also known as a Philly Special.

2 oz. bourbon
1 oz. dark crème de cacao
½ oz. heavy cream

Fill a cocktail shaker ½ full with ice. Pour in bourbon, dark crème de cacao, and heavy cream. Give it a good shake, and strain into an old-fashioned glass full of ice.

Oh Henry

1½ oz. bourbon
1 oz. Benedictine
½ oz. ginger ale
1 maraschino cherry

Fill a cocktail shaker ½ full with ice. Pour in bourbon, Benedictine, and ginger ale. Give it a good stir, and strain into a cocktail glass. Garnish with maraschino cherry.

Old Pal

1 oz. bourbon
1 oz. dry vermouth
1 oz. *Campari*

Fill a cocktail shaker ½ full with ice. Pour in bourbon, dry vermouth, and Campari. Give it a good shake, and strain into a cocktail glass.

Liquor Lingo

Campari—also known as Campari bitters—is a slightly bitter herbal Italian aperitif. It contains 24 percent alcohol and is often used as an ingredient in various classic cocktails such as the Negroni or the Americano.

The Peg

2 oz. bourbon
4 oz. cola
1 TB. lime juice
1 lime wedge

Fill a Collins glass ¾ full with crushed ice. Pour in bourbon, cola, and lime juice. Give it a good stir, and garnish with lime wedge.

Presbyterian

2 oz. bourbon
2 oz. ginger ale
3 oz. club soda
1 lemon twist

Fill a highball glass ¾ full with ice.
Pour in bourbon, ginger ale, and club
soda. Give it a good stir, and garnish
with lemon twist.

Quickie

1 oz. bourbon
1 oz. light rum
1 tsp. triple sec

Fill a cocktail shaker ½ full with ice.
Pour in bourbon, rum, and triple sec.
Give it a good stir, and strain into a
cocktail glass.

Ragged Company

2 oz. bourbon
½ oz. sweet vermouth
1 tsp. Benedictine
2 dashes bitters
1 lemon twist

Fill a cocktail shaker ½ full with ice.
Pour in bourbon, sweet vermouth, and
Benedictine, and add bitters. Give it a
good stir, and strain into a cocktail
glass. Garnish with lemon twist.

Red Raider

2 oz. bourbon
1 oz. triple sec
1 tsp. lemon juice
1 dash grenadine

Fill a cocktail shaker ½ full with ice.
Pour in bourbon, triple sec, lemon
juice, and grenadine. Give it a good
shake, and strain into a cocktail glass.

Riprock

2 oz. bourbon
2 oz. orange juice

Fill a cocktail shaker ½ full with ice.
Pour in bourbon and orange juice.
Give it a good shake, and strain into
a cocktail glass.

Robicheaux

2 oz. bourbon
1 oz. lime juice
1 tsp. cherry juice
3 oz. cola
1 maraschino cherry

Fill a cocktail shaker ½ full with ice.
Pour in bourbon, lime juice, and
cherry juice. Give it a good shake, and
strain into a highball glass ¾ full of
crushed ice. Top with cola and garnish
with maraschino cherry.

Santa Barbara

2½ oz. bourbon
½ oz. apricot brandy
1 oz. grapefruit juice
¼ tsp. sugar

Fill a cocktail shaker ½ full with ice. Pour in bourbon, apricot brandy, and grapefruit juice, and add sugar. Give it a good shake, and strain into a cocktail glass.

Sazarec

1 tsp. superfine sugar or 1 sugar cube
2 dashes bitters (preferably Peychaud)
2 oz. bourbon
1 tsp. pastis
1 lemon twist

Add sugar and bitters in a cocktail shaker. Pour in bourbon, and give it a good stir until sugar is dissolved. Pour pastis into an old-fashioned glass full of ice, and add in bourbon mixture. Garnish with lemon twist.

Cocktail Conversation

Some claim the early derivation of the Sazarec to be the first cocktail invented. This tidbit is most certainly up for debate, but one thing *is* true: the drink was born in that lovely city by the river, New Orleans, at the Sazarec Coffee House, now known as just Sazarec House, where you can still go to get the original version (well, almost original—one original ingredient, absinthe, was outlawed in the eighteenth century, so now we substitute pastis).

Soul Kiss Cocktail

1 oz. bourbon
1 oz. dry vermouth
¾ oz. Dubonnet
2 tsp. orange juice

Fill a cocktail shaker ½ full with ice. Pour in bourbon, dry vermouth, Dubonnet, and orange juice. Give it a good shake, and strain into a cocktail glass.

Stirrup

2½ oz. bourbon
1½ oz. orange juice
2 dashes bitters
1 lemon twist

Fill a cocktail shaker ½ full with ice. Pour in bourbon and orange juice, and add bitters. Give it a good shake, and strain into a cocktail glass. Garnish with lemon twist.

Trilby

2 oz. bourbon
1 oz. sweet vermouth
2 dashes orange bitters

Fill a cocktail shaker ½ full with ice. Pour in bourbon and sweet vermouth, and add orange bitters. Give it a good stir, and strain into a cocktail glass.

Trolley

2 oz. bourbon
1½ oz. pineapple juice
1½ oz. cranberry juice

Fill a highball glass with ice. Pour in bourbon, pineapple juice, and cranberry juice. Give it a good stir.

Up to Date

1½ oz. bourbon
1½ oz. sweet vermouth
½ oz. Grand Marnier
1 tsp. lemon juice
1 dash bitters
1 lemon twist

Fill a cocktail shaker ½ full with ice. Pour in bourbon, sweet vermouth, Grand Marnier, and lemon juice, and add bitters. Give it a good shake, and strain into a cocktail glass. Garnish with lemon twist.

Velvet Presley

3 oz. bourbon
2 oz. chocolate milk

Fill a highball glass ½ full with ice. Pour in bourbon and chocolate milk. Give it a good stir.

Villa Park

3 oz. bourbon
1 oz. pineapple juice
1 oz. orange juice

Fill a cocktail shaker ½ full with ice. Pour in bourbon, pineapple juice, and orange juice. Give it a good shake, and strain into a highball glass full of ice.

Waldorf

1½ oz. bourbon
¾ oz. pastis
½ oz. sweet vermouth
1 dash Angostura bitters

Fill a cocktail shaker ½ full with ice. Pour in bourbon, pastis, and sweet vermouth, and add bitters. Give it a good stir, and strain into a cocktail glass.

Whirlaway

2 oz. bourbon
1 oz. orange curaçao
1 dash bitters
2 oz. club soda
1 maraschino cherry

Fill a cocktail shaker ½ full with ice. Pour in bourbon and orange curaçao, and add bitters. Give it a good shake, and strain into an old-fashioned glass ½ full of ice. Add in club soda, and garnish with maraschino cherry.

Chapter 6

Gin

A good heavy book holds you down. It's an anchor that keeps you from getting up and having another gin and tonic.

—Roy Blount Jr.

Abbey Cocktail

2 oz. gin
1 oz. orange juice
1 dash orange bitters
1 maraschino cherry

Fill a cocktail shaker ½ full with ice. Pour in gin and orange juice, and add orange bitters. Give it a good shake, and strain into a cocktail glass. Garnish with maraschino cherry.

Alaska

2 oz. gin
1 oz. yellow Chartreuse
2 dashes orange bitters
1 lemon twist

Fill a cocktail shaker ½ full with ice. Pour in gin and yellow Chartreuse, and add orange bitters. Give it a good stir, and strain into a cocktail glass. Garnish with lemon twist.

Alexander's Sister

1½ oz. gin
1 oz. green crème de menthe
1 oz. heavy cream
1 cucumber slice

Fill a cocktail shaker ½ full with ice. Pour in gin, green crème de menthe, and heavy cream. Give it a good shake, and strain into a cocktail glass. Garnish with cucumber slice.

Angel Face

2 oz. gin
¾ oz. apricot brandy
¾ oz. apple brandy

Fill a cocktail shaker ½ full with ice. Pour in gin, apricot brandy, and apple brandy. Give it a good shake, and strain into a cocktail glass.

Arthur Tompkins

2 oz. gin
½ oz. Grand Marnier
2 tsp. lemon juice
1 lemon twist

Fill a cocktail shaker ½ full with ice. Pour in gin, Grand Marnier, and lemon juice. Give it a good shake, and strain into a sour glass. Garnish with lemon twist.

Artillery

2 oz. gin
½ oz. sweet vermouth
1 dash bitters

Fill a cocktail shaker ½ full with ice. Pour in gin and vermouth, and add bitters. Give it a good stir, and strain into a cocktail glass.

Aviation

2 oz. gin
1 tsp. cherry brandy
¾ oz. lemon juice

Fill a cocktail shaker ½ full with ice. Pour in gin, cherry brandy, and lemon juice. Give it a good shake, and strain into a cocktail glass.

Barbary Coast

½ oz. gin
½ oz. light rum
½ oz. Scotch whisky
½ oz. crème de cacao
½ oz. light cream

Fill a cocktail shaker ½ full with ice. Pour in gin, light rum, Scotch whisky, crème de cacao, and light cream. Give it a good shake, and strain into a cocktail glass.

Barking Dog

2 oz. gin
¾ oz. sweet vermouth
¾ oz. dry vermouth
1 tsp. strega
1 green cherry

Fill a cocktail shaker ½ full with ice. Pour in gin, sweet vermouth, dry vermouth, and strega. Give it a good shake, and strain into a cocktail glass. Garnish with green cherry.

Beauty Spot

1½ oz. gin
½ oz. sweet vermouth
½ oz. dry vermouth
¼ oz. orange juice
1 tsp. grenadine

Fill a cocktail shaker ½ full with ice. Pour in gin, sweet vermouth, dry vermouth, and orange juice. Give it a good shake, and strain into a cocktail glass. Drip grenadine into center of cocktail.

Belles of St. Mary's

1½ oz. gin
1 oz. triple sec
1 oz. apricot brandy
2 tsp. lemon juice

Fill a cocktail shaker ½ full with ice. Pour in gin, triple sec, apricot brandy, and lemon juice. Give it a good shake, and strain into a cocktail glass.

Bennett Cocktail

1½ oz. gin
½ oz. lime juice
¾ oz. simple syrup
1 dash orange bitters

Fill a cocktail shaker ½ full with ice. Pour in gin, lime juice, and simple syrup, and add orange bitters. Give it a good shake, and strain into a cocktail glass.

Bermuda Highball

1 oz. gin
1 oz. brandy
½ oz. dry vermouth
4 oz. ginger ale

Fill a highball glass ½ full with ice. Pour in gin, brandy, and dry vermouth. Fill to the top with ginger ale, and give it a good stir.

Bermuda Rose

2 oz. gin
¼ oz. apricot brandy
1 tsp. lime juice
1 tsp. grenadine

Fill a cocktail shaker ½ full with ice. Pour in gin, apricot brandy, lime juice, and grenadine. Give it a good shake, and strain into a cocktail glass.

Bernardo

2 oz. gin
½ oz. triple sec
1 TB. lemon juice
2 dashes bitters
1 lemon twist

Fill a cocktail shaker ½ full with ice. Pour in gin, triple sec, and lemon juice, and add bitters. Give it a good shake, and strain into a cocktail glass. Garnish with lemon twist.

Bitch on Wheels

2 oz. gin
½ oz. dry vermouth
½ oz. crème de menthe
1 tsp. pastis

Fill a cocktail shaker ½ full with ice. Pour in gin, dry vermouth, crème de menthe, and pastis. Give it a good stir, and strain into a cocktail glass.

Blue Cowboy

2 oz. gin
½ oz. blue curaçao

Fill a cocktail shaker ½ full with ice. Pour in gin and blue curaçao. Give it a good stir, and strain into a cocktail glass.

Blue Devil

2 oz. gin
½ oz. *maraschino liqueur*
½ oz. *parfait amour*
1 oz. lime juice
1 maraschino cherry

Fill a cocktail shaker ½ full with ice. Pour in gin, maraschino liqueur, parfait amour, and lime juice. Give it a good shake, and strain into a cocktail glass. Garnish with maraschino cherry.

Liquor Lingo

Maraschino liqueur is a neutral-spirit-based liqueur that gets its flavor from marasca cherries. **Parfait amour** is a vanilla-flavored liqueur with hints of marshmallow and citrus. You can use it as a substitute for liqueur de violette or crème de violette, which can be difficult to find.

Blue Flyer

2 oz. gin
½ oz. blue curaçao
½ oz. lime juice

Fill a cocktail shaker ½ full with ice. Pour in gin, curaçao, and lime juice. Give it a good shake, and strain into a cocktail glass.

Blue Moon

2 oz. gin
½ oz. blue curaçao
1 tsp. dry vermouth

Fill a cocktail shaker ½ full with ice. Pour in gin, blue curaçao, and dry vermouth. Give it a good shake, and strain into a cocktail glass.

Bluebird

2 oz. gin
½ oz. blue curaçao
2 dashes bitters
1 lemon twist

Fill a cocktail shaker ½ full with ice. Pour in gin and blue curaçao, and add bitters. Give it a good stir, and strain into a cocktail glass. Garnish with lemon twist.

Boomerang

2 oz. gin
½ oz. dry vermouth
1 tsp. maraschino liqueur
2 dashes orange bitters
1 lemon twist

Fill a cocktail shaker ½ full with ice. Pour in gin, dry vermouth, and maraschino liqueur, and add orange bitters. Give it a good shake, and strain into a cocktail glass. Garnish with lemon twist.

Boxcar

1½ oz. gin
½ oz. triple sec
¼ oz. grenadine
½ oz. lime juice
1 egg white

Fill a cocktail shaker ½ full with ice. Pour in gin, triple sec, grenadine, lime juice, and egg white. Give it a good, vigorous shake, and strain into a cocktail glass.

Bronx Cocktail

Legend has it that mixologist Johnny Solon of New York's Waldorf-Astoria Bar created and named the Bronx Cocktail after a visit to the Bronx Zoo.

2 oz. gin
1 oz. orange juice
1 tsp. lemon juice
1 tsp. dry vermouth
1 tsp. sweet vermouth
1 orange slice

Fill a cocktail shaker ½ full with ice. Pour in gin, orange juice, lemon juice, dry vermouth, and sweet vermouth. Give it a good shake, and strain into a cocktail glass. Garnish with orange slice.

Bronx River Cocktail

2 oz. gin
½ oz. sweet vermouth
¼ oz. lemon juice
1 tsp. simple syrup
1 lemon twist

Fill a cocktail shaker ½ full with ice. Pour in gin, sweet vermouth, lemon juice, and simple syrup. Give it a good shake, and strain into a cocktail glass. Garnish with lemon twist.

Bronx Silver

1½ oz. gin
2 tsp. dry vermouth
¼ oz. orange juice
1 egg white

Fill a cocktail shaker ½ full with ice. Pour in gin, dry vermouth, orange juice, and egg white. Give it a good shake, and strain into a sour glass.

Cabaret

2 oz. gin
¼ oz. dry vermouth
¼ oz. Benedictine
2 dashes bitters
1 maraschino cherry

Fill a cocktail shaker ½ full with ice. Pour in gin, dry vermouth, and Benedictine, and add bitters. Give it a good shake, and strain into a cocktail glass. Garnish with maraschino cherry.

Café de Paris

2 oz. gin
½ oz. pastis
½ oz. heavy cream
1 egg white

Fill a cocktail shaker ½ full with ice. Pour in gin, pastis, heavy cream, and egg white. Give it a good shake, and strain into a sour glass full of ice.

Campobello

2 oz. gin
1 oz. sweet vermouth
1 oz. Campari

Fill a cocktail shaker ½ full with ice. Pour in gin, sweet vermouth, and Campari. Give it a good shake, and strain into a cocktail glass.

Caprice

2½ oz. gin
½ oz. Benedictine
½ oz. dry vermouth
2 dashes orange bitters
1 lemon twist

Fill a cocktail shaker ½ full with ice. Pour in gin, Benedictine, and dry vermouth, and add orange bitters. Give it a good stir, and strain into a cocktail glass. Garnish with lemon twist.

Captain's Table

2 oz. gin
½ oz. Campari
1 tsp. grenadine
1 oz. orange juice
4 oz. ginger ale
1 maraschino cherry

Fill a cocktail shaker ½ full with ice. Pour in gin, Campari, grenadine, and orange juice. Give it a good shake, and strain into a Collins glass full of ice. Pour in ginger ale, and garnish with maraschino cherry.

Caruso

2 oz. gin 1 oz. dry vermouth 1 oz. crème de menthe	Fill a cocktail shaker ½ full with ice. Pour in gin, dry vermouth, and crème de menthe. Give it a good stir, and strain into a cocktail glass.

Casino

2 oz. gin 1 tsp. maraschino liqueur 1 tsp. lemon juice 1 dash orange bitters 1 maraschino cherry	Fill a cocktail shaker ½ full with ice. Pour in gin, maraschino liqueur, and lemon juice, and add orange bitters. Give it a good shake, and strain into a cocktail glass. Garnish with maraschino cherry.

Casino Royale

2 oz. gin 1 tsp. maraschino liqueur ½ oz. lemon juice 1 dash orange bitters 1 egg yolk 1 orange slice	Fill a cocktail shaker ½ full with ice. Pour in gin, maraschino liqueur, and lemon juice, and add orange bitters and egg yolk. Give it a very good, vigorous shake, and strain into a cocktail glass. Garnish with orange slice.

Chelsea Hotel

2 oz. gin ½ oz. triple sec 2 tsp. lemon juice	Fill a cocktail shaker ½ full with ice. Pour in gin, triple sec, and lemon juice. Give it a good shake, and strain into a cocktail glass.

Chelsea Sidecar

1 oz. gin 1 oz. triple sec Juice from ¼ lemon	Fill a cocktail shaker ½ full with ice. Pour in gin, triple sec, and lemon juice. Give it a good shake, and strain into a cocktail glass.

Claridge

1 oz. gin 1 oz. sweet vermouth ½ oz. apricot brandy ½ oz. triple sec	Fill a cocktail shaker ½ full with ice. Pour in gin, sweet vermouth, apricot brandy, and triple sec. Give it a good shake, and strain into a cocktail glass.

Clover Club

2 oz. gin
2 tsp. grenadine
Juice of ½ lemon
1 egg white

Fill a cocktail shaker ½ full with ice. Pour in gin, grenadine, lemon juice, and egg white. Give it a good shake, and strain into a cocktail glass.

Clover Leaf

2 oz. gin
2 tsp. grenadine
Juice of ½ lemon
1 egg white
1 mint sprig

Fill a cocktail shaker ½ full with ice. Pour in gin, grenadine, lemon juice, and egg white. Give it a good shake, and strain into a cocktail glass. Garnish with mint sprig.

Come Again

3 oz. gin
2 dashes peach bitters
1 mint sprig

Fill a cocktail shaker ½ full with ice. Pour in gin, and add peach bitters. Give it a good stir, and strain into a cocktail glass. Garnish with mint sprig.

Confirmed Bachelor

2 oz. gin
1 tsp. grenadine
½ tsp. Rose's lime juice
1 egg white

Fill a cocktail shaker ½ full with ice. Pour in gin, grenadine, Rose's lime juice, and egg white. Give it a good shake, and strain into a cocktail glass.

Crimson Sunset

2 oz. gin
2 tsp. lemon juice
½ tsp. grenadine
½ oz. tawny port

Fill a cocktail shaker ½ full with ice. Pour in gin and lemon juice. Give it a good shake, and strain into a cocktail glass. Drip grenadine into center of cocktail, and float tawny port on top.

Damn the Weather

1½ oz. gin
1 TB. sweet vermouth
1 tsp. triple sec
1 TB. orange juice

Fill a cocktail shaker ½ full with ice. Pour in gin, sweet vermouth, triple sec, and orange juice. Give it a good shake, and strain into a cocktail glass.

Darb Cocktail

1 oz. gin
1 oz. dry vermouth
1 oz. apricot brandy
2 tsp. lemon juice

Fill a cocktail shaker ½ full with ice. Pour in gin, dry vermouth, apricot brandy, and lemon juice. Give it a good shake, and strain into a cocktail glass.

Darby

2 oz. gin
½ oz. grapefruit juice
½ oz. lime juice
¾ oz. simple syrup
1 TB. club soda
1 maraschino cherry

Fill a cocktail shaker ½ full with ice. Pour in gin, grapefruit juice, lime juice, and simple syrup. Give it a good shake, and strain into a cocktail glass. Add club soda, and garnish with maraschino cherry.

Delmonico Cocktail

1 oz. gin
½ oz. dry vermouth
½ oz. sweet vermouth
½ oz. brandy
1 dash bitters
1 lemon peel

Fill a cocktail shaker ½ full with ice. Pour in gin, dry vermouth, sweet vermouth, and brandy, and add bitters. Give it a good shake, and strain into a Delmonico glass. Garnish with lemon peel.

Dempsey

1 oz. gin
1 oz. apple brandy
1 tsp. pastis
½ tsp. grenadine

Fill a cocktail shaker ½ full with ice. Pour in gin, apple brandy, pastis, and grenadine. Give it a good shake, and strain into a cocktail glass.

Diamond Fizz

2 oz. gin
¼ oz. lemon juice
½ oz. simple syrup
2 oz. champagne

Fill a cocktail shaker ½ full with ice. Pour in gin, lemon juice, and simple syrup. Give it a good shake, and strain into a highball glass with a few ice cubes. Fill to the top with champagne.

Diamond Head

2 oz. gin
½ oz. apricot brandy
½ oz. lemon juice
1 oz. simple syrup
½ egg white

Fill a cocktail shaker ½ full with ice. Pour in gin, apricot brandy, lemon juice, simple syrup, and egg white. Give it a good, vigorous shake, and strain into a cocktail glass.

Dirty Dick's Downfall

2 oz. gin
½ oz. dry vermouth
½ oz. Campari
1 lemon twist

Fill a cocktail shaker ½ full with ice. Pour in gin, dry vermouth, and Campari. Give it a good stir, and strain into a cocktail glass. Garnish with lemon twist.

Dirty Martini

3 oz. gin
1 dash dry vermouth
1 TB. olive juice
2 cocktail olives

Fill a cocktail shaker ½ full with ice. Pour in gin, dry vermouth, and olive juice. Give it a good stir, and strain into a cocktail glass. Garnish with cocktail olives.

Dragonfly

2 oz. gin
4 oz. ginger ale
1 lime wedge

Fill a highball glass ¾ full with ice. Pour in gin and ginger ale. Give a good stir, and garnish with lime wedge.

Dreyer's G&T

Sometimes I wonder if my very charming and handsome friend Chris Dreyer was not transported from a more classic and genteel time. His delicious version of a G&T adds an inventive twist to an old favorite: Key limes. Dreyer recommends using Tanqueray gin. "My gin and tonic isn't really all that special," he humbly tells me. "It's really quite simple." Spoken like a bona fide connoisseur of good taste.

2 Key limes, cut into 8 wedges
1½ oz. gin
4 oz. tonic

Squeeze juice of limes into a highball glass, drop in spent lime wedges, and muddle wedges with juice. Add 3 ice cubes. Pour in gin and add tonic. Give it a good stir.

Earthquake

1 oz. gin
1 oz. whisky
1 oz. pastis

Fill a cocktail shaker ½ full with ice. Pour in gin, whiskey, and pastis. Give it a good shake, and strain into a cocktail glass.

Emerald Forest

2 oz. gin
1 tsp. green crème de menthe
1 tsp. white crème de menthe

Fill a cocktail shaker ½ full with crushed ice. Pour in gin, green crème de menthe, and white crème de menthe. Give it a good shake, and strain into a cocktail glass.

Emerald Isle

2 oz. gin
1 tsp. green crème de menthe
2 dashes bitters

Fill a cocktail shaker ½ full with ice. Pour in gin and green crème de menthe, and add bitters. Give it a good stir, and strain into a cocktail glass.

Emerald Martini

3 oz. gin
½ oz. dry vermouth
2 tsp. green Chartreuse
1 lime twist

Fill a cocktail shaker ½ full with ice. Pour in gin, dry vermouth, and green Chartreuse. Give it a good stir, and strain into a cocktail glass. Garnish with lime twist.

Emerson

2 oz. gin
1 oz. sweet vermouth
1 tsp. maraschino liqueur
2 tsp. lime juice

Fill a cocktail shaker ½ full with ice. Pour in gin, sweet vermouth, maraschino liqueur, and lime juice. Give it a good shake, and strain into a cocktail glass.

English Rose

2 oz. gin
1 oz. dry vermouth
1 oz. apricot brandy
1 tsp. grenadine
½ tsp. lemon juice
1 maraschino cherry

Fill a cocktail shaker ½ full with ice. Pour in gin, dry vermouth, apricot brandy, grenadine, and lemon juice. Give it a good shake, and strain into a cocktail glass. Garnish with maraschino cherry.

European

1 oz. gin
½ oz. cream sherry
½ oz. Dubonnet Rouge
½ oz. dry vermouth
½ tsp. Grand Marnier
1 maraschino cherry

Fill an old-fashioned glass ¾ full with ice. Pour in gin, cream sherry, Dubonnet Rouge, dry vermouth, and Grand Marnier. Give it a good stir, and garnish with maraschino cherry.

Fairy Bell

2 oz. gin
1 oz. apricot brandy
¼ oz. grenadine
1 egg white

Fill a cocktail shaker ½ full with ice. Pour in gin, apricot brandy, grenadine, and egg white. Give it a good, vigorous shake, and strain into a cocktail glass.

Fallen Angel

2 oz. gin
½ tsp. white crème de menthe
¼ oz. lemon juice
1 dash bitters
1 maraschino cherry

Fill a cocktail shaker ½ full with ice. Pour in gin, white crème de menthe, and lemon juice, and add bitters. Give it a good shake, and strain into a cocktail glass. Garnish with maraschino cherry.

Fare-Thee-Well

2 oz. gin
½ oz. dry vermouth
1 tsp. sweet vermouth
1 tsp. triple sec

Fill a cocktail shaker ½ full with ice. Pour in gin, dry vermouth, sweet vermouth, and triple sec. Give it a good shake, and strain into a cocktail glass.

Farmer Giles

2 oz. gin
½ oz. dry vermouth
½ oz. sweet vermouth
2 dashes bitters
1 lemon twist

Fill a cocktail shaker ½ full with ice. Pour in gin, dry vermouth, and sweet vermouth, and add bitters. Give it a good stir, and strain into a cocktail glass. Garnish with lemon twist.

Fastlap

2 oz. gin
½ oz. dry vermouth
½ tsp. grenadine
1 oz. orange juice

Fill a cocktail shaker ½ full with ice. Pour in gin, dry vermouth, grenadine, and orange juice. Give it a good shake, and strain into an old-fashioned glass full of ice.

Fat Face

1½ oz. gin
½ oz. apricot brandy
1 tsp. grenadine
1 egg white

Fill a cocktail shaker ½ full with ice.
Pour in gin, apricot brandy, and grenadine, and add egg white. Give it a
good shake, and strain into a sour glass
full of ice.

Favorite

1 oz. gin
1 oz. dry vermouth
1 oz. apricot brandy
½ tsp. lemon juice

Fill a cocktail shaker ½ full with ice.
Pour in gin, dry vermouth, apricot
brandy, and lemon juice. Give it a
good shake, and strain into an old-
fashioned glass full of ice.

Fibber McGee

2 oz. gin
½ oz. grapefruit juice
½ oz. sweet vermouth
2 dashes bitters

Fill a cocktail shaker ½ full with ice.
Pour in gin, grapefruit juice, and sweet
vermouth, and add bitters. Give it a
good stir, and strain into a cocktail
glass.

Fifty-Fifty

1½ oz. gin
1½ oz. dry vermouth
3 cocktail olives

Fill a cocktail shaker ½ full with ice.
Pour in gin and dry vermouth. Give it
a good stir, and strain into a cocktail
glass. Garnish with olives skewered on
a toothpick.

Fine and Dandy

2 oz. gin
½ oz. triple sec
½ oz. lemon juice
1 dash bitters
1 maraschino cherry

Fill a cocktail shaker ½ full with ice.
Pour in gin, triple sec, and lemon
juice, and add bitters. Give it a good
shake, and strain into a cocktail glass.
Garnish with maraschino cherry.

Fino Martini

2½ oz. gin
1½ oz. fino sherry
1 lemon twist

Fill a cocktail shaker ½ full with ice.
Pour in gin and fino sherry. Give it a
good stir, and strain into a cocktail
glass. Garnish with lemon twist.

Flamingo

2 oz. gin
¾ oz. brandy
1 tsp. grenadine
¾ oz. lime juice

Fill a cocktail shaker ½ full with ice. Pour in gin, brandy, grenadine, and lime juice. Give it a good shake, and strain into a cocktail glass.

Fleet Street

1½ oz. gin
½ oz. sweet vermouth
1 tsp. dry vermouth
1 tsp. triple sec
1 tsp. lemon juice

Fill a cocktail shaker ½ full with ice. Pour in gin, sweet vermouth, dry vermouth, triple sec, and lemon juice. Give it a good stir, and strain into a cocktail glass.

Florida

½ oz. gin
1½ tsp. *kirschwasser*
1½ tsp. triple sec
1 oz. orange juice
1 tsp. lemon juice

Fill a cocktail shaker ½ full with ice. Pour in gin, kirschwasser, triple sec, orange juice, and lemon juice. Give it a good shake, and strain into a cocktail glass.

Liquor Lingo

Kirschwasser is an unaged cherry brandy usually made in Germany, France, and Switzerland, although it is also produced in the United States.

Flying Dutchman

2 oz. gin
½ oz. triple sec

Fill an old-fashioned glass ¾ full with ice. Pour in gin and triple sec. Give it a good stir.

Fog Horn

2 oz. gin
Juice of ½ lime
Ginger ale
1 lime wedge

Fill a highball glass ¾ full with ice. Pour in gin and lime juice. Fill to the top with ginger ale. Give it a good stir, and garnish with lime wedge.

Frankenjack Cocktail

1 oz. gin
¾ oz. dry vermouth
½ oz. apricot brandy
1 tsp. triple sec
1 maraschino cherry

Fill a cocktail shaker ½ full with ice. Pour in gin, dry vermouth, apricot brandy, and triple sec. Give it a good shake, and strain into a cocktail glass. Garnish with maraschino cherry.

French "75" (Gin)

2 oz. gin
1½ oz. lemon juice
2 tsp. superfine sugar
4 oz. champagne
1 orange slice
1 maraschino cherry

Fill a cocktail shaker ½ full with ice. Pour in gin and lemon juice, and add superfine sugar. Give it a good shake, and strain into a Collins glass. Fill to the top with champagne, and garnish with orange slice and maraschino cherry.

Froth Blower

2 oz. gin
1 tsp. grenadine
1 egg white

Fill a cocktail shaker ½ full with ice. Pour in gin, grenadine, and egg white. Give it a good shake, and strain into a cocktail glass.

Gent of the Jury

2 oz. gin
½ tsp. dry vermouth
3 cocktail onions

Fill a cocktail shaker ½ full with ice. Pour in gin and dry vermouth. Give it a good stir, and strain into a cocktail glass. Garnish with cocktail onions.

Gentleman's Club

1½ oz. gin
1 oz. brandy
1 oz. sweet vermouth
1 oz. club soda

Fill an old-fashioned glass ¾ full with ice. Pour in gin, brandy, sweet vermouth, and club soda. Give it a good stir.

Gibson

As with many classic cocktails, the Gibson has dueling stories concerning its origins. Some say it was named for boxing promoter Billie Gibson; some offer that it was named for turn-of-the-twentieth-century illustrator Charles Gibson. Whichever story you believe, don't forget the cocktail onion when you drink it!

3 oz. gin	Fill a cocktail shaker ½ full with ice. Pour in gin, and add dry vermouth. Give it a good stir, and strain into a cocktail glass. Garnish with cocktail onion.
1 dash dry vermouth	
1 cocktail onion	

Gilroy

1½ oz. gin	Fill a cocktail shaker ½ full with ice. Pour in gin, cherry brandy, dry vermouth, and lemon juice, and add orange bitters. Give it a good shake, and strain into a cocktail glass.
1 oz. cherry brandy	
½ oz. dry vermouth	
¼ oz. lemon juice	
1 dash orange bitters	

Gimlet

2 oz. gin	Fill a cocktail shaker ½ full with ice. Pour in gin and lime juice. Give it a good shake, and strain into an old-fashioned glass full of ice. Garnish with lime wedge.
¼ oz. Rose's lime juice	
1 lime wedge	

Gin Alexander

2 oz. gin	Fill a cocktail shaker ½ full with ice. Pour in gin, white crème de cacao, and heavy cream. Give it a good shake, and strain into a cocktail glass. Garnish with grated nutmeg.
1 oz. white crème de cacao	
½ oz. heavy cream	
Grated nutmeg	

Gin and Bitter Lemon

2 oz. gin	Fill a cocktail shaker ½ full with ice. Pour in gin, lemon juice, and superfine sugar. Give it a good shake, and strain into a highball glass ¾ full of ice. Pour in tonic water.
½ oz. lemon juice	
½ tsp. superfine sugar	
4 oz. tonic water	

Gin and Pink

2 oz. gin
5 oz. tonic water
2 dashes bitters
1 lemon twist

Fill a highball glass ¾ full with ice. Pour in gin and tonic water, and add bitters. Give it a good stir. Garnish with lemon twist.

Gin and Sin

2 oz. gin
2 tsp. grenadine
1 oz. orange juice
½ oz. lemon juice
1 lemon twist

Fill a cocktail shaker ½ full with ice. Pour in gin, grenadine, orange juice, and lemon juice. Give it a good shake, and strain into a cocktail glass. Garnish with lemon twist.

Gin and Tonic

2 oz. gin
4 oz. tonic water
1 lime wedge

Fill a highball glass ¾ full with ice. Pour in gin and tonic water. Give it a good stir, and garnish with lemon wedge.

Gin Buck

2 oz. gin
¼ oz. lemon juice
4 oz. ginger ale
1 lemon twist

Fill a highball glass ¾ full with ice. Pour in gin, lemon juice, and ginger ale. Give it a good stir, and garnish with lemon twist.

Gin-Cassis

2 oz. gin
¾ oz. crème de cassis
½ oz. lemon juice

Fill a cocktail shaker ½ full with ice. Pour in gin, crème de cassis, and lemon juice. Give it a good shake, and strain into an old-fashioned glass full of ice.

Gin-Cassis Fizz

2 oz. gin
½ oz. lemon juice
1 oz. simple syrup
1 oz. club soda
½ oz. crème de cassis

Fill a cocktail shaker ½ full with ice. Pour in gin, lemon juice, and simple syrup. Give it a good shake, and strain into a Delmonico glass. Pour in club soda and then drip crème de cassis into center of cocktail.

Gin Cobbler

1 tsp. superfine sugar
3 oz. club soda
2 oz. gin
1 lemon slice
1 orange slice
1 maraschino cherry

Dissolve sugar in club soda in an old-fashioned glass. Fill the glass ¾ full with crushed ice. Pour in gin, and give it a good stir. Garnish with lemon slice, orange slice, and maraschino cherry.

Gin Cooler

2 oz. gin
4 oz. lemon-lime soda
1 lime wedge

Fill a highball glass ¾ full with ice. Pour in gin and lemon-lime soda. Give it a good stir, and garnish with lime wedge.

Gin Daisy

2 oz. gin
½ tsp. grenadine
1 oz. lemon juice
1 oz. simple syrup
1 orange slice
1 maraschino cherry

Fill a cocktail shaker with ice. Pour in gin, grenadine, lemon juice, and simple syrup. Give it a good shake, and strain into an old-fashioned glass filled ¾ full of ice. Garnish with orange slice and maraschino cherry.

Gin Fix

2 oz. gin
¾ oz. lemon juice
1 oz. simple syrup
1 lemon slice
1 maraschino cherry

Fill a cocktail shaker with ice. Pour in gin, lemon juice, and simple syrup. Give it a good shake, and strain into a highball glass full of ice. Garnish with lemon slice and maraschino cherry.

Gin Rickey

2 oz. gin
½ oz. lime juice
1 tsp. simple syrup
4 oz. club soda
1 lime wedge

Fill a cocktail shaker ½ full with ice. Pour in gin, lime juice, and simple syrup. Give it a good shake, and strain into a highball glass full of ice. Pour in club soda, and garnish with lime wedge.

Gin Sangaree

2 oz. gin
1 tsp. simple syrup
2 oz. club soda
½ oz. tawny port
1 lemon twist
½ tsp. grated nutmeg

Fill an old-fashioned glass ¾ full with ice. Pour in gin and simple syrup. Pour in club soda, and float port on top. Garnish with lemon twist and nutmeg.

Gin Sling

2 oz. gin
¾ oz. lemon juice
1 oz. simple syrup
1 lemon twist

Fill a cocktail shaker with ice. Pour in gin, lemon juice, and simple syrup. Give it a good shake, and strain into an old-fashioned glass full of ice. Garnish with lemon twist.

Gin Smash

5 mint sprigs
1 tsp. superfine sugar
1 oz. club soda
2 oz. gin
1 lemon twist

Muddle 4 mint sprigs, superfine sugar, and club soda in an old-fashioned glass. Fill glass ¾ full with ice, and pour in gin. Give it a good stir, and garnish with remaining mint sprig and lemon twist.

Gin Sour

2 oz. gin
¾ oz. lemon juice
1 oz. simple syrup
1 orange slice
1 maraschino cherry

Fill a cocktail shaker with ice. Pour in gin, lemon juice, and simple syrup. Give it a good shake, and strain into a highball glass ¾ full of ice. Garnish with orange slice and maraschino cherry.

Gin Squirt

2 oz. gin
1 tsp. grenadine
1 TB. superfine sugar
4 oz. club soda
3 pineapple chunks
2 strawberries

Fill a cocktail shaker ½ full with ice. Pour in gin, grenadine, and superfine sugar. Give it a good stir, and strain into a highball glass full of ice. Pour in club soda. Stir again and garnish with pineapple chunks and strawberries.

Gin Swizzle

2 oz. gin
1 oz. lime juice
1 oz. simple syrup
1 dash bitters
3 oz. club soda

Fill a cocktail shaker with ice. Pour in gin, lime juice, and simple syrup, and add bitters. Give it a good shake, and strain into a highball glass ¾ full of ice. Pour in club soda, and serve with (of course) a swizzle stick.

Golden Bronx

2 oz. gin
1 tsp. dry vermouth
1 tsp. sweet vermouth
½ oz. orange juice
1 egg yolk

Fill a cocktail shaker ½ full with ice. Pour in gin, dry vermouth, sweet vermouth, orange juice, and egg yolk. Give it a good, vigorous shake, and strain into a sour glass full of ice.

Golden Daze

2 oz. gin
¾ oz. peach brandy
½ oz. orange juice

Fill a cocktail shaker ½ full with ice. Pour in gin, peach brandy, and orange juice. Give it a good shake, and strain into a highball glass full of ice.

Golden Fizz

2 oz. gin
2 TB. lemon juice
1 TB. sugar
1 egg yolk
4 oz. club soda

Fill a cocktail shaker ½ full with ice. Pour in gin, lemon juice, sugar, and egg yolk. Give it a good, vigorous shake, and strain into a Collins glass full of ice. Pour in club soda.

Golden Girl

2½ oz. gin
1 oz. sherry
1 dash orange bitters
1 dash Angostura bitters
1 lemon twist

Fill a cocktail shaker ½ full with ice. Pour in gin and sherry, and add orange bitters and Angostura bitters. Give it a good stir, and strain into a cocktail glass. Garnish with lemon twist.

Golf Cocktail

2 oz. gin
½ oz. dry vermouth
2 dashes bitters

Fill a cocktail shaker ½ full with ice. Pour in gin and dry vermouth, and add bitters. Give it a good stir, and strain into a cocktail glass.

Grand Passion

2 oz. gin
1 oz. passion fruit nectar
1 dash bitters

Fill a cocktail shaker ½ full with ice. Pour in gin and passion fruit nectar, and add bitters. Give it a good, vigorous shake, and strain into a cocktail glass.

Grapefruit Cocktail

2 oz. gin
2 oz. grapefruit juice
1 tsp. maraschino liqueur
1 maraschino cherry

Fill a cocktail shaker ½ full with ice. Pour in gin, grapefruit juice, and maraschino liqueur. Give it a good shake, and strain into an old-fashioned glass full of ice. Garnish with maraschino cherry.

Grass Skirt

2 oz. gin
1 oz. triple sec
1 oz. pincapple juice
½ tsp. grenadine
1 pineapple slice

Fill a cocktail shaker ½ full with ice. Pour in gin, triple sec, pineapple juice, and grenadine. Give it a good shake, and strain into an old-fashioned glass full of ice. Garnish with pineapple slice.

Great Secret

2 oz. gin
1 oz. Lillet blanc
1 dash bitters
1 orange twist

Fill a cocktail shaker ½ full with ice. Pour in gin and Lillet blanc, and add bitters. Give it a good shake, and strain into a cocktail glass. Garnish with orange twist.

Greehham's Grotto

2 oz. gin
1 oz. brandy
2 tsp. *orgeat syrup*
2 tsp. lemon juice

Fill a cocktail shaker ½ full with ice. Pour in gin, brandy, orgeat syrup, and lemon juice. Give it a good shake, and strain into an old-fashioned glass full of ice.

Liquor Lingo

Orgeat syrup is a nonalcoholic almond-flavored syrup with hints of orange flower water used to flavor drinks.

Green Dragon

2 oz. gin
½ oz. crème de menthe
½ oz. kummel
2 TB. lemon juice
2 dashes orange bitters

Fill a cocktail shaker ½ full with ice. Pour in gin, crème de menthe, kummel, and lemon juice, and add orange bitters. Give it a good shake, and strain into an old-fashioned glass full of ice.

Greenback

2 oz. gin
2 TB. lemon juice
½ oz. green crème de menthe

Fill a cocktail shaker ½ full with ice. Pour in gin, lemon juice, and green crème de menthe. Give it a good shake, and strain into an old-fashioned glass full of ice.

Gypsy

2 oz. gin
1½ oz. sweet vermouth
1 maraschino cherry

Fill a cocktail shaker ½ full with ice. Pour in gin and sweet vermouth. Give it a good stir, and strain into a cocktail glass. Garnish with maraschino cherry.

Harlem Cocktail

2 oz. gin
1 oz. pineapple juice
¼ oz. maraschino liqueur
2 pineapple chunks

Fill a cocktail shaker ½ full with ice. Pour in gin, pineapple juice, and maraschino liqueur. Give it a good shake, and strain into a cocktail glass. Garnish with pineapple chunks.

Hasty Cocktail

1½ oz. gin
¾ oz. dry vermouth
¼ tsp. pastis
1 tsp. grenadine

Fill a cocktail shaker ½ full with ice. Pour in gin, dry vermouth, pastis, and grenadine. Give it a good shake, and strain into a cocktail glass.

Hawaiian

2 oz. gin
½ oz. triple sec
1 TB. pineapple juice

Fill a cocktail shaker ½ full with ice. Pour in gin, triple sec, and pineapple juice. Give it a good shake, and strain into a cocktail glass.

Hillsboro

2½ oz. gin
1 oz. dry vermouth
1 dash orange bitters
1 dash Angostura bitters
1 lemon twist

Fill a cocktail shaker ½ full with ice. Pour in gin and dry vermouth, and add orange bitters and Angostura bitters. Give it a good stir, and strain into a cocktail glass. Garnish with lemon twist.

Hoffman House

3 oz. gin
1 TB. dry vermouth
2 dashes bitters
1 cocktail olive

Fill a cocktail shaker ½ full with ice. Pour in gin and dry vermouth, and add bitters. Give it a good shake, and strain into a cocktail glass. Garnish with olive.

Homestead

2 oz. gin
1 oz. sweet vermouth
1 orange slice

Fill a cocktail shaker ½ full with ice. Pour in gin and sweet vermouth. Give it a good stir, and strain into a cocktail glass. Garnish with orange slice.

Hornpipe

2 oz. gin
3 tsp. cherry brandy
1 egg white

Fill a cocktail shaker ½ full with ice. Pour in gin, cherry brandy, and egg white. Give it a good, vigorous shake, and strain into a cocktail glass.

Horsley's Honor

1½ oz. gin
½ oz. dry vermouth
½ oz. applejack brandy
½ oz. triple sec
1 apple slice

Fill an old-fashioned glass ¾ full with ice. Pour in gin, dry vermouth, applejack brandy, and triple sec. Give it a good stir, and garnish with apple slice.

Hudson Bay

1 oz. gin
½ oz. cherry brandy
2 tsp. *151 proof rum*
1 TB. orange juice
2 tsp. lemon juice

Fill a cocktail shaker ½ full with ice. Pour in gin, cherry brandy, 151 proof rum, orange juice, and lemon juice. Give it a good shake, and strain into a cocktail glass.

Liquor Lingo

151 proof rum is a highly alcoholic rum used in flamed or specialty drinks, such as the Zombie.

Hula-Hula

¼ tsp. superfine sugar
2 oz. gin
1 oz. orange juice

Fill an old-fashioned glass with ice. Add superfine sugar, gin, and orange juice. Give it a good stir.

Ideal Cocktail

1 oz. gin
1 oz. dry vermouth
¼ tsp. maraschino liqueur
½ tsp. grapefruit juice
1 maraschino cherry

Fill a cocktail shaker ½ full with ice. Pour in gin, dry vermouth, maraschino liqueur, and grapefruit juice. Give it a good shake, and strain into a cocktail glass. Garnish with maraschino cherry.

Income Tax Cocktail

2 oz. gin
2 tsp. dry vermouth
2 tsp. sweet vermouth
1 oz. orange juice
2 dashes bitters

Fill a cocktail shaker ½ full with ice. Pour in gin, dry vermouth, sweet vermouth, and orange juice, and add bitters. Give it a good shake, and strain into an old-fashioned glass full of ice.

James Bond Martini

3 oz. gin
1 oz. vodka
½ oz. *Lillet*

Fill a cocktail shaker ½ full with ice. Pour in gin, vodka, and Lillet. Give it a good shake, and strain into a cocktail glass.

Liquor Lingo

Lillet is a *quinquina* (a sweetened aperitif wine) that comes in rouge (or red), which is the sweetest, and blanc, which is semi-sweet.

Java Cooler

1½ oz. gin
2 tsp. lime juice
3 dashes bitters
4 oz. tonic water

Fill a highball glass with ice. Pour in gin and lime juice, and add bitters. Give it a good stir. Pour in tonic water, and stir.

Jet Black

1½ oz. gin
1 tsp. black Sambuca
2 tsp. sweet vermouth

Fill a cocktail shaker ½ full with ice. Pour in gin, black Sambuca, and sweet vermouth. Give it a good stir, and strain into a cocktail glass.

Jewel

1 oz. gin
1 oz. sweet vermouth
¾ oz. green Chartreuse
2 dashes orange bitters
1 maraschino cherry

Fill a cocktail shaker ½ full with ice. Pour in gin, sweet vermouth, and green Chartreuse, and add orange bitters. Give it a good shake, and strain into a cocktail glass. Garnish with maraschino cherry.

Jewel of the Nile

2 oz. gin
½ oz. green Chartreuse
½ oz. yellow Chartreuse

Fill a cocktail shaker ½ full with ice. Pour in gin, green Chartreuse, and yellow Chartreuse. Give it a good stir, and strain into a cocktail glass.

Jockey Club

2 oz. gin
1 tsp. white crème de cacao
2 TB. lemon juice
1 dash bitters

Fill a cocktail shaker ½ full with ice. Pour in gin, white crème de cacao, and lemon juice, and add bitters. Give it a good stir, and strain into a cocktail glass.

Joulouville

1 oz. gin
½ oz. apple brandy
2 tsp. sweet vermouth
2 tsp. lemon juice
3 drops grenadine

Fill a cocktail shaker ½ full with ice. Pour in gin, apple brandy, sweet vermouth, and lemon juice, and add grenadine. Give it a good shake, and strain into an old-fashioned glass full of ice.

Jupiter Martini

2 oz. gin
¼ oz. dry vermouth
1 tsp. *crème de violette*
1 tsp. orange juice

Fill a cocktail shaker ½ full with ice. Pour in gin, dry vermouth, crème de violette, and orange juice. Give it a good shake, and strain into a cocktail glass.

> **Liquor Lingo**
>
> **Crème de violette,** or liqeur de violet, is a violet-flavored liqueur. It can be difficult to find; you can sometimes use parfait amour as a substitute.

Kensler's Father-in-Law Killer

When I told my friend Chris Kensler I was writing a book on cocktails, he responded with such an enthusiastic and particular recitation of a recipe for a martini, I had to include it. The most important thing about this drink is that the entire thing be prepared *in your freezer*. So if you plan on making Kensler's Father-in-Law Killer, clear a spot between the frozen peas and ice cream.

3 oz. gin
½ oz. dry vermouth
1 thinly sliced apple piece

Chill your favorite gin overnight or for at least 2 hours. Rinse a martini glass under cold water. Do not dry it—leave wet and place in the freezer. Pour vermouth into the glass, and leave in the freezer for 10 minutes. Remove the glass from the freezer, swirl vermouth so it coats the glass, and then dump out vermouth. Put the glass back on the freezer shelf, pour in gin, and garnish with apple slice. Remove from freezer and drink.

K.G.B.

½ tsp. superfine sugar
2 oz. gin
½ oz. kirschwasser
1 tsp. apricot brandy
2 TB. lemon juice

Fill a cocktail shaker ½ full with ice. Add superfine sugar and then pour in gin, kirschwasser, apricot brandy, and lemon juice. Give it a good shake, and strain into an ice-filled highball glass.

Kiss in the Dark

1 oz. gin
1 oz. cherry brandy
1 oz. dry vermouth

Fill a cocktail shaker ½ full with ice. Pour in gin, cherry brandy, and dry vermouth. Give it a good shake, and strain into a cocktail glass.

Knickerbocker

1½ oz. gin
¾ oz. dry vermouth
¼ tsp. sweet vermouth
1 lemon twist

Fill a cocktail shaker ½ full with ice. Pour in gin, dry vermouth, and sweet vermouth. Give it a good shake, and strain into a cocktail glass. Garnish with lemon twist.

Knock-Out Cocktail

1 oz. gin
¾ oz. dry vermouth
½ oz. pastis
¼ oz. white crème de menthe

Fill a cocktail shaker ½ full with ice. Pour in gin, dry vermouth, pastis, and white crème de menthe. Give it a good shake, and strain into a cocktail glass.

Ladyfinger

½ tsp. superfine sugar
1½ oz. gin
1 oz. kirschwasser
½ oz. cherry brandy
1 oz. lemon juice

Fill a cocktail shaker ½ full with ice. Add superfine sugar and then pour in gin, kirschwasser, cherry brandy, and lemon juice. Give it a good shake, and strain into a cocktail glass.

Lasky

1 oz. gin	Fill a cocktail shaker ½ full with ice.
1 oz. *Swedish punsch*	Pour in gin, Swedish punsch, and
1 oz. grape juice	grape juice. Give it a good shake, and
	strain into an old-fashioned glass full
	of ice.

Liquor Lingo

Swedish punsch is a Scandinavian liqueur made from Batavia Arak rum, tea, lemon, spices, sugar, and even sometimes wine.

Leaning Tower

2 oz. gin	Fill a cocktail shaker with crushed ice.
1 tsp. dry vermouth	Pour in gin and dry vermouth, and
2 dashes orange bitters	add orange bitters. Give it a good
	shake, and strain into a cocktail glass.

Leap Frog

2 oz. gin	Fill a highball glass with ice. Pour in
2 TB. lemon juice	gin and lemon juice. Give it a good
4 oz. ginger ale	stir, and fill with ginger ale.

Leap Year

2 oz. gin	Fill a cocktail shaker ½ full with ice.
½ oz. Grand Marnier	Pour in gin, Grand Marnier, sweet
½ oz. sweet vermouth	vermouth, and lemon juice. Give it a
1 TB. lemon juice	good stir, and strain into a cocktail
1 lemon twist	glass. Garnish with lemon twist.

Leave It to Me

1½ oz. gin	Fill a cocktail shaker ½ full with ice.
½ oz. dry vermouth	Pour in gin, dry vermouth, apricot
½ oz. apricot brandy	brandy, grenadine, and lemon juice.
½ tsp. grenadine	Give it a good shake, and strain into a
½ tsp. lemon juice	cocktail glass.

Lilly Cocktail

1 oz. gin
1 oz. Lillet blanc
1 oz. crème de noyaux
¼ oz. lemon juice

Fill a cocktail shaker ½ full with ice. Pour in gin, Lillet blanc, crème de noyaux, and lemon juice. Give it a good stir, and strain into a cocktail glass.

Little Devil

1 oz. gin
1 oz. gold rum
½ oz. triple sec
½ oz. lemon juice

Fill a cocktail shaker ½ full with ice. Pour in gin, gold rum, triple sec, and lemon juice. Give it a good shake, and strain into an old-fashioned glass full of ice.

London Buck

2 oz. gin
½ tsp. maraschino liqueur
½ tsp. simple syrup
2 dashes orange bitters
1 lemon twist

Fill a cocktail shaker ½ full with ice. Pour in gin, maraschino liqueur, and simple syrup, and add orange bitters. Give it a good shake, and strain into a highball glass full of ice. Garnish with lemon twist.

London Fog

2 oz. gin
¼ oz. pastis

Fill a cocktail shaker ½ full with ice. Pour in gin and pastis. Give it a good shake, and strain into a wine glass.

London Town

2 oz. gin
½ oz. maraschino liqueur
2 dashes bitters

Fill a cocktail shaker ½ full with ice. Pour in gin and maraschino liqueur, and add bitters. Give it a good shake, and strain into a cocktail glass.

Lone Tree

1½ oz. gin
½ oz. sweet vermouth

Fill a cocktail shaker ½ full with ice. Pour in gin and sweet vermouth. Give it a good shake, and strain into a cocktail glass.

Lucky Stiff

2 oz. gin
2 oz. orange curaçao
4 oz. cranberry juice

Pour gin, orange curaçao, and cranberry juice into an ice-filled highball glass and stir.

Maiden No More

1½ oz. gin
½ oz. triple sec
1 tsp. brandy
1 oz. lemon juice

Fill a cocktail shaker ½ full with ice. Pour in gin, triple sec, brandy, and lemon juice. Give it a good shake, and strain into a cocktail glass.

Maiden's Blush

1½ oz. gin
½ oz. triple sec
1 tsp. cherry brandy
1 oz. lemon juice
1 maraschino cherry

Fill a cocktail shaker ½ full with ice. Pour in gin, triple sec, cherry brandy, and lemon juice. Give it a good shake, and strain into a cocktail glass. Garnish with maraschino cherry.

Maiden's Prayer

1½ oz. gin
½ oz. triple sec
1 oz. lemon juice

Fill a cocktail shaker ½ full with ice. Pour in gin, triple sec, and lemon juice. Give it a good shake, and strain into a cocktail glass.

Mainbrace

2 oz. gin
1 oz. triple sec
1½ TB. grape juice

Fill a cocktail shaker ½ full with ice. Pour in gin, triple sec, and grape juice. Give it a good shake, and strain into a highball glass full of ice.

Marguerite

2½ oz. gin
1 oz. dry vermouth
2 dashes orange bitters
1 orange twist

Fill a cocktail shaker ½ full with ice. Pour in gin and dry vermouth, and add orange bitters. Give it a good stir, and strain into a cocktail glass. Garnish with orange twist.

Martinez

1 oz. gin
1 oz. dry vermouth
¼ tsp. maraschino liqueur
1 dash bitters

Fill a cocktail shaker ½ full with ice. Pour in gin, dry vermouth, and maraschino liqueur, and add bitters. Give it a good stir, and strain into a cocktail glass.

Martini

3 oz. gin
1 dash dry vermouth
2 cocktail olives

Fill a cocktail shaker ½ full with ice. Pour in gin and dry vermouth. Give it a good stir, and strain into a cocktail glass. Garnish with cocktail olives.

Matinee

1½ oz. gin
1 oz. sweet vermouth
½ oz. green Chartreuse
1 oz. orange juice
2 dashes orange bitters

Fill a cocktail shaker ½ full with ice. Pour in gin, sweet vermouth, green Chartreuse, and orange juice, and add orange bitters. Give it a good shake, and strain into a cocktail glass.

Cocktail Conversation

The only cocktail debate more rousing than the origins of the martini is the proper way to make one. Everyone thinks his way is the best way. With this in mind, I give you the following caveat: this martini recipe is the way I like to drink mine. It's not right or wrong—it's simply my preference. I like it dry, and I think they should be stirred, not shaken. I am Italian, so maybe that's why I'm partial to olives. Occasionally I get in the mood for a vodka martini and forego gin entirely (gasp!). If you prefer yours less dry, add more vermouth. If you think even a drop of vermouth is too much, that's fine, too. But whatever you do, drink that baby cold.

Maxim

1½ oz. gin
1 oz. dry vermouth
1 dash white crème de cacao

Fill a cocktail shaker ½ full with ice. Pour in gin, dry vermouth, and white crème de cacao. Give it a good shake, and strain into a cocktail glass.

Melon Cocktail

2 oz. gin
¼ tsp. maraschino liqueur
¼ tsp. lemon juice

Fill a cocktail shaker ½ full with ice. Pour in gin, maraschino liqueur, and lemon juice. Give it a good stir, and strain into a cocktail glass.

Merry Widow

1½ oz. gin
1½ oz. dry vermouth
1 tsp. Benedictine
1 tsp. pastis
1 dash orange bitters
1 lemon twist

Fill a cocktail shaker ½ full with ice. Pour in gin, dry vermouth, Benedictine, and pastis, and add orange bitters. Give it a good shake, and strain into a cocktail glass. Garnish with lemon twist.

Mississippi Mule

1½ oz. gin
1 tsp. crème de cassis
1 tsp. lemon juice

Fill a cocktail shaker ½ full with ice. Pour in gin, crème de cassis, and lemon juice. Give it a good shake, and strain into an old-fashioned glass full of ice.

Monkey Gland Cocktail

2 oz. gin
1 tsp. Benedictine
1 tsp. grenadine
½ oz. orange juice

Fill a cocktail shaker ½ full with ice. Pour in gin, Benedictine, grenadine, and orange juice. Give it a good shake, and strain into a cocktail glass.

Montmarte

2 oz. gin
½ oz. sweet vermouth
½ oz. triple sec

Fill a cocktail shaker ½ full with ice. Pour in gin, sweet vermouth, and triple sec. Give it a good shake, and strain into an old-fashioned glass full of ice.

Montreal Club Bouncer

1½ oz. gin
1½ oz. pastis

Fill an old-fashioned glass with ice. Pour in gin and pastis, and give it a good stir.

Napoleon

2 oz. gin
½ Dubonnet Rouge
½ Grand Marnier

Fill a cocktail shaker ½ full with ice. Pour in gin, Dubonnet Rouge, and Grand Marnier. Give it a good stir, and strain into a cocktail glass.

Newbury

1½ oz. gin
1½ oz. sweet vermouth
¼ tsp. curaçao
1 lemon twist

Fill a cocktail shaker ½ full with ice. Pour in gin, sweet vermouth, and curaçao. Give it a good shake, and strain into a cocktail glass. Garnish with lemon twist.

North Pole Cocktail

1 oz. gin
½ oz. maraschino liqueur
½ oz. lemon juice
1 egg white
Whipped cream

Fill a cocktail shaker ½ full with ice. Pour in gin, maraschino liqueur, lemon juice, and egg white. Give it a good, vigorous shake, and strain into a cocktail glass. Garnish with whipped cream.

Oaxaca Jim

2 oz. gin
1 oz. orange juice
1 oz. grapefruit juice
2 dashes bitters
1 lemon twist
1 maraschino cherry

Fill a cocktail shaker ½ full with ice. Pour in gin, orange juice, and grapefruit juice, and add bitters. Give it a good shake, and strain into an old-fashioned glass ¾ full with ice. Garnish with lemon twist and maraschino cherry.

Old Etonian

1½ oz. gin
1½ oz. Lillet
¼ tsp. *crème de noyaux*
2 dashes orange bitters

Fill a cocktail shaker ½ full with ice. Pour in gin, Lillet, and crème de noyaux, and add orange bitters. Give it a good stir, and strain into a cocktail glass.

Liquor Lingo

Crème de noyaux is a brandy-based almond-flavored liqueur.

Once Upon a Time

1½ oz. gin
½ oz. apricot brandy
½ oz. Lillet

Fill a cocktail shaker ½ full with ice. Pour in gin, apricot brandy, and Lillet. Give it a good stir, and strain into a cocktail glass.

Opal Cocktail

2 oz. gin
½ oz. triple sec
½ oz. orange juice
2 dashes orange bitters

Fill a cocktail shaker ½ full with ice. Pour in gin, triple sec, and orange juice, and add orange bitters. Give it a good shake, and strain into a cocktail glass.

Opera Cocktail

2 oz. gin
½ oz. Dubonnet Rouge
½ oz. maraschino liqueur
1 maraschino cherry

Fill a cocktail shaker ½ full with ice. Pour in gin, Dubonnet Rouge, and maraschino liqueur. Give it a good stir, and strain into a cocktail glass. Garnish with maraschino cherry.

Orange Bloom

1½ oz. gin
2 tsp. sweet vermouth
2 tsp. triple sec
1 maraschino cherry

Fill a cocktail shaker ½ full with ice. Pour in gin, sweet vermouth, and triple sec. Give it a good stir, and strain into a cocktail glass. Garnish with maraschino cherry.

Orange Blossom

1 tsp. superfine sugar
2 oz. gin
1 oz. orange juice
1 orange slice

Fill a cocktail shaker ½ full with ice. Add superfine sugar, and pour in gin and orange juice. Give it a good shake, and strain into a cocktail glass. Garnish with orange slice.

Orange Buck

1½ oz. gin
1 oz. orange juice
1 TB. lime juice
3 oz. ginger ale

Fill a cocktail shaker ½ full with ice. Pour in gin, orange juice, and lime juice. Give it a good shake, and strain into a highball glass full of ice. Pour in ginger ale.

Orange Fizz

2 oz. gin
2 tsp. triple sec
1 oz. orange juice
2 TB. lemon juice
1 tsp. simple syrup
2 oz. club soda
1 orange slice

Fill a cocktail shaker ½ full with ice. Pour in gin, triple sec, orange juice, lemon juice, and simple syrup. Give it a good shake, and strain into a Delmonico glass. Pour in club soda, and garnish with orange slice.

Orchid

3 oz. gin
¼ tsp. Lillet
1 egg white

Fill a cocktail shaker ½ full with ice. Pour in gin, Lillet, and egg white. Give it a good, vigorous shake, and strain into a cocktail glass.

Paisley Martini

3 oz. gin
¼ oz. dry vermouth
1 tsp. Scotch whisky

Fill a cocktail shaker ½ full with ice. Pour in gin, dry vermouth, and Scotch whisky. Give it a good shake, and strain into a cocktail glass.

Pall Mall Martini

3 oz. gin
½ oz. dry vermouth
½ oz. sweet vermouth
1 tsp. white crème de menthe
1 dash orange bitters

Fill a cocktail shaker ½ full with ice. Pour in gin, dry vermouth, sweet vermouth, and white crème de menthe, and add orange bitters. Give it a good shake, and strain into a cocktail glass.

Palm Beach Cocktail

2 oz. gin
2 tsp. sweet vermouth
2 tsp. grapefruit juice

Fill a cocktail shaker ½ full with ice. Pour in gin, sweet vermouth, and grapefruit juice. Give it a good shake, and strain into a cocktail glass.

Parisian

1 oz. gin
1 oz. dry vermouth
¼ oz. crème de cassis

Fill a cocktail shaker ½ full with ice. Pour in gin, dry vermouth, and crème de cassis. Give it a good shake, and strain into a cocktail glass.

Park Avenue

2 oz. gin
¾ oz. sweet vermouth
2 TB. pineapple juice

Fill a cocktail shaker ½ full with ice. Pour in gin, sweet vermouth, and pineapple juice. Give it a good stir, and strain into a cocktail glass.

Patty's Violet Martini

This martini is the signature drink of Patty, the bartender at Sel de la Terre in Boston, whose favorite color is purple.

3 oz. Bombay Sapphire gin
2 oz. sour mix
1 oz. grenadine
1 oz. blue curaçao
Candied violet for garnish

Fill a cocktail shaker ½ full with ice. Pour in Bombay Sapphire gin, sour mix, grenadine, and blue curaçao. Give it a good shake, and strain into a chilled martini glass over a candied violet.

Peggy Cocktail

2 oz. gin
¾ oz. dry vermouth
½ oz. Dubonnet Rouge
½ tsp. pastis

Fill a cocktail shaker ½ full with ice. Pour in gin, dry vermouth, Dubonnet Rouge, and pastis. Give it a good shake, and strain into a cocktail glass.

Pegu Club

1½ oz. gin
½ oz. triple sec
½ oz. lime juice
2 dashes bitters

Fill a cocktail shaker ½ full with ice. Pour in gin, triple sec, and lime juice, and add bitters. Give it a good shake, and strain into a cocktail glass.

Petticoat Lane

2 oz. gin
½ oz. sweet vermouth
½ oz. Campari
1 lemon twist

Fill a cocktail shaker ½ full with ice. Pour in gin, sweet vermouth, and Campari. Give it a good stir, and strain into a cocktail glass. Garnish with lemon twist.

Piccadilly Cocktail

2 oz. gin
¾ oz. dry vermouth
½ tsp. pastis
½ tsp. grenadine

Fill a cocktail shaker ½ full with ice. Pour in gin, dry vermouth, pastis, and grenadine. Give it a good stir, and strain into a cocktail glass.

Pink Cream Fizz

1 tsp. superfine sugar
2 oz. gin
1 tsp. grenadine
1 oz. lemon juice
1 oz. light cream
4 oz. club soda

Fill a cocktail shaker ½ full with ice. Add superfine sugar, and pour in gin, grenadine, lemon juice, and light cream. Give it a good shake, and strain into a Collins glass ¾ full of ice. Pour in club soda.

Pink Gin

2 oz. gin
3 dashes bitters

Fill a cocktail shaker ½ full with ice. Pour in gin and shake. Add bitters to a wine glass, and swirl around to coat the inside of the glass. Strain in gin.

Pink Lady

2 oz. gin
1 tsp. grenadine
1 tsp. light cream
1 egg white

Fill a cocktail shaker ½ full with ice. Pour in gin, grenadine, light cream, and egg white. Give it a good, vigorous shake, and strain into a cocktail glass.

Pink Pussycat

2 oz. gin
4 oz. pineapple juice
1 tsp. cherry brandy

Fill a cocktail shaker ½ full with ice. Pour in gin, pineapple juice, and cherry brandy. Give it a good shake, and strain into a cocktail glass.

Pink Rose

2 oz. gin
¼ tsp. grenadine
1 tsp. lemon juice
1 tsp. heavy cream
1 egg white

Fill a cocktail shaker ½ full with ice. Pour in gin, grenadine, lemon juice, heavy cream, and egg white. Give it a good, vigorous shake, and strain into a cocktail glass.

Plaza Cocktail

1 oz. gin
1 oz. dry vermouth
1 oz. sweet vermouth
1 tsp. pineapple juice

Fill a cocktail shaker ½ full with ice. Pour in gin, dry vermouth, sweet vermouth, and pineapple juice. Give it a good shake, and strain into a cocktail glass.

Polo

2 oz. gin
2 TB. lemon juice
2 TB. orange juice

Fill a cocktail shaker ½ full with ice. Pour in gin, lemon juice, and orange juice. Give it a good shake, and strain into an old-fashioned glass full of ice.

Pompano

1½ oz. gin
2 tsp. dry vermouth
1½ oz. grapefruit juice

Fill a cocktail shaker ½ full with ice. Pour in gin, dry vermouth, and grapefruit juice. Give it a good shake, and strain into a cocktail glass.

Poppy Cocktail

2 oz. gin
1 oz. white crème de cacao

Fill a cocktail shaker ½ full with ice. Pour in gin and white crème de cacao. Give it a good shake, and strain into a cocktail glass.

Princeton Cocktail

2 oz. gin
1 oz. dry vermouth
1 oz. lime juice

Fill a cocktail shaker ½ full with ice. Pour in gin, dry vermouth, and lime juice. Give it a good shake, and strain into a cocktail glass.

Princeton Pride

2 oz. gin
¾ oz. tawny port
2 dashes orange bitters

Fill a cocktail shaker ½ full with ice. Pour in gin, tawny port, and orange bitters. Give it a good shake, and strain into a cocktail glass.

Prohibition Cocktail

2 oz. gin
2 oz. Lillet
½ tsp. apricot brandy
½ tsp. orange juice

Fill a cocktail shaker ½ full with ice. Pour in gin, Lillet, apricot brandy, and orange juice. Give it a good shake, and strain into a cocktail glass.

Queen Elizabeth

2 oz. gin
½ oz. dry vermouth
2 tsp. Benedictine

Fill a cocktail shaker ½ full with ice. Pour in gin, dry vermouth, and Benedictine. Give it a good shake, and strain into a cocktail glass.

Red Cloud

1½ oz. gin
½ oz. apricot brandy
1 tsp. grenadine
1 TB. lemon juice

Fill a cocktail shaker ½ full with ice. Pour in gin, apricot brandy, grenadine, and lemon juice. Give it a good shake, and strain into a highball glass full of ice.

Red Gin

2 oz. gin
1 tsp. *cherry Heering*
1 maraschino cherry

Fill a cocktail shaker ½ full with ice. Pour in gin and cherry Heering. Give it a good stir, and strain into a cocktail glass. Garnish with maraschino cherry.

 Liquor Lingo

Cherry Heering is a Danish brandy-based dark cherry liqueur.

Red Lion

1½ oz. gin
1½ oz. Grand Marnier
½ oz. lemon juice
½ oz. orange juice
1 lemon twist

Fill a cocktail shaker ½ full with ice. Pour in gin, Grand Marnier, lemon juice, and orange juice. Give it a good shake, and strain into an old-fashioned glass full of ice. Garnish with maraschino cherry.

Red Ruby

2 oz. gin
½ oz. dry vermouth
½ oz. cherry brandy

Fill a cocktail shaker ½ full with ice. Pour in gin, dry vermouth, and cherry brandy. Give it a good shake, and strain into a cocktail glass.

Rolls Royce

1½ oz. gin
½ oz. dry vermouth
½ oz. sweet vermouth
½ tsp. Benedictine

Fill a cocktail shaker ½ full with ice. Pour in gin, dry vermouth, sweet vermouth, and Benedictine. Give it a good shake, and strain into a cocktail glass.

Root Beer Fizz

2 oz. gin
1 oz. lemon juice
1 tsp. superfine sugar
4 oz. root beer
1 maraschino cherry

Fill a cocktail shaker ½ full with ice. Pour in gin, lemon juice, and superfine sugar. Give it a good shake, and strain into a Collins glass ¾ full of ice. Pour in root beer, stir, and garnish with maraschino cherry.

Rose Cocktail

1 oz. gin
½ oz. dry vermouth
½ oz. apricot brandy
½ oz. grenadine
½ oz. lemon juice
½ oz. Rose's lime juice

Fill a cocktail shaker ½ full with ice. Pour in gin, dry vermouth, apricot brandy, grenadine, lemon juice, and Rose's lime juice. Give it a good shake, and strain into a cocktail glass.

Rouge Martini

3 oz. gin
1½ tsp. Chambord

Fill cocktail shaker ½ full with ice. Pour in gin and Chambord. Give it a good stir, and strain into a cocktail glass.

Royal Gin Fizz

2 oz. gin
½ oz. Grand Marnier
2 TB. lemon juice
1 tsp. simple syrup
1 egg
3 oz. club soda

Fill a cocktail shaker ½ full with ice. Pour in gin, Grand Marnier, lemon juice, simple syrup, and egg. Give it a good, vigorous shake, and strain into a highball glass ½ full of ice. Pour in club soda.

Ruby in the Rough

1½ oz. gin
½ oz. cherry brandy
1 tsp. sweet vermouth

Fill a cocktail shaker ½ full with ice. Pour in gin, cherry brandy, and sweet vermouth. Give it a good shake, and strain into a cocktail glass.

Saketini

2½ oz. gin
½ oz. sake
1 cucumber slice

Fill a cocktail shaker ½ full with ice. Pour in gin and sake. Give it a good shake, and strain into a cocktail glass. Garnish with cucumber slice.

San Sebastian

2 oz. gin
½ oz. light rum
½ oz. triple sec
1 TB. grapefruit juice
1 tsp. lemon juice

Fill a cocktail shaker ½ full with ice. Pour in gin, light rum, triple sec, grapefruit juice, and lemon juice. Give it a good shake, and strain into a cocktail glass.

Savannah

2 oz. gin
1 tsp. white crème de cacao
½ oz. orange juice
1 egg white

Fill a cocktail shaker ½ full with ice. Pour in gin, white crème de cacao, orange juice, and egg white. Give it a good, vigorous shake, and strain into a cocktail glass.

Self-Starter

2 oz. gin
1 oz. Lillet
½ oz. apricot brandy
¼ tsp. pastis

Fill a cocktail shaker ½ full with ice. Pour in gin, Lillet, apricot brandy, and pastis. Give it a good stir, and strain into a cocktail glass.

Silver Bronx

2 oz. gin
½ oz. dry vermouth
½ oz. sweet vermouth
1 tsp. orange juice
1 egg white

Fill a cocktail shaker ½ full with ice. Pour in gin, dry vermouth, sweet vermouth, orange juice, and egg white. Give it a good, vigorous shake, and strain into a cocktail glass.

Silver Bullet

3 oz. gin
2 tsp. Scotch whisky
1 lemon twist

Fill a cocktail shaker ½ full with ice. Pour in gin and Scotch whisky. Give it a good shake, and strain into a cocktail glass. Garnish with lemon twist.

Singapore Sling

1 oz. gin
1 oz. Benedictine
1 oz. cherry brandy
3 oz. club soda
1 maraschino cherry

Fill a cocktail shaker ½ full with ice. Pour in gin, Benedictine, and cherry brandy. Give it a good shake, and strain into a Collins glass full of ice. Pour in club soda, and garnish with maraschino cherry.

Smart Christine

2 oz. gin
½ oz. Benedictine
2 oz. orange juice
1 maraschino cherry

Fill a cocktail shaker ½ full with ice. Pour in gin, Benedictine, and orange juice. Give it a good shake, and strain into an old-fashioned glass full of ice. Garnish with maraschino cherry.

Smile Cocktail

1½ oz. gin
1½ oz. grenadine
1 tsp. lemon juice

Fill a cocktail shaker ½ full with ice. Pour in gin, grenadine, and lemon juice. Give it a good shake, and strain into a cocktail glass.

Southern Bride

2 oz. gin
1 oz. grapefruit juice
¼ tsp. maraschino liqueur

Fill a cocktail shaker ½ full with ice. Pour in gin, grapefruit juice, and maraschino liqueur. Give it a good shake, and strain into a cocktail glass.

Southern Gin Cocktail

2 oz. gin
½ tsp. triple sec
2 dashes bitters
1 lemon twist

Fill a cocktail shaker ½ full with ice. Pour in gin and triple sec, and add bitters. Give it a good shake, and strain into a cocktail glass. Garnish with lemon twist.

Sphinx

2 oz. gin
2 tsp. dry vermouth
2 tsp. sweet vermouth
1 lemon slice

Fill a cocktail shaker ½ full with ice. Pour in gin, dry vermouth, and sweet vermouth. Give it a good stir, and strain into a cocktail glass. Garnish with lemon slice.

Spring Feeling

1¼ oz. gin
¾ oz. green Chartreuse
1 TB. lemon juice

Fill a cocktail shaker ½ full with ice. Pour in gin, green Chartreuse, and lemon juice. Give it a good shake, and strain into a cocktail glass.

Stanley Cocktail

1 oz. gin
½ oz. light rum
1 tsp. grenadine
2 TB. lemon juice
1 lemon twist

Fill a cocktail shaker ½ full with ice. Pour in gin, light rum, grenadine, and lemon juice. Give it a good shake, and strain into a cocktail glass. Garnish with lemon twist.

Star

1½ oz. gin
1½ oz. calvados
1 tsp. sweet vermouth
1 tsp. grapefruit juice

Fill a cocktail shaker ½ full with ice. Pour in gin, calvados, sweet vermouth, and grapefruit juice. Give it a good shake, and strain into a cocktail glass.

Star Daisy

1 oz. gin
1 oz. apple brandy
1 tsp. grenadine
1 oz. lemon juice
1 tsp. simple syrup

Fill a cocktail shaker ½ full with ice. Pour in gin, apple brandy, grenadine, lemon juice, and simple syrup. Give it a good shake, and strain into a cocktail glass.

Starlight

2½ oz. gin
1 oz. orange curaçao
1 dash bitters
1 orange twist

Fill a cocktail shaker ½ full with ice. Pour in gin and orange curaçao, and add bitters. Give it a good shake, and strain into a cocktail glass. Garnish with orange twist.

Strawberry Martini

2 strawberries
1 tsp. sugar
1½ oz. gin
1 tsp. grenadine
1 tsp. dry vermouth

Cut 1 strawberry in ½, and rub the rim of a cocktail glass with inside of berry. Dip the rim in sugar. Fill a cocktail shaker ½ full with ice. Pour in gin, grenadine, and dry vermouth. Give it a good shake, and strain into the cocktail glass. Garnish with remaining uncut strawberry.

Sugar Daddy

2 oz. gin
2 tsp. maraschino liqueur
1 oz. pineapple juice
1 dash bitters

Fill a cocktail shaker ½ full with ice. Pour in gin, maraschino liqueur, and pineapple juice, and add bitters. Give it a good shake, and strain into a cocktail glass.

Sweet Patootie

2 oz. gin
1 oz. triple sec
1 oz. orange juice

Fill a cocktail shaker ½ full with ice. Pour in gin, triple sec, and orange juice. Give it a good shake, and strain into a highball glass ¾ full of ice.

Tango

1 oz. gin
½ oz. dry vermouth
½ oz. sweet vermouth
½ tsp. triple sec
1 TB. orange juice

Fill a cocktail shaker ½ full with ice. Pour in gin, dry vermouth, sweet vermouth, triple sec, and orange juice. Give it a good shake, and strain into a cocktail glass.

Ten Quidder

1½ oz. gin
1 oz. triple sec
1 dash bitters
1 tsp. blue curaçao

Fill an old-fashioned glass ¾ full with ice. Pour in gin and triple sec, and add bitters. Give it a good stir, and drip blue curaçao into center of cocktail.

Three Stripes

1 oz. gin
½ oz. dry vermouth
1 TB. orange juice

Fill a cocktail shaker ½ full with ice. Pour in gin, dry vermouth, and orange juice. Give it a good shake, and strain into a cocktail glass.

Tom Collins

1 tsp. superfine sugar
2 oz. gin
1 oz. lemon juice
3 oz. club soda
1 maraschino cherry
1 orange slice

Fill a cocktail shaker ½ full with ice. Add superfine sugar and then pour in gin and lemon juice. Give it a good shake, and strain into a Collins glass ¾ full of ice. Pour in club soda, and garnish with maraschino cherry and orange slice.

Trinity

¾ oz. gin
¾ oz. dry vermouth
¾ oz. sweet vermouth

Fill a cocktail shaker ½ full with ice.
Pour in gin, dry vermouth, and sweet
vermouth. Give it a good stir, and
strain into a cocktail glass.

Turf

1 oz. gin
1 oz. dry vermouth
1 tsp. pastis
2 dashes bitters
1 orange twist

Fill a cocktail shaker ½ full with ice.
Pour in gin, dry vermouth, and pastis,
and add bitters. Give it a good shake,
and strain into a cocktail glass. Garnish with orange twist.

Twenty Thousand Leagues

1½ oz. gin
1 oz. dry vermouth
1 tsp. pastis
2 dashes orange bitters

Fill a cocktail shaker with crushed ice.
Pour in gin, vermouth, and pastis, and
add orange bitters. Give it a good stir,
and strain into a cocktail glass.

Ulanda

1½ oz. gin
¾ oz. triple sec
¼ tsp. pastis

Fill a cocktail shaker with crushed ice.
Pour in gin, triple sec, and pastis.
Give it a good shake, and strain into
a cocktail glass.

Union Jack

1½ oz. gin
¾ oz. *sloe gin*
½ tsp. grenadine

Fill a cocktail shaker ½ full with ice.
Pour in gin, sloe gin, and grenadine.
Give it a good shake, and strain into
a cocktail glass.

Liquor Lingo

Sloe gin is a liqueur made from steeping blackthorn plums—sloe
berries—in a neutral spirit. The *gin* portion of the name, although
at one time a main ingredient, is rare these days.

Vesper

3 oz. gin
1 oz. vodka
½ oz. Lillet

Fill a cocktail shaker ½ full with ice. Pour in gin, vodka, and Lillet. Give it a good stir, and strain into a cocktail glass.

Virgin

1½ oz. gin
½ oz. white crème de menthe
1 oz. *Forbidden Fruit liqueur*

Fill a cocktail shaker ½ full with ice. Pour in gin, white crème de menthe, and Forbidden Fruit liqueur. Give it a good shake, and strain into a cocktail glass.

Liquor Lingo

Forbidden Fruit liqueur is a brandy-based, honey-flavored liqueur with citrus notes. Sadly, it's no longer manufactured, but I've left it in the recipe if only because its inclusion in the Virgin cocktail was an integral choice. If you can't find Forbidden Fruit, try using parfait amour as a substitute.

Weekly Special

1½ oz. gin
½ oz. kummel
½ oz. maraschino liqueur
1 oz. grapefruit juice
1 maraschino cherry

Fill a cocktail shaker ½ full with ice. Pour in gin, kummel, maraschino liqueur, and grapefruit juice. Give it a good shake, and strain into a cocktail glass. Garnish with maraschino cherry.

Whisper Martini

Our technical editor, John James, logged many an hour behind the bar while working his way through college. He found the Whisper to be an incredibly popular form of the martini, and I liked the idea so much I wanted to add his input. For a "dirty" version, add olive juice when you add the vermouth; if gin's not your thing, feel free to substitute vodka.

2 dashes dry vermouth
3 oz. gin
2 cocktail olives

Fill a cocktail shaker ½ full with ice. Pour in dry vermouth. Give it a good shake, and strain. Pour gin into the shaker, give it a good shake, and strain into a cocktail glass. Garnish with cocktail olives.

White Lady

1 tsp. superfine sugar
2 oz. gin
1 oz. light cream
1 egg white

Fill a cocktail shaker ½ full with ice. Add superfine sugar and then pour in gin, light cream, and egg white. Give it a good, vigorous shake, and strain into a cocktail glass.

Will Rogers

1½ oz. gin
½ oz. dry vermouth
¼ tsp. triple sec
1 TB. orange juice

Fill a cocktail shaker ½ full with ice. Pour in gin, dry vermouth, triple sec, and orange juice. Give it a good shake, and strain into a cocktail glass.

Yale Cocktail

2 oz. gin
½ oz. dry vermouth
1 tsp. blue curaçao
1 dash bitters

Fill a cocktail shaker ½ full with ice. Pour in gin, dry vermouth, and blue curaçao, and add bitters. Give it a good shake, and strain into a cocktail glass.

Yellow Rattler

1 oz. gin
½ oz. dry vermouth
½ oz. sweet vermouth
1 TB. orange juice
1 cocktail onion

Fill a cocktail shaker ½ full with ice. Pour in gin, dry vermouth, sweet vermouth, and orange juice. Give it a good shake, and strain into a cocktail glass. Garnish with cocktail onion.

Chapter 7

Rum

There's naught, no doubt, so much the spirit calms as rum and true religion.

—Lord Byron

Abilene

2 oz. rum	Fill a highball glass ¾ full with ice. Pour in rum, peach nectar, and orange juice. Give it a good stir.
2 oz. peach nectar	
3 oz. orange juice	

Acapulco

1 tsp. superfine sugar	Fill a cocktail shaker ½ full with ice. Add superfine sugar and then pour in light rum, triple sec, lime juice, and egg white. Give it a good, vigorous shake, and strain into an old-fashioned glass ¾ full of ice. Garnish with mint sprig.
2 oz. light rum	
¼ oz. triple sec	
3 TB. lime juice	
1 egg white	
1 mint sprig	

Adam

2½ oz. dark rum	Fill a cocktail shaker ½ full with ice. Pour in dark rum, lemon juice, and grenadine. Give it a good shake, and strain into cocktail glass.
1 oz. lemon juice	
1 tsp. grenadine	

Almond Hot Chocolate

2 oz. dark rum
1 TB. orgeat syrup
4 oz. hot chocolate

Pour dark rum and orgeat syrup into an Irish coffee glass. Top with hot chocolate, and give it a good stir.

Amy's Tattoo

1½ oz. dark rum
1½ oz. light rum
2 oz. orange juice
2 oz. pineapple juice
¼ tsp. grenadine

Fill a cocktail shaker ½ full with ice. Pour in dark rum, light rum, orange juice, pineapple juice, and grenadine. Give it a good shake, and strain into a Collins glass ¾ full of ice.

Ann Sheridan

Born in Texas, Ann Sheridan won Paramount Picture's "Search for Beauty" contest in the early 1930s, which carried a screen test as part of the prize. By 19, she'd signed a movie contract and would become one of the many legendary "discovered" starlets of filmdom's golden years and would enjoy a career that spanned several decades. Sheridan worked right up to 1967, the year she died.

2 oz. light rum
½ oz. orange curaçao
½ oz. lime juice

Fill a cocktail shaker ½ full with ice. Pour in light rum, orange curaçao, and lime juice. Give it a good shake, and strain into a cocktail glass.

Apple Pie

2 oz. light rum
½ oz. sweet vermouth
½ oz. applejack brandy
1 tsp. lemon juice
½ tsp. grenadine

Fill a cocktail shaker ½ full with ice. Pour in light rum, sweet vermouth, applejack brandy, lemon juice, and grenadine. Give it a good shake, and strain into a cocktail glass.

Appled Rum Cooler

2 oz. añejo rum
½ oz. applejack brandy
2 tsp. lime juice
2½ oz. club soda

Fill a cocktail shaker ½ full with ice. Pour in añejo rum, applejack brandy, and lime juice. Give it a good shake, and strain into an old-fashioned glass ¾ full of ice. Pour in club soda on top.

Astronaut

1½ oz. rum
1½ oz. vodka
2 tsp. lemon juice
3 tsp. passion fruit juice
2 oz. club soda

Fill a cocktail shaker ½ full with ice. Pour in rum, vodka, lemon juice, and passion fruit juice. Give it a good shake, and strain into a highball glass ¾ full of ice. Top it off with club soda.

Atlantic Breeze

2 oz. light rum
½ oz. apricot brandy
½ oz. Galliano
¼ tsp. grenadine
4 oz. pineapple juice
½ oz. lemon juice

Fill a cocktail shaker ½ full with ice. Pour in light rum, apricot brandy, Galliano, grenadine, pineapple juice, and lemon juice. Give it a good shake, and strain into a Collins glass ¾ full of ice.

Aunt Agatha

2 oz. light rum
3 oz. orange juice
2 dashes bitters

Fill a cocktail shaker ½ full with ice. Pour in light rum and orange juice, and add bitters. Give it a good shake, and strain into an old-fashioned glass ¾ full of ice.

Bacardi Cocktail

2 oz. Bacardi light rum
1 oz. lime juice
1 tsp. simple syrup
¼ tsp. grenadine

Fill a cocktail shaker ½ full with ice. Pour in light rum, lime juice, simple syrup, and grenadine. Give it a good shake, and strain into a cocktail glass.

Bahama Mama

1 oz. light rum
1 oz. dark rum
1 oz. coconut liqueur
¼ tsp. grenadine
2 oz. pineapple juice
2 oz. orange juice
1 pineapple slice
1 maraschino cherry

Fill a cocktail shaker ½ full with ice. Pour in light rum, dark rum, coconut liqueur, grenadine, pineapple juice, and orange juice. Give it a good shake, and strain into a goblet. Garnish with pineapple slice and maraschino cherry.

Banana Rum Cream

2 oz. dark rum
½ oz. crème de bananes
1 oz. light cream

Fill a cocktail shaker ½ full with ice. Pour in dark rum, crème de bananes, and light cream. Give it a good shake, and strain into a cocktail glass.

Barbados Cocktail

2 oz. dark rum
½ oz. triple sec
1½ oz. pineapple juice

Fill a cocktail shaker ½ full with ice. Pour in dark rum, triple sec, and pineapple juice. Give it a good shake, and strain into a cocktail glass.

Barrier Breaker

2 oz. dark rum
½ oz. Galliano
2 tsp. dark crème de cacao
4 oz. cold coffee

Fill an Irish coffee glass ¾ full with crushed ice. Pour in dark rum, Galliano, dark crème de cacao, and cold coffee. Give it a good stir.

Basic Bill

2 oz. añejo rum
½ oz. Dubonnet Rouge
½ oz. Grand Marnier
2 dashes bitters

Fill a cocktail shaker ½ full with ice. Pour in añejo rum, Dubonnet Rouge, and Grand Marnier, and add bitters. Give it a good stir, and strain into a cocktail glass.

Beachcomber

1 lime wedge
1 tsp. superfine sugar
2 oz. light rum
½ oz. triple sec
2 tsp. maraschino liqueur
½ oz. lime juice

Gently rub the rim of a cocktail glass with lime wedge. Sprinkle superfine sugar in a small dish, and place the glass upside down in the dish so the rim is coated with sugar. Fill a cocktail shaker ½ full with ice. Pour in light rum, triple sec, maraschino liqueur, and lime juice. Give it a good stir, and strain into a cocktail glass.

Bee's Kiss

1½ oz. light rum
1½ oz. dark rum
¼ oz. light cream
2 tsp. honey

Fill a cocktail shaker with crushed ice. Pour in light rum, dark rum, light cream, and honey. Give it a good shake, and strain into a cocktail glass.

Bee's Knees

1 lemon wedge
2 tsp. superfine sugar
2 oz. light rum
¼ oz. lemon juice
1 tsp. honey

Gently rub the rim of a cocktail glass with lemon wedge. Sprinkle superfine sugar in a small dish, and place the glass upside down in the dish so the rim is coated with sugar. Fill a cocktail shaker with crushed ice. Pour in light rum, lemon juice, and honey. Give it a good stir, and strain into the cocktail glass.

Bee-Stung Lips

2 oz. light rum
2 tsp. light cream
1 tsp. honey

Fill a cocktail shaker ½ full with ice. Pour in light rum, light cream, and honey. Give it a good stir, and strain into a cocktail glass.

Black Devil

3 oz. light rum
1 tsp. dry vermouth
1 black olive

Fill a cocktail shaker ½ full with ice. Pour in light rum and dry vermouth. Give it a good stir, and strain into a cocktail glass. Garnish with black olive.

Black Maria

1 tsp. superfine sugar
2 oz. dark rum
¾ oz. brandy
¼ oz. coffee liqueur
1 oz. cold espresso coffee

Fill a brandy snifter ½ full with crushed ice. Add superfine sugar and then pour in dark rum, brandy, coffee liqueur, and cold espresso coffee. Give it a good stir.

Black Monday

1½ oz. dark rum
½ oz. black Sambuca
1½ tsp. cherry brandy
½ oz. lemon juice

Fill a cocktail shaker ½ full with ice. Pour in dark rum, black Sambuca, cherry brandy, and lemon juice. Give it a good stir, and strain into an old-fashioned glass ¾ full of ice.

Black Stripe

3 oz. dark rum
1 tsp. molasses
1 tsp. honey
1 cinnamon stick
3 oz. boiling water

Add dark rum, molasses, honey, and cinnamon stick to an Irish coffee glass. Pour in boiling water, and give it a good stir.

Black Stripe Cold

3 oz. dark rum
1 tsp. molasses
1 tsp. honey
1 cinnamon stick

Add dark rum, molasses, honey, and cinnamon stick to a cocktail shaker. Stir until molasses and honey are dissolved. Strain into an old-fashioned glass full of ice.

Black Witch

1½ oz. gold rum
1 oz. dark rum
¼ oz. apricot brandy
1 oz. pineapple juice

Fill a cocktail shaker ½ full with ice. Pour in gold rum, dark rum, apricot brandy, and pineapple juice. Give it a good shake, and strain into a cocktail glass.

Blue Mountain

2 oz. añejo rum
½ oz. vodka
½ oz. coconut liqueur
1 oz. orange juice
1 tsp. lemon juice

Fill a cocktail shaker ½ full with ice. Pour in añejo rum, vodka, coconut liqueur, orange juice, and lemon juice. Give it a good shake, and strain into an old-fashioned glass ¾ full of ice.

Boardwalk Breeze

2 oz. coconut rum
½ oz. añejo rum
1 oz. almond liqueur
½ oz. orange juice
4 oz. pineapple juice
¼ tsp. grenadine

Fill a cocktail shaker ½ full with ice. Pour in coconut rum, añejo rum, almond liqueur, orange juice, and pineapple juice. Give it a good shake, and strain into a goblet. Gently drip grenadine in center of cocktail.

Bob Marley

2 oz. dark rum
4 oz. pineapple juice
¼ tsp. grenadine

Fill a cocktail shaker ½ full with ice. Pour in dark rum, pineapple juice, and grenadine. Give it a good shake, and strain into a highball glass ½ full of ice.

Bolero

2 oz. light rum
¾ oz. apple brandy
2 tsp. sweet vermouth
1 dash bitters

Fill a cocktail shaker ½ full with ice. Pour in light rum, apple brandy, and sweet vermouth, and add bitters. Give it a good shake, and strain into an old-fashioned glass ¾ full of ice.

Boston Sidecar

1½ oz. light rum
¾ oz. brandy
¾ oz. triple sec
½ oz. lemon juice

Fill a cocktail shaker ½ full with ice. Pour in light rum, brandy, triple sec, and lemon juice. Give it a good shake, and strain into a cocktail glass.

Brass Monkey

1½ oz. light rum
1½ oz. vodka
4 oz. orange juice

Fill a highball glass ¾ full with ice. Pour in light rum, vodka, and orange juice. Give it a good stir.

Brooklynite

2½ oz. dark rum
½ oz. honey
2 tsp. lime juice
1 dash bitters

Fill a cocktail shaker ½ full with ice. Pour in dark rum, honey, and lime juice, and add bitters. Give it a good, vigorous shake, and strain into a cock-tail glass.

Brown Cocktail

1½ oz. rum
1½ oz. gin
½ oz. dry vermouth
1 dash orange bitters

Fill a cocktail shaker ½ full with ice. Pour in rum, gin, and dry vermouth, and add orange bitters. Give it a good stir, and strain into a cocktail glass.

Burgundy Bishop

1 tsp. superfine sugar
1½ oz. light rum
2 TB. lemon juice
2 oz. red wine (try a burgundy/
  pinot noir)

Fill a cocktail shaker ½ full with ice. Add superfine sugar and then pour in light rum and lemon juice. Give it a good shake, and strain into a highball glass full of ice. Top off with red wine and stir.

Burnt Embers

2 oz. añejo rum
¾ oz. apricot brandy
1¼ oz. pineapple juice

Fill a cocktail shaker ½ full with ice. Pour in añejo rum, apricot brandy, and pineapple juice. Give it a good shake, and strain into a cocktail glass.

Butter's Painkiller

This substitute for ibuprofen comes from Nolita House in New York City's East Village. The Painkiller is actually a drink famous in the Virgin Islands. Nolita House is nicknamed after a bar-owner friend in St. John who provided them with her own recipe.

2 oz. Bacardi Lite rum
1 oz. coconut rum
½ tsp. *Coco López*
1 tsp. pineapple juice
1 tsp. orange juice
1 pineapple wedge
1 maraschino cherry
⅛ tsp. ground nutmeg

Fill a cocktail shaker ½ full with ice. Pour in Bacardi Lite rum, coconut rum, Coco López, pineapple juice, and orange juice. Give it a good shake, and strain into a highball glass full of ice. Garnish with pineapple wedge, maraschino cherry, and nutmeg.

Liquor Lingo

Coco López is a nonalcoholic cream of coconut mixer.

Caipirinha

1 lime, cut into 7 or 8 wedges
2 tsp. sugar
2½ oz. Brazilian (or light) rum

Place lime wedges pulp side up in an old-fashioned glass. Pour sugar over the top, and muddle until lime juice dissolves sugar. Fill the glass with ice, and pour in rum. Give it a good stir.

Calypso

1½ oz. dark rum
1½ oz. coffee liqueur
1 tsp. sugar (optional)
3 oz. hot coffee

Pour dark rum and coffee liqueur into an Irish coffee glass. Add sugar (if using) and then pour in hot coffee. Give it a good stir.

Calypso Cooler

1 oz. spiced rum
½ oz. dark rum
1 oz. apricot schnapps
½ oz. grenadine
3 oz. orange juice
1 orange slice

Fill a cocktail shaker ½ full with ice. Pour in spiced rum, dark rum, apricot schnapps, grenadine, and orange juice. Give it a good shake, and strain into a highball glass ¾ full of ice. Garnish with orange slice.

Cape of Good Will

2 oz. light rum
1 oz. apricot brandy
1½ oz. orange juice
½ oz. lime juice
2 dashes orange bitters

Fill a cocktail shaker ½ full with ice. Pour in light rum, apricot brandy, orange juice, and lime juice, and add orange bitters. Give it a good shake, and strain into a cocktail glass.

Captain's Blood

2½ oz. dark rum
1 oz. lime juice
2 dashes bitters

Fill a cocktail shaker ½ full with ice. Pour in dark rum and lime juice, and add bitters. Give it a good shake, and strain into a cocktail glass.

Cardinal

2 oz. añejo rum
½ oz. maraschino liqueur
2 tsp. triple sec
1 tsp. grenadine

Fill a cocktail shaker ½ full with ice. Pour in añejo rum, maraschino liqueur, triple sec, and grenadine. Give it a good shake, and strain into a cocktail glass.

Caribbean Cruise

1 oz. light rum
1 oz. dark rum
½ oz. coffee liqueur
½ oz. coconut cream
2 oz. orange juice
2 oz. pineapple juice
1 orange slice
1 pineapple slice

Fill a cocktail shaker ½ full with ice. Pour in light rum, dark rum, coffee liqueur, coconut cream, orange juice, and pineapple juice. Give it a good shake, and strain into a hurricane glass. Garnish with orange slice and pineapple slice.

Casablanca

2 oz. light rum
½ oz. triple sec
1½ tsp. cherry liqueur
2 tsp. lime juice

Fill a cocktail shaker ½ full with ice. Pour in light rum, triple sec, cherry liqueur, and lime juice. Give it a good shake, and strain into a cocktail glass.

Catherine of Sheridan Square

2 oz. dark rum
½ oz. coffee liqueur
½ oz. light cream
4 oz. cold coffee

Fill a cocktail shaker ½ full with ice. Pour in dark rum, coffee liqueur, light cream, and cold coffee. Give it a good shake, and strain into an Irish coffee glass ¾ full of crushed ice.

Celebration

2 oz. rum
1 oz. cognac
1 oz. triple sec
1 oz. lemon juice
1 tsp. simple syrup
2 dashes orange bitters

Fill cocktail shaker with ice. Pour in rum, cognac, triple sec, lemon juice, simple syrup, and add the bitters. Give it a good shake, and strain into a cocktail glass.

Cherried Cream Rum

2 oz. light rum
½ oz. cherry brandy
½ oz. light cream

Fill a cocktail shaker ½ full with ice. Pour in light rum, cherry brandy, and light cream. Give it a good shake, and strain into a cocktail glass.

Cherry Cola

2 oz. dark rum
½ oz. cherry brandy
2 oz. cola
1 maraschino cherry

Fill a highball glass ¾ full with ice. Pour in dark rum, cherry brandy, and cola. Give it a good stir, and garnish with maraschino cherry.

Chinese Cocktail

2 oz. dark rum
1 TB. grenadine
1 tsp. maraschino liqueur
1 tsp. triple sec
1 dash bitters

Fill a cocktail shaker ½ full with ice. Pour in dark rum, grenadine, maraschino liqueur, and triple sec, and add bitters. Give it a good shake, and strain into a cocktail glass.

Chocolate Minty Rum

2 oz. dark rum
2 tsp. 151 proof rum
½ oz. crème de cacao
¼ oz. white crème de menthe
1 TB. light cream

Fill a cocktail shaker ½ full with ice. Pour in dark rum, 151 proof rum, crème de cacao, white crème de menthe, and light cream. Give it a good shake, and strain into a cocktail glass.

Coco-Loco

1½ oz. light rum
1½ oz. dark rum
½ oz. coconut rum
¾ oz. vodka
½ oz. coconut cream
2 oz. pineapple juice

Fill a cocktail shaker ½ full with ice. Pour in light rum, dark rum, coconut rum, vodka, coconut cream, and pineapple juice. Give it a good shake, and strain into a hurricane glass.

Cocomacoque

1½ oz. light rum
3 TB. lemon juice
2 oz. pineapple juice
2 oz. orange juice
1½ oz. red wine
1 pineapple slice

Fill a Collins glass ¾ full with ice. Fill a cocktail shaker ½ full with ice, and pour in light rum, lemon juice, pineapple juice, and orange juice. Give it a good shake, and strain into the Collins glass. Pour in red wine, and garnish with pineapple slice.

Spills

Although the Cocomacoque recipe calls for "red wine," you really shouldn't use just any red wine you happen to have around. Opt for a fruit-driven, low-tannic wine like a Beaujolais (gamay grape), burgundy (pinot noir grape), Chianti (sangiovese grape), or a Rioja (tempranillo grape) *crianza* (which just means it's younger and not aged as long).

Columbia Cocktail

2 oz. light rum
½ oz. raspberry syrup
½ oz. lemon juice
1 lemon twist

Fill a cocktail shaker ½ full with ice. Pour in light rum, raspberry syrup, and lemon juice. Give it a good shake, and strain into a cocktail glass. Garnish with lemon twist.

Continental

½ tsp. superfine sugar
2 oz. light rum
1 TB. green crème de menthe
2 TB. lime juice
1 TB. lemon juice
1 lemon twist

Fill a cocktail shaker ½ full with ice. Add superfine sugar and then pour in light rum, green crème de menthe, lime juice, and lemon juice. Give it a good shake, and strain into a cocktail glass. Garnish with lemon twist.

Coral

2½ oz. light rum
¼ oz. apricot brandy
½ oz. grapefruit juice
2 TB. lemon juice
1 lemon twist

Fill a cocktail shaker ½ full with ice. Pour in light rum, apricot brandy, grapefruit juice, and lemon juice. Give it a good shake, and strain into a cocktail glass. Garnish with lemon twist.

Corkscrew

2 oz. light rum
½ oz. peach schnapps
2 tsp. dry vermouth
1 lemon twist

Fill a cocktail shaker ½ full with ice. Pour in light rum, peach schnapps, and dry vermouth. Give it a good shake, and strain into a cocktail glass. Garnish with lemon twist.

Cosmos

1 tsp. superfine sugar
2 oz. light rum
1 oz. lime juice
1 lemon twist

Fill a cocktail shaker with crushed ice. Add superfine sugar and then pour in rum and lime juice. Give it a good shake, and strain into a cocktail glass. Garnish with lemon twist.

Cream Puff

1 tsp. superfine sugar
2 oz. light rum
2 TB. light cream
4 oz. club soda

Fill a highball glass ½ full with ice. Fill a cocktail shaker ½ full with ice, add sugar, and then pour in light rum and light cream. Give it a good shake, and strain into the highball glass. Top with club soda.

Creole Cocktail

2 oz. light rum
3 oz. beef bouillon
⅛ tsp. Tabasco sauce
1 tsp. lemon juice
1 pinch salt
1 pinch black pepper
1 lemon twist

Fill an old-fashioned glass ¾ full with ice. Fill a cocktail shaker ½ full with ice, and pour in light rum, beef bouillon, Tabasco sauce, lemon juice, salt, and pepper. Give it a good shake, and strain into a cocktail glass. Garnish with lemon twist.

Cruise Control

2 oz. light rum
½ oz. apricot brandy
½ oz. triple sec
¼ oz. lemon juice
3 oz. club soda

Fill a highball glass ½ full with ice. Fill a cocktail shaker ½ full with ice, and pour in light rum, apricot brandy, triple sec, and lemon juice. Give it a good shake, and strain into the highball glass. Top with club soda.

Cuba Libre

2 oz. light rum
4 oz. cola
1 lime wedge

Fill a highball glass ¾ full with ice. Pour in light rum and cola. Give it a good stir, and garnish with lime wedge.

Cuban Cocktail

2 oz. light rum
3 TB. lime juice
1 TB. lemon juice
1 tsp. simple syrup

Fill a cocktail shaker ½ full with ice. Pour in light rum, lime juice, lemon juice, and simple syrup. Give it a good shake, and strain into a cocktail glass.

Cuban Cooler

2½ oz. light rum
4 oz. ginger ale
1 lime wedge

Fill a highball glass ¾ full with ice. Pour in light rum and ginger ale. Garnish with lime wedge.

Cuban Manhattan

3 oz. white rum
¾ oz. sweet vermouth
1 dash bitters
1 maraschino cherry

Fill a cocktail shaker ½ full with ice. Pour in white rum and sweet vermouth, and add bitters. Give it a good stir, and strain into a cocktail glass. Garnish with maraschino cherry.

Culross

2 oz. rum
½ oz. Lillet
½ oz. apricot brandy
1 tsp. lime juice

Fill a cocktail shaker ½ full with ice. Pour in rum, Lillet, apricot brandy, and lime juice. Give it a good shake, and strain into a cocktail glass.

Daiquiri

2 oz. light rum
1 oz. lime juice
1 oz. simple syrup

Fill a cocktail shaker ½ full with ice. Pour in light rum, lime juice, and simple syrup. Give it a good shake, and strain into a cocktail glass.

Cocktail Conversation

The daiquiri got its name from the eponymous town in Cuba where it was created by two mining engineers—one Cuban, one American—in the late nineteenth century.

Dambuster

3 oz. rum
1 oz. Kahlúa
1 oz. ginger ale
2 oz. milk

Fill a highball glass ¾ full with ice. Pour in rum, Kahlúa, ginger ale, and milk. Give it a good stir.

Damn Your Eyes

2 oz. añejo rum
¾ oz. Dubonnet Blanc
1 tsp. dry vermouth
1 lemon twist

Fill a cocktail shaker with crushed ice. Pour in añejo rum, Dubonnet Blanc, and dry vermouth. Give it a good shake, and strain into a cocktail glass. Garnish with lemon twist.

Dark 'n' Stormy

My first encounter with a Dark 'n' Stormy was, fittingly, on a dark and stormy night in ye olde town of Marblehead, Massachusetts (right next to spooky Salem), at the home of our good friends Jeff Baker and Cynthia Roberts. Jeff, who is very particular about his cocktails, prefers to use 151 proof rum. But be forewarned—the 151 might make you feel a little extra dark and stormy the morning after.

2½ oz. dark rum
5 oz. ginger beer
1 lime wedge

Fill a Collins glass ¾ full with ice.
Pour in dark rum and ginger beer.
Give it a good stir, and garnish with lime wedge.

Davis

2 oz. light rum
¾ oz. dry vermouth
1 oz. lime juice
¼ tsp. raspberry syrup

Fill a cocktail shaker ½ full with ice.
Pour in light rum, dry vermouth, lime juice, and raspberry syrup. Give it a good shake, and strain into a cocktail glass.

Deep, Dark Secret

1½ oz. dark rum
½ oz. añejo rum
½ oz. coffee liqueur
½ oz. heavy cream

Fill a cocktail shaker ½ full with ice.
Pour in dark rum, añejo rum, coffee liqueur, and heavy cream. Give it a good shake, and strain into a cocktail glass.

Deep South

1 tsp. molasses
4 oz. pineapple juice
2 oz. dark rum
¼ tsp. cherry syrup
1 pineapple slice

Fill a Collins glass with ice. Fill a cocktail shaker ½ full with ice, and pour in molasses and pineapple juice. Give it a good, vigorous shake, and strain into the highball glass. Pour in dark rum (do not stir). Then drip cherry syrup in center of cocktail. Garnish with pineapple slice.

Derailer

1 oz. light rum
1 oz. dark rum
2 TB. 151 proof rum
2 oz. orange juice
2 oz. lemon-lime soda

Fill a highball glass ¾ full with ice. Fill a cocktail shaker ½ full with ice, and pour in light rum, dark rum, 151 proof rum, and orange juice. Give it a good shake, and strain into a cocktail glass. Top with lemon-lime soda.

Derby Special

2 oz. light rum
½ oz. triple sec
1 oz. orange juice
½ oz. lime juice

Fill a highball glass ½ full with ice. Fill a cocktail shaker ½ full with ice, and pour in light rum, triple sec, orange juice, and lime juice. Give it a good shake, and strain into the highball glass.

DeRosier

1½ oz. añejo rum
½ oz. bourbon
½ oz. dark crème de cacao
½ oz. cherry brandy
1 oz. heavy cream

Fill a cocktail shaker ½ full with ice. Pour in añejo rum, bourbon, dark crème de cacao, cherry brandy, and heavy cream. Give it a good shake, and strain into a cocktail glass.

Dianne on the Tower

2 oz. light rum
½ oz. bourbon
1 tsp. dark crème de cacao
1 tsp. cherry brandy

Fill a cocktail shaker ½ full with ice. Pour in light rum, bourbon, dark crème de cacao, and cherry brandy. Give it a good shake, and strain into an old-fashioned glass full of ice.

Don Juan

1½ oz. dark rum
1 oz. white tequila
1 oz. pineapple juice
1 oz. orange juice
1 pineapple slice

Fill a cocktail shaker ½ full with ice. Pour in dark rum, white tequila, pineapple juice, and orange juice. Give it a good shake, and strain into an old-fashioned glass ¾ full of ice. Garnish with pineapple slice.

Dr. Funk

1 lime, cut in half
2 tsp. superfine sugar
2½ oz. dark rum
¼ oz. pastis
1 tsp. grenadine
½ oz. lemon juice
3 oz. club soda

Fill a cocktail shaker ½ full with ice. Squeeze 2 lime halves into shaker. Add superfine sugar, and pour in dark rum, pastis, grenadine, and lemon juice. Give it a good shake, and pour into a Collins glass ¾ full of ice. Pour in club soda, and give it a good stir.

Dunlop

3 oz. light rum
¾ oz. sherry
2 dashes bitters

Fill a cocktail shaker ½ full with ice. Pour in light rum and sherry, and add bitters. Give it a good shake, and strain into an old-fashioned glass ¾ full of ice.

El Floridita

2 oz. rum
½ oz. sweet vermouth
¼ tsp. white crème de cacao
¼ tsp. grenadine
½ oz. lime juice
1 lime wedge

Fill a cocktail shaker ½ full with ice. Pour in rum, sweet vermouth, white crème de cacao, grenadine, and lime juice. Give it a good shake, and strain into a Collins glass ¾ full of ice. Garnish with lime wedge.

El Presidente

2 oz. light rum
1 oz. sweet vermouth
¼ tsp. grenadine
1 orange twist

Fill a cocktail shaker ½ full with ice. Pour in light rum, sweet vermouth, and grenadine. Give it a good shake, and strain into a cocktail glass. Garnish with orange twist.

El Salvador

2 oz. gold rum
½ oz. Frangelico
½ oz. lime juice
¼ tsp. grenadine

Fill a cocktail shaker ½ full with ice. Pour in gold rum, Frangelico, lime juice, and grenadine. Give it a good shake, and strain into a cocktail glass.

Elephant Lips

2 oz. dark rum
½ oz. crème de bananes
¼ oz. lemon juice

Fill a cocktail shaker ½ full with ice. Pour in dark rum, crème de bananes, and lemon juice. Give it a good shake, and strain into an old-fashioned glass ¾ full of ice.

Entwistle's Error

2 oz. dark rum
½ oz. lemon juice
4 oz. tonic water

Fill a highball glass ¾ full with ice. Pour in dark rum, lemon juice, and tonic water. Give it a good stir.

Everglades Special

2 oz. light rum
1 oz. white crème de cacao
2 tsp. coffee liqueur
½ oz. light cream

Fill a cocktail shaker ½ full with ice. Pour in light rum, white crème de cacao, coffee liqueur, and light cream. Give it a good shake, and strain into a cocktail glass.

Eye-Opener

3 oz. light rum
¼ oz. pastis
¼ oz. orange curaçao
¼ oz. crème de cacao
1 egg
1 tsp. sugar

Fill a cocktail shaker ½ full with ice. Pour in light rum, pastis, orange curaçao, and crème de cacao, and add egg and sugar. Give it a good, vigorous shake, and strain into a cocktail glass.

Fair and Warmer

2½ oz. light rum
½ oz. sweet vermouth
2 dashes orange curaçao

Fill a cocktail shaker ½ full with ice. Pour in light rum, sweet vermouth, and orange curaçao. Give it a good stir, and strain into an old-fashioned glass ¾ full of ice.

Fern Gully

1 oz. light rum
1 oz. dark rum
¾ oz. almond liqueur
½ oz. cream of coconut
1 oz. orange juice
2 tsp. lime juice

Fill a cocktail shaker ½ full with ice. Pour in light rum, dark rum, almond liqueur, cream of coconut, orange juice, and lime juice. Give it a good shake, and strain into a highball glass ¾ full of ice.

Fiesta

1 oz. light rum
1 oz. calvados
¾ oz. dry vermouth
¼ tsp. grenadine
1 tsp. lime juice

Fill a cocktail shaker ½ full with ice. Pour in light rum, calvados, dry vermouth, grenadine, and lime juice. Give it a good shake, and strain into a cocktail glass.

Fiji Fizz

2 oz. dark rum
¾ oz. bourbon
1 tsp. cherry brandy
3 dashes orange bitters
4 oz. cola
1 lime wedge

Fill a cocktail shaker ½ full with ice. Pour in dark rum, bourbon, and cherry brandy, and add orange bitters. Give it a good shake, and strain into a Collins glass ½ full of ice. Top with cola, and garnish with lime wedge.

Fireman's Sour

2 oz. light rum
2 oz. lime juice
½ oz. grenadine
2 oz. club soda
1 lime wedge
1 maraschino cherry

Fill a cocktail shaker ½ full with ice. Pour in light rum, lime juice, and grenadine. Give it a good shake, and strain into a highball glass ¾ full of ice. Pour in club soda, and garnish with lime wedge and maraschino cherry.

Flim Flam

2 oz. light rum
1 oz. triple sec
½ oz. lemon juice
¾ oz. orange juice

Fill a cocktail shaker ½ full with ice. Pour in light rum, triple sec, lemon juice, and orange juice. Give it a good shake, and strain into a cocktail glass.

Florida Punch Cocktail

2 oz. dark rum
½ oz. cognac
1 oz. grapefruit juice
1 oz. orange juice

Fill a cocktail shaker ½ full with ice. Pour in dark rum, cognac, grapefruit juice, and orange juice. Give it a good shake, and strain into a highball glass ¾ full of ice.

Fogcutter

2 oz. light rum
½ oz. brandy
½ oz. gin
2 tsp. orgeat syrup
1 oz. orange juice
2 TB. lemon juice
1 tsp. sweet sherry

Fill a cocktail shaker ½ full with ice. Pour in light rum, brandy, gin, orgeat syrup, orange juice, and lemon juice. Give it a good shake, and strain into a Collins glass ¾ full of ice. Drop sweet sherry into center of cocktail.

Fort Lauderdale Cocktail

3 oz. gold rum
½ oz. sweet vermouth
1 TB. orange juice
1 TB. lemon juice
1 orange slice

Fill a cocktail shaker ½ full with ice. Pour in gold rum, sweet vermouth, orange juice, and lemon juice. Give it a good shake, and strain into an old-fashioned glass ¾ full of ice. Garnish with orange slice.

Fox Trot

2 oz. light rum
½ oz. lime juice
¼ tsp. curaçao

Fill a cocktail shaker ½ full with ice. Pour in light rum, lime juice, and curaçao. Give it a good shake, and strain into a cocktail glass.

French Pirate

½ oz. orange curaçao
1½ oz. dark rum
2 oz. champagne

Pour orange curaçao into a champagne flute. Add dark rum, and follow with champagne.

Full Moon Fever

2 oz. coconut rum
1 oz. spiced rum
1 oz. melon liqueur
1 tsp. sour mix
3 oz. pineapple juice
1 maraschino cherry

Fill a highball glass ¾ full with ice. Pour in coconut rum, spiced rum, melon liqueur, and sour mix, and top off with pineapple juice. Give a good stir, and garnish with maraschino cherry.

Ginger Breeze

2 oz. light rum
1 tsp. cherry liqueur
4 oz. orange juice
1 oz. ginger ale

Fill a cocktail shaker ½ full with ice. Pour in light rum, cherry liqueur, and orange juice. Give it a good shake, and strain into a highball glass ¾ full of ice. Pour in ginger ale.

Good Golly

2 oz. dark rum
½ oz. Galliano
2 tsp. dark crème de cacao
4 oz. hot coffee
¼ oz. whipped cream

Pour dark rum, Galliano, dark crème de cacao, and hot coffee into an Irish coffee glass. Give it a good stir, and top with whipped cream.

Gradeal Special

1½ oz. light rum
1 oz. apricot brandy
¾ oz. gin

Fill a cocktail shaker ½ full with ice. Pour in light rum, apricot brandy, and gin. Give it a good shake, and strain into a cocktail glass.

Grass Is Greener

2 oz. light rum
1 TB. green crème de menthe
½ oz. lemon juice

Fill a cocktail shaker ½ full with ice. Pour in light rum, green crème de menthe, and lemon juice. Give it a good shake, and strain into a cocktail glass.

Grog

2 tsp. sugar
2 oz. dark rum
1 TB. lemon juice
4 oz. boiling water

Add sugar in an Irish coffee glass and then pour in dark rum and lemon juice. Pour in boiling water and stir.

Hammerhead

2 oz. gold rum
1 oz. amaretto
1 oz. curaçao
¼ tsp. Southern Comfort

Fill a cocktail shaker ½ full with ice. Pour in gold rum, amaretto, curaçao, and Southern Comfort. Give it a good shake, and strain into a cocktail glass.

Hat Trick

¾ oz. light rum
¾ oz. dry vermouth
2 dashes bitters
1 lemon peel

Fill a cocktail shaker ½ full with ice. Pour in light rum and dry vermouth, and add bitters. Give it a good stir, and strain into a cocktail glass. Garnish with lemon peel.

Havana Beach Cocktail

½ tsp. superfine sugar
2 oz. light rum
1 oz. pineapple juice
¼ oz. lime juice

Fill a cocktail shaker ½ full with ice. Add superfine sugar and then pour in light rum, pineapple juice, and lime juice. Give it a good shake, and strain into a cocktail glass.

Havana Club

2 oz. light rum
1 tsp. dry vermouth

Fill a cocktail shaker ½ full with ice. Pour in light rum and dry vermouth. Give it a good shake, and strain into a cocktail glass.

Havana Sidecar

1½ oz. gold rum
¾ oz. triple sec
¾ oz. lemon juice
1 lemon twist

Fill a cocktail shaker ½ full with ice. Pour in gold rum, triple sec, and lemon juice. Give it a good shake, and strain into a cocktail glass. Garnish with lemon twist.

Havana Special

2 oz. light rum
1 TB. maraschino liqueur
2 oz. pineapple juice
½ tsp. lime juice
1 maraschino cherry

Fill a cocktail shaker ½ full with ice. Pour in light rum, maraschino liqueur, pineapple juice, and lime juice. Give it a good shake, and strain into a cocktail glass. Garnish with maraschino cherry.

Hemingway Daiquiri

The Hemingway Daiquiri (or Hemingway Special) was named for the famous and beloved Ernest during one of his extended stays in Cuba. Constantino Ribailagua at the El Floridita Bar in Havana created the Hemingway when he added maraschino liqueur and grapefruit juice to the original daiquiri recipe.

1½ oz. light rum
¼ oz. maraschino liqueur
¾ oz. lime juice
¼ oz. grapefruit juice

Fill a cocktail shaker ½ full with ice. Pour in light rum, maraschino liqueur, lime juice, and grapefruit juice. Give it a good shake, and strain into a cocktail glass.

Henry Morgan's Cocktail

2 oz. white rum
3 oz. orange juice
1 tsp. grenadine
2 oz. club soda

Fill a cocktail shaker ½ full with ice. Pour in white rum, orange juice, and grenadine. Give it a good shake, and strain into a highball glass ¾ full of ice. Pour in club soda.

High Jamaican Wind

2 oz. dark rum
½ oz. coffee liqueur
1 TB. heavy cream

Fill an old-fashioned glass with ice. Pour in dark rum and then add coffee liqueur. Gently drip heavy cream on top.

Honey Bee

2 tsp. honey
2 oz. gold rum
½ oz. lemon juice
1 lemon twist

Fill a cocktail shaker ½ full with ice. Spoon in honey and then pour in gold rum and lemon juice. Give it a good, vigorous shake, and strain into a cocktail glass. Garnish with lemon twist.

Hop Toad

1½ oz. rum
1½ oz. apricot brandy
2 TB. lime juice

Fill a cocktail shaker ½ full with ice. Pour in rum, apricot brandy, and lime juice. Give it a good shake, and strain into a cocktail glass.

Horse and Jockey

1½ oz. añejo rum
1½ oz. Southern Comfort
½ oz. sweet vermouth
2 dashes bitters
1 maraschino cherry

Fill a cocktail shaker ½ full with ice. Pour in añejo rum, Southern Comfort, and sweet vermouth, and add bitters. Give it a good shake, and strain into a cocktail glass. Garnish with maraschino cherry.

Hot Buttered Rum

1 tsp. brown sugar
1 cinnamon stick
2 oz. dark rum
4 oz. boiling water
½ TB. butter

Add brown sugar and cinnamon stick to an Irish coffee glass. Pour in dark rum and boiling water. Give it a good stir, and top with butter.

Hot Rum Toddy

1 TB. honey
2 oz. rum
1 TB. lemon juice
4 oz. boiling water

Add honey to an Irish coffee glass. Pour in rum, lemon juice, and boiling water. Give it a good stir.

Hurricane

My husband Dan and I are big fans of New Orleans. In fact, we've traveled there enough that we even have little rituals we must perform while there. One is making Pat O'Brien's our first stop for a hurricane, where the drink was invented. Of course, O'Brien's churns out enough of these very potent drinks now that they simply use a mix to keep up with the demand, but for this recipe (and every recipe in this book!), use fresh juices for a simply sublime sipping experience.

1½ oz. dark rum
½ oz. 151 proof rum
2 oz. orange juice
2 oz. pineapple juice
½ oz. lime juice
½ oz. grenadine
1 TB. passion fruit syrup
1 orange slice
1 maraschino cherry

Fill a cocktail shaker ½ full with ice. Pour in dark rum, 151 proof rum, orange juice, pineapple juice, lime juice, grenadine, and passion fruit syrup. Give it a good shake, and strain into a hurricane glass. Garnish with orange slice and maraschino cherry.

Ice Palace

1½ oz. light rum
¼ oz. Galliano
¼ oz. apricot brandy
2 oz. pineapple juice
½ oz. lemon juice
1 maraschino cherry

Fill a cocktail shaker ½ full with ice. Pour in light rum, Galliano, apricot brandy, pineapple juice, and lemon juice. Give it a good shake, and strain into a highball glass ½ full of ice. Garnish with maraschino cherry.

Immaculata

1 tsp. superfine sugar
2 oz. light rum
½ oz. amaretto
½ oz. lime juice
½ oz. lemon juice

Fill a cocktail shaker ½ full with ice. Add superfine sugar and then pour in light rum, amaretto, lime juice, and lemon juice. Give it a good shake, and strain into a cocktail glass.

Isle of Pines

2 oz. light rum
3 oz. grapefruit juice

Fill a highball glass with ice. Pour in rum and grapefruit juice. Give it a good stir.

Jade

1 tsp. superfine sugar
2 oz. gold rum
1 tsp. green curaçao
½ oz. lime juice
1 lime slice

Fill a cocktail shaker ½ full with ice. Add superfine sugar and then pour in gold rum, green curaçao, and lime juice. Give it a good shake, and strain into a cocktail glass. Garnish with lime slice.

Jamaica Cooler

2½ oz. dark rum
½ oz. orange juice
2 TB. lemon juice
2 dashes orange bitters
3 oz. lemon-lime soda

Fill a cocktail shaker ½ full with ice. Pour in dark rum, orange juice, and lemon juice, and add orange bitters. Give it a good shake, and strain into a highball glass ¾ full of ice. Top off with lemon-lime soda.

Jamaican Fizz

1 tsp. superfine sugar
2½ oz. rum
1 oz. pineapple juice
4 oz. club soda

Fill a cocktail shaker ½ full with ice. Add superfine sugar and then pour in rum and pineapple juice. Give it a good shake, and strain into a Collins glass ¾ full of ice. Top off with club soda, and give it a good stir.

Jamaican Martini

2½ oz. light rum
½ oz. dry sherry

Fill a cocktail shaker ½ full with ice. Pour in light rum and dry sherry. Give it a good stir, and strain into a cocktail glass.

Jamaican's Ginger

3 oz. dark rum
1 dash bitters
5 oz. ginger beer
1 lime wedge

Fill a Collins glass ¾ full with ice. Pour in dark rum, and add bitters. Pour in ginger beer, and garnish with lime wedge.

Jean Gabin

Jean Gabin (born Jean-Alexis Moncourge) made his career debut in 1915 on the stage of the famous Moulin Rouge in Paris. He made a multitude of performances on the stage and screen until his death in 1976, and in 1998 the French Post Office honored him by placing his likeness on a stamp.

1 TB. maple syrup
2 oz. dark rum
½ oz. calvados
4 oz. hot milk
½ tsp. grated nutmeg

Add maple syrup to an Irish coffee glass. Pour in dark rum, calvados, and hot milk. Give it a good stir, and garnish with grated nutmeg.

Joburg

1½ oz. light rum
1½ oz. Dubonnet Blanc
2 dashes orange bitters

Fill a cocktail shaker ½ full with ice. Pour in light rum and Dubonnet Blanc, and add orange bitters. Give it a good shake, and strain into a cocktail glass.

Joy to the World

2 oz. añejo rum
½ oz. bourbon
½ oz. dark crème de cacao

Fill a cocktail shaker ½ full with ice.
Pour in añejo rum, bourbon, and dark
crème de cacao. Give it a good shake,
and strain into a cocktail glass.

Judge Jr.

½ tsp. superfine sugar
1 oz. light rum
1 oz. gin
¼ tsp. grenadine
½ oz. lemon juice

Fill a cocktail shaker ½ full with ice.
Add superfine sugar and then pour in
light rum, gin, grenadine, and lemon
juice. Give it a good shake, and strain
into a cocktail glass.

Kialoa

1 oz. spiced rum
1 oz. coffee liqueur
1 oz. light cream

Fill a cocktail shaker ½ full with ice.
Pour in spiced rum, coffee liqueur, and
light cream. Give it a good shake, and
strain into an old-fashioned glass full
of ice.

Kick in the Face

¼ tsp. superfine sugar
2½ oz. rum
4 oz. lemon juice
1 oz. club soda

Fill a cocktail shaker ½ full with ice.
Add superfine sugar and then pour in
rum and lemon juice. Give it a good
shake, and strain into a Collins glass
¾ full of ice. Pour in club soda, and
give it a good stir.

Kingston

2 oz. dark rum
1 oz. gin
1 tsp. grenadine
½ oz. lime juice

Fill a cocktail shaker ½ full with ice.
Pour in dark rum, gin, grenadine, and
lime juice. Give it a good shake, and
strain into a cocktail glass.

Knickerbocker Special

2 oz. spiced rum
1 TB. orange curaçao
½ oz. orange juice
½ oz. lime juice
1 tsp. raspberry syrup

Fill a cocktail shaker ½ full with ice. Pour in spiced rum, orange curaçao, orange juice, lime juice, and raspberry syrup. Give it a good shake, and strain into a cocktail glass.

Kona Cocktail

2 oz. light rum
¼ oz. maraschino liqueur
1 oz. pineapple juice
½ oz. lemon juice

Fill a cocktail shaker ½ full with ice. Pour in light rum, maraschino liqueur, pineapple juice, and lemon juice. Give it a good shake, and strain into a cocktail glass.

Krazee Keith

2 oz. light rum
2 tsp. cherry brandy
1 tsp. anisette
½ oz. lemon juice
4 oz. cola
1 lemon slice

Fill a cocktail shaker ½ full with ice. Pour in light rum, cherry brandy, anisette, and lemon juice. Give it a good shake, and strain into a highball glass ¾ full of ice. Pour in cola, and garnish with lemon slice.

Lady Cello

1 lemon wedge
2 tsp. sugar
1½ oz. gold rum
1½ oz. *Limoncello*
1 tsp. grenadine
½ oz. lemon juice
1 maraschino cherry

Gently rub the rim of a highball glass with lemon wedge. Sprinkle sugar in a small dish, and place the glass upside down in the dish so the rim is coated with sugar. Fill a cocktail shaker ½ full with ice. Pour in gold rum, Limoncello, grenadine, and lemon juice. Give it a good shake, and strain into the highball glass ¾ full of ice. Garnish with maraschino cherry.

Liquor Lingo

Limoncello is an Italian lemon liqueur.

Lallah Rookh

1¾ oz. dark rum
¾ oz. cognac
1 tsp. vanilla extract
1 tsp. simple syrup
¼ cup whipped cream

Fill a cocktail shaker ½ full with ice. Pour in dark rum, cognac, vanilla extract, and simple syrup. Give it a good shake, and strain into a brandy snifter. Dollop whipped cream on top.

Landed Gentry

2 oz. dark rum
1 oz. coffee liqueur
½ oz. heavy cream

Fill a cocktail shaker ½ full with ice. Pour in dark rum, coffee liqueur, and heavy cream. Give it a good shake, and strain into a cocktail glass.

Latin Perfect Manhattan

2 oz. dark rum
½ oz. sweet vermouth
½ oz. dry vermouth
1 dash bitters
1 maraschino cherry

Fill a cocktail shaker ½ full with ice. Pour in dark rum, sweet vermouth, and dry vermouth, and add bitters. Give it a good stir, and strain into a cocktail glass. Garnish with maraschino cherry.

Leeward

2 oz. light rum
2 tsp. calvados
2 tsp. sweet vermouth
1 lemon twist

Fill a cocktail shaker ½ full with ice. Pour in light rum, calvados, and sweet vermouth. Give it a good shake, and strain into an old-fashioned glass full of ice. Garnish with lemon twist.

Liberty Cocktail

2 oz. light rum
1 oz. apple brandy
1 oz. lime juice
1 tsp. simple syrup

Fill a cocktail shaker ½ full with ice. Pour in light rum, apple brandy, lime juice, and simple syrup. Give it a good shake, and strain into a cocktail glass.

Limbo

2 oz. rum
½ oz. banana liqueur
1 oz. orange juice
2 tsp. pineapple juice

Fill a cocktail shaker ½ full with ice. Pour in rum, banana liqueur, orange juice, and pineapple juice. Give it a good shake, and strain into a cocktail glass.

Limey

2 oz. light rum
2 TB. lime liqueur
2 tsp. triple sec
2 TB. lime juice
1 tsp. simple syrup
1 lime twist

Fill a cocktail shaker with crushed ice. Pour in light rum, lime liqueur, triple sec, lime juice, and simple syrup. Give it a good shake, and strain into an old-fashioned glass full of ice. Garnish with lime twist.

Little Princess Cocktail

2 oz. light rum
1 oz. sweet vermouth

Fill a cocktail shaker ½ full with ice. Pour in light rum and sweet vermouth. Give it a good stir, and strain into a cocktail glass.

Long Island Iced Tea

½ oz. light rum
½ oz. gin
½ oz. vodka
½ oz. tequila
½ oz. triple sec
1 oz. sour mix
2 oz. cola

Fill a cocktail shaker ½ full with ice. Pour in light rum, gin, vodka, tequila, triple sec, and sour mix. Give it a good shake, and strain into a Collins glass ½ full of ice. Pour in cola.

Look Out Below

1½ oz. 151 proof rum
1 tsp. grenadine
1 TB. lime juice

Fill a cocktail shaker ½ full with ice. Pour in 151 proof rum, grenadine, and lime juice. Give it a good shake, and strain into an old-fashioned glass full of ice.

Lord and Lady

2 oz. dark rum
¾ oz. coffee liqueur

Pour dark rum and coffee liqueur into an old-fashioned glass full of ice. Give it a good stir.

Louisiana Lullaby

2 oz. dark rum
3 tsp. Dubonnet Rouge
¼ tsp. Grand Marnier
1 orange twist

Fill a cocktail shaker ½ full with ice. Pour in dark rum, Dubonnet Rouge, and Grand Marnier. Give it a good shake, and strain into a cocktail glass. Garnish with orange twist.

Love for Toby

2 oz. light rum
½ oz. brandy
½ oz. cherry brandy
2 tsp. lime juice

Fill a cocktail shaker ½ full with ice.
Pour in light rum, brandy, cherry
brandy, and lime juice. Give it a good
shake, and strain into a cocktail glass.

Madison Avenue Cocktail

3 mint leaves
1½ oz. white rum
¾ oz. triple sec
½ oz. lime juice
1 dash orange bitters
1 lime slice

Fill a cocktail shaker ½ full with ice.
Add mint leaves; pour in white rum,
triple sec, and lime juice; and add
orange bitters. Give it a good shake,
and strain into an old-fashioned glass
¾ full of ice. Garnish with lime slice.

Maestro

2 oz. añejo rum
½ oz. sherry
¼ oz. lime juice
4 oz. ginger ale
1 lemon twist

Fill a cocktail shaker ½ full with ice.
Pour in añejo rum, sherry, and lime
juice. Give it a good shake, and strain
into a Collins glass ¾ full of ice. Pour
in ginger ale, and garnish with lemon
twist.

Mai Tai

The Mai Tai was created and named by bartender Victor Bergeron, of the
famous Trader Vic's, in 1944. The name came from the Tahitian saying, "Mai tai
roa ae!" or "Out of this world!"

2 oz. aged rum
½ oz. orange curaçao
½ oz. orgeat syrup
½ oz. lime juice
¼ oz. simple syrup
1 lime wedge
1 mint sprig

Fill a cocktail shaker with crushed ice.
Pour in aged rum, orange curaçao,
orgeat syrup, lime juice, and simple
syrup. Give it a good shake, and strain
into an old-fashioned glass ¾ full of
ice. Garnish with lime wedge and mint
sprig.

Mallelieu

2 oz. light rum
½ oz. Grand Marnier
2 oz. orange juice

Fill a cocktail shaker ½ full with ice.
Pour in light rum, Grand Marnier,
and orange juice. Give it a good shake,
and strain into an old-fashioned glass
¾ full of ice.

Mandeville

1½ oz. light rum
1 oz. dark rum
1 tsp. pastis
½ tsp. grenadine
¼ oz. lemon juice
1 oz. cola

Fill a cocktail shaker ½ full with ice. Pour in light rum, dark rum, pastis, grenadine, and lemon juice. Give it a good shake, and strain into an old-fashioned glass ¾ full of ice. Pour in cola, and give it a good stir.

Mariposa

1½ oz. light rum
½ oz. brandy
¼ tsp. grenadine
1 TB. lemon juice
1 TB. orange juice

Fill a cocktail shaker ½ full with ice. Pour in light rum, brandy, grenadine, lemon juice, and orange juice. Give it a good shake, and strain into a cocktail glass.

Mary Pickford Cocktail

2 oz. light rum
½ tsp. maraschino liqueur
½ tsp. grenadine
1½ oz. pineapple juice
1 maraschino cherry

Fill a cocktail shaker ½ full with ice. Pour in light rum, maraschino liqueur, grenadine, and pineapple juice. Give it a good shake, and strain into an old-fashioned glass ¾ full of ice. Garnish with maraschino cherry.

Mary's Dream

2 oz. light rum
1 oz. triple sec
3 oz. orange juice
2 dashes orange bitters
1 orange slice

Fill a cocktail shaker ½ full with ice. Pour in light rum, triple sec, and orange juice, and add orange bitters. Give it a good shake, and strain into a highball glass ¾ full of ice. Garnish with orange slice.

Ménage à Trois

1 oz. dark rum
1 oz. triple sec
1 oz. light cream

Fill a cocktail shaker ½ full with ice. Pour in dark rum, triple sec, and light cream. Give it a good shake, and strain into a cocktail glass.

Mexicano

2 oz. light rum
2 tsp. kummel
2 tsp. orange juice
3 dashes bitters

Fill a cocktail shaker ½ full with ice. Pour in light rum, kummel, orange juice, and bitters. Give it a good shake, and strain into an old-fashioned glass ¾ full of ice.

Miami Cocktail

2 oz. light rum
½ oz. white crème de menthe
1 tsp. lemon juice

Fill a cocktail shaker ½ full with ice. Pour in light rum, white crème de menthe, and lemon juice. Give it a good shake, and strain into a cocktail glass.

Miss Belle

2 oz. dark rum
½ oz. Grand Marnier
2 tsp. dark crème de cacao

Fill a cocktail shaker ½ full with ice. Pour in dark rum, Grand Marnier, and dark crème de cacao. Give it a good shake, and strain into a cocktail glass.

Mister Christian

2 oz. light rum
½ oz. brandy
1 tsp. grenadine
1 oz. orange juice
¼ oz. lemon juice
¼ oz. lime juice

Fill a cocktail shaker ½ full with ice. Pour in light rum, brandy, grenadine, orange juice, lemon juice, and lime juice. Give it a good shake, and strain into a cocktail glass.

Mojito

2 mint sprigs
1 oz. simple syrup
½ oz. lime juice
2 oz. light rum
3 to 4 oz. club soda

Muddle 1 mint sprig with simple syrup and lime juice in a highball glass. Fill glass ¾ full with crushed ice, and pour in light rum. Give it a good stir. Pour in club soda, and garnish with remaining mint sprig.

Monkey Wrench

2½ oz. light rum
1 dash bitters
4 oz. ginger ale

Pour light rum, bitters, and ginger ale into a highball glass filled ¾ full with ice. Give it a good stir.

Monsoon

2 oz. light rum
1 oz. pineapple juice
1 tsp. passion fruit syrup
3 oz. sour mix
½ oz. dark rum

Fill a cocktail shaker ½ full with ice. Pour in light rum, pineapple juice, passion fruit syrup, and sour mix. Give it a good shake, and strain into a Collins glass ¾ full of ice. Float dark rum on top.

Morgan's Mountain

2 oz. light rum
½ white crème de cacao
¼ oz. heavy cream
1 TB. coffee liqueur

Fill a cocktail shaker ½ full with ice. Pour in light rum, white crème de cacao, and heavy cream. Give it a good shake, and strain into a cocktail glass. Drip coffee liqueur into center of cocktail.

Mozart

2 oz. añejo rum
½ oz. sweet vermouth
1 tsp. triple sec
2 dashes orange bitters
1 lemon twist

Fill a cocktail shaker ½ full with ice. Pour in añejo rum, sweet vermouth, and triple sec, and add orange bitters. Give it a good shake, and strain into a cocktail glass. Garnish with lemon twist.

Mutiny

2 oz. dark rum
½ oz. Dubonnet Rouge
2 dashes bitters
1 maraschino cherry

Fill a cocktail shaker ½ full with ice. Pour in dark rum and Dubonnet Rouge, and add bitters. Give it a good shake, and strain into a cocktail glass. Garnish with maraschino cherry.

The Naked Lady

1 oz. light rum
1 oz. dark rum
½ oz. amaretto
½ oz. peach schnapps
2 oz. orange juice
1 TB. lemon-lime soda

Fill a cocktail shaker ½ full with ice. Pour in light rum, dark rum, amaretto, peach schnapps, and orange juice. Give it a good shake, and strain into a Collins glass ¾ full of ice. Pour in lemon-lime soda, and give it a good stir.

Navy Grog

1 oz. light rum
1 oz. dark rum
1 oz. gold rum
½ oz. guava nectar
½ oz. orange juice
½ oz. pineapple juice
¼ oz. lime juice
1 orange slice
1 mint sprig

Fill a cocktail shaker ½ full with ice. Pour in light rum, dark rum, gold rum, guava nectar, orange juice, pineapple juice, and lime juice. Give it a good shake, and strain into a Collins glass ¾ full of ice. Garnish with orange slice and mint sprig.

Nevada Cocktail

2 tsp. superfine sugar
2 oz. light rum
1½ oz. grapefruit juice
½ oz. lime juice
1 dash bitters

Fill a cocktail shaker ½ full with ice. Add superfine sugar; pour in light rum, grapefruit juice, and lime juice; and add bitters. Give it a good shake, and strain into a cocktail glass.

New Orleans Buck

2 oz. rum
½ oz. orange juice
½ oz. lime juice
3 oz. ginger ale

Fill a cocktail shaker ½ full with ice. Pour in rum, orange juice, and lime juice. Give it a good shake, and strain into a Collins glass ¾ full of ice. Pour in ginger ale, and give it a good stir.

A Night in Old Mandalay

1½ oz. light rum
1½ oz. añejo rum
1 oz. orange juice
¼ oz. lemon juice
1 tsp. grenadine
2 oz. ginger ale
1 lemon twist

Fill a cocktail shaker ½ full with ice. Pour in light rum, añejo rum, orange juice, lemon juice, and grenadine. Give it a good shake, and strain into a Collins glass ¾ full of ice. Pour ginger ale on top. Garnish with lemon twist.

Olympia

3 oz. dark rum
½ oz. cherry brandy
1 oz. lime juice

Fill a cocktail shaker ½ full with ice. Pour in dark rum, cherry brandy, and lime juice. Give it a good shake, and strain into a cocktail glass.

Orang-a-Tang

1 oz. vodka
½ oz. triple sec
1 tsp. grenadine
1 tsp. sour mix
2 oz. orange juice
1 oz. 151 proof rum

Fill a cocktail shaker ½ full with ice. Pour in vodka, triple sec, grenadine, sour mix, and orange juice. Give it a good shake, and strain into a brandy snifter. Float 151 proof rum on top.

Owen Moore

2 oz. light rum
½ oz. white crème de cacao
¼ oz. heavy cream
1 tsp. blue curaçao

Fill a cocktail shaker ½ full with ice. Pour in light rum, white crème de cacao, and heavy cream. Give it a good shake, and strain into a cocktail glass. Drip blue curaçao into center of cocktail.

Palmetto

1½ oz. light rum
1½ oz. dry vermouth
2 dashes bitters

Fill a cocktail shaker ½ full with ice. Pour in light rum and dry vermouth, and add bitters. Give it a good shake, and strain into a cocktail glass.

Panama

2 oz. dark rum
½ oz. dark crème de cacao
1 TB. heavy cream

Fill a cocktail shaker ½ full with ice. Pour in dark rum, dark crème de cacao, and heavy cream. Give it a good shake, and strain into an old-fashioned glass ¾ full of ice.

Pancho Villa

1 oz. light rum
1 oz. gin
1 oz. apricot brandy
1 tsp. cherry brandy
1 TB. pineapple juice
1 maraschino cherry

Fill a cocktail shaker ½ full with ice. Pour in light rum, gin, apricot brandy, cherry brandy, and pineapple juice. Give it a good shake, and strain into a cocktail glass. Garnish with maraschino cherry.

Parisian Blonde

1 oz. gold rum
1 oz. curaçao
1 TB. heavy cream
1 tsp. simple syrup

Fill a cocktail shaker ½ full with ice. Pour in gold rum, curaçao, heavy cream, and simple syrup. Give it a good shake, and strain into an old-fashioned glass ¾ full of ice.

Pedro Collins

2½ oz. light rum
1 oz. lemon juice
1 tsp. simple syrup
3 oz. club soda

Fill a cocktail shaker ½ full with ice. Pour in light rum, lemon juice, and simple syrup. Give it a good shake, and strain into a Collins glass ¾ full of ice. Pour in club soda, and give it a good stir.

Pilot Boat

2 oz. dark rum
1 oz. crème de bananes
1 oz. lime juice

Fill a cocktail shaker ½ full with ice. Pour in dark rum, crème de bananes, and lime juice. Give it a good shake, and strain into a cocktail glass.

Pineapple Cocktail

2 oz. dark rum
4 oz. pineapple juice
1 tsp. lemon juice
1 pineapple chunk

Fill a highball glass ¾ full with ice. Pour in dark rum, pineapple juice, and lemon juice. Give it a good stir, and garnish with pineapple chunk.

Pineapple Fizz

½ tsp. superfine sugar
2 oz. light rum
1 oz. pineapple juice
2 oz. club soda

Fill a cocktail shaker ½ full with ice. Add superfine sugar and then pour in light rum and pineapple juice. Give it a good shake, and strain into a highball glass ¾ full of ice. Pour in club soda, and give it a good stir.

Pink Pearl

2 oz. white rum
¼ oz. grenadine
1 oz. grapefruit juice
¼ oz. lemon juice
1 egg white

Fill a cocktail shaker ½ full with ice. Pour in white rum, grenadine, grapefruit juice, lemon juice, and egg white. Give it a good, vigorous shake, and strain into a cocktail glass.

Pink Veranda

1 tsp. superfine sugar
1½ oz. gold rum
½ oz. dark rum
2 oz. cranberry juice
¼ oz. lime juice
1 egg white

Fill a cocktail shaker ½ full with ice. Add superfine sugar and then pour in gold rum, dark rum, cranberry juice, lime juice, and egg white. Give it a good, vigorous shake, and strain into an old-fashioned glass ¾ full of ice.

Planter's Punch

2 oz. dark rum
1 oz. añejo rum
¼ oz. orange curaçao
2 oz. pineapple juice
2 oz. orange juice
2 TB. lime juice
1 tsp. simple syrup
2 dashes orange bitters
1 pineapple chunk
1 maraschino cherry

Fill a cocktail shaker ½ full with ice. Pour in dark rum, añejo rum, orange curaçao, pineapple juice, orange juice, lime juice, and simple syrup, and add orange bitters. Give it a good shake, and strain into a Collins glass ¾ full of ice. Garnish with pineapple chunk and maraschino cherry.

Platinum Blonde

1½ oz. light rum
½ oz. triple sec
¼ oz. heavy cream

Fill a cocktail shaker ½ full with ice. Pour in light rum, triple sec, and heavy cream. Give it a good shake, and strain into a brandy snifter.

Poker

1½ oz. gold rum
1½ oz. dry vermouth

Fill a cocktail shaker ½ full with ice. Pour in gold rum and dry vermouth. Give it a good shake, and strain into a cocktail glass.

Port Antonio

1 oz. gold rum
1 oz. dark rum
½ oz. coffee liqueur
½ oz. lime juice
4 oz. ginger ale

Fill a cocktail shaker ½ full with ice. Pour in gold rum, dark rum, coffee liqueur, and lime juice. Give it a good shake, and strain into a highball glass ¾ full of ice. Pour in the ginger ale, and give it a good stir.

Portland Coffee

1 tsp. sugar
1 oz. 151 proof rum
1 oz. coffee liqueur
1 tsp. triple sec
3 oz. hot coffee
¼ cup whipped cream
¼ tsp. cinnamon

Add superfine sugar to an Irish coffee glass and then pour in 151 proof rum, coffee liqueur, and triple sec. Pour in hot coffee, and top with a dollop of whipped cream. Garnish with cinnamon.

Presidente

1½ oz. light rum
¾ oz. curaçao
½ oz. dry vermouth
¼ tsp. grenadine

Fill a cocktail shaker ½ full with ice. Pour in light rum, curaçao, dry vermouth, and grenadine. Give it a good shake, and strain into a cocktail glass.

Puffer

2 oz. light rum
2 oz. orange juice
2 oz. grapefruit juice
1 tsp. grenadine

Pour light rum, orange juice, and grapefruit juice into a highball glass ¾ full of ice. Give it a good stir and then drip grenadine into center of cocktail.

Quaker

1 oz. light rum
1 oz. brandy
½ oz. lemon juice
1 tsp. raspberry syrup

Fill a cocktail shaker ½ full with ice. Pour in light rum, brandy, lemon juice, and raspberry syrup. Give it a good shake, and strain into a cocktail glass.

Quarter Deck

1½ oz. light rum
½ oz. dark rum
1 TB. sherry
½ oz. lime juice

Fill a cocktail shaker ½ full with ice. Pour in light rum, dark rum, sherry, and lime juice. Give it a good shake, and strain into a cocktail glass.

Redcoat

1½ oz. light rum
½ oz. vodka
¼ oz. apricot brandy
1 tsp. grenadine
½ oz. lime juice
1 tsp. simple syrup

Fill a cocktail shaker ½ full with ice. Pour in light rum, vodka, apricot brandy, grenadine, lime juice, and simple syrup. Give it a good shake, and strain into a cocktail glass.

Riley

1½ oz. añejo rum
½ oz. triple sec
½ oz. orange juice
½ oz. lemon juice
½ oz. lime juice
½ tsp. raspberry syrup

Fill a cocktail shaker ½ full with ice. Pour in añejo rum, triple sec, orange juice, lemon juice, and lime juice. Give it a good shake, and strain into a cocktail glass. Drip raspberry syrup into center of cocktail.

Robson

2 oz. dark rum
1 tsp. grenadine
¼ oz. orange juice
1 tsp. lemon juice

Fill a cocktail shaker ½ full with ice. Pour in dark rum, grenadine, orange juice, and lemon juice. Give it a good shake, and strain into a cocktail glass.

Rockaway Beach

1½ oz. light rum
½ oz. dark rum
½ oz. tequila
1½ tsp. crème de noyaux
1 oz. pineapple juice
1 oz. orange juice
1 oz. cranberry juice
1 maraschino cherry

Fill a cocktail shaker ½ full with ice. Pour in light rum, dark rum, tequila, crème de noyaux, pineapple juice, orange juice, and cranberry juice. Give it a good shake, and strain into a Collins glass ¾ full of ice. Garnish with maraschino cherry.

Rum and Tonic

2 oz. light rum
4 oz. tonic water
1 lime wedge

Fill a highball glass with ice. Pour in light rum and tonic water. Give it a good stir, and garnish with lime wedge.

Rum Cobbler

2 pineapple chunks
2 orange slices
1 tsp. simple syrup
2 oz. dark rum
3 oz. club soda
1 maraschino cherry

Muddle 1 pineapple chunk and 1 orange slice with simple syrup in an old-fashioned glass. Fill the glass ¾ full with ice, and pour in dark rum and club soda. Give it a good stir. Garnish with maraschino cherry and remaining pineapple chunk and orange slice.

Rum Collins

2½ oz. dark rum
1 tsp. simple syrup
1 oz. lemon juice
4 oz. club soda
1 orange slice
1 maraschino cherry

Fill a cocktail shaker ½ full with ice. Pour in dark rum, simple syrup, and lemon juice. Give it a good shake, and strain into a Collins glass ¾ full of ice. Pour in club soda, and garnish with orange slice and maraschino cherry.

Rum Cooler

2 oz. light rum
4 oz. lemon-lime soda
1 lemon wedge

Fill a highball glass ¾ full with ice. Pour in light rum and lemon-lime soda. Give it a good stir, and garnish with lemon wedge.

Rum Curaçao Cooler

2 oz. dark rum
1 oz. curaçao
½ oz. lime juice
3 oz. club soda
1 orange slice
1 lime slice

Fill a cocktail shaker ½ full with ice. Pour in dark rum, curaçao, and lime juice. Give it a good shake, and strain into a highball glass ¾ full of ice. Pour in club soda, and garnish with orange slice and lime slice.

Rum Daisy

2 oz. dark rum
½ tsp. grenadine
1 oz. lemon juice
½ tsp. simple syrup
1 orange slice
1 maraschino cherry

Fill a cocktail shaker ½ full with ice. Pour in dark rum, grenadine, lemon juice, and simple syrup. Give it a good shake, and strain into an old-fashioned glass ¾ full of ice. Garnish with orange slice and maraschino cherry.

Rum Fix

2 oz. light rum
1 oz. lemon juice
1 tsp. simple syrup
1 lemon slice
1 maraschino cherry

Fill a cocktail shaker ½ full with ice. Pour in light rum, lemon juice, and simple syrup. Give it a good shake, and strain into a highball glass full of ice. Garnish with lemon slice and maraschino cherry.

Rum Gimlet

2½ oz. light rum
½ oz. lime juice
1 lime slice

Fill a cocktail shaker ½ full with ice. Pour in light rum and lime juice. Give it a good stir, and strain into a cocktail glass. Garnish with lime slice.

Rum Martini

3 oz. light rum
¼ tsp. dry vermouth
1 lemon twist

Fill a cocktail shaker ½ full with ice. Pour in light rum and dry vermouth. Give it a good stir, and strain into a cocktail glass. Garnish with lemon twist.

Rum Rickey

2 oz. light rum
½ oz. lime juice
1 tsp. simple syrup
4 oz. club soda
1 lime wedge

Fill a cocktail shaker ½ full with ice. Pour in light rum, lime juice, and simple syrup. Give it a good shake, and strain into a highball glass full of ice. Pour in club soda, and garnish with lime wedge.

Rum Runner

1½ oz. light rum
1½ oz. dark rum
2 oz. pineapple juice
½ oz. lime juice
1 TB. simple syrup
1 dash bitters
1 maraschino cherry

Fill a cocktail shaker ½ full with ice. Pour in light rum, dark rum, pineapple juice, lime juice, and simple syrup, and add bitters. Give it a good shake, and strain into a highball glass ¾ full of ice. Garnish with maraschino cherry.

Rum Sour

2 oz. light rum
1 oz. lemon juice
1 oz. simple syrup
1 orange slice
1 maraschino cherry

Fill a cocktail shaker ½ full with ice. Pour in light rum, lemon juice, and simple syrup. Give it a good shake, and strain into a highball glass ¾ full of ice. Garnish with orange slice and maraschino cherry.

Rum Swizzle

2 oz. light rum
½ oz. lime juice
1 tsp. simple syrup
1 dash bitters
3 oz. club soda

Fill a cocktail shaker ½ full with ice. Pour in light rum, lime juice, and simple syrup, and add bitters. Give it a good shake, and strain into a highball glass ¾ full of ice. Pour in club soda, and serve with (of course) a swizzle stick.

Santiago

3 oz. light rum
1 tsp. grenadine
½ oz. lime juice
1 tsp. simple syrup

Fill a cocktail shaker ½ full with ice. Pour in light rum, grenadine, lime juice, and simple syrup. Give it a good shake, and strain into a cocktail glass.

Scorpion

1 oz. light rum
1 oz. dark rum
1 oz. brandy
2 oz. orange juice
½ oz. lime juice
¼ oz. orgeat syrup
1 orange slice
1 maraschino cherry

Fill a cocktail shaker ½ full with ice. Pour in light rum, dark rum, brandy, orange juice, lime juice, and orgeat syrup. Give it a good shake, and strain into a highball glass ¾ full of ice. Garnish with orange slice and maraschino cherry.

Secret Place

2 oz. dark rum
½ oz. cherry brandy
1 TB. dark crème de cacao
3 oz. cold coffee

Fill an Irish coffee glass with crushed ice. Pour in dark rum, cherry brandy, dark crème de cacao, and cold coffee. Give it a good stir.

September Morning

2 oz. light rum
1 tsp. cherry brandy
1 tsp. grenadine
½ oz. lime juice
1 egg white

Fill a cocktail shaker ½ full with ice. Pour in light rum, cherry brandy, grenadine, lime juice, and egg white. Give it a good, vigorous shake, and strain into a cocktail glass.

Sevilla

1½ oz. dark rum
1 oz. sweet vermouth
1 orange slice

Fill a cocktail shaker ½ full with ice. Pour in dark rum and sweet vermouth. Give it a good shake, and strain into an old-fashioned glass full of ice. Garnish with orange slice.

Shanghai

1½ oz. dark rum
1 oz. anisette
¼ tsp. grenadine
¼ oz. lemon juice

Fill a cocktail shaker ½ full with ice. Pour in dark rum, anisette, grenadine, and lemon juice. Give it a good shake, and strain into a cocktail glass.

Shark's Tooth

2 oz. dark rum
¼ oz. grenadine
½ oz. lime juice
½ oz. lemon juice
4 oz. club soda

Fill a cocktail shaker ½ full with ice. Pour in dark rum, grenadine, lime juice, and lemon juice. Give it a good shake, and strain into a highball glass ¾ full of ice. Pour in club soda.

Sir Walter

1 oz. añejo rum
1 oz. brandy
½ oz. curaçao
1 tsp. grenadine
1 TB. lime juice

Fill a cocktail shaker ½ full with ice. Pour in añejo rum, brandy, curaçao, grenadine, and lime juice. Give it a good shake, and strain into an old-fashioned glass ¾ full of ice.

Sledgehammer

¾ oz. gold rum
¾ oz. brandy
¾ oz. calvados
¼ tsp. pastis
1 lemon twist

Fill a cocktail shaker ½ full with ice. Pour in gold rum, brandy, calvados, and pastis. Give it a good shake, and strain into a cocktail glass. Garnish with lemon twist.

Sloppy Joe

¾ oz. light rum
¾ oz. dry vermouth
½ tsp. triple sec
½ tsp. grenadine
½ oz. lime juice

Fill a cocktail shaker ½ full with ice. Pour in light rum, dry vermouth, triple sec, grenadine, and lime juice. Give it a good shake, and strain into an old-fashioned glass full of ice.

Sonny Gets Kissed

1 tsp. superfine sugar
2 oz. rum
½ oz. apricot brandy
¼ oz. lime juice
¼ oz. lemon juice
1 lemon twist

Fill a cocktail shaker ½ full with ice. Add superfine sugar, and then pour in rum, apricot brandy, lime juice, and lemon juice. Give it a good shake, and strain into a cocktail glass. Garnish with lemon twist.

Space Odyssey

1 oz. 151 proof rum
1 oz. coconut rum
1 tsp. grenadine
½ oz. pineapple juice
2 oz. orange juice
1 maraschino cherry

Fill a cocktail shaker ½ full with ice. Pour in 151 proof rum, coconut rum, grenadine, pineapple juice, and orange juice. Give it a good shake, and strain into a highball glass ¾ full of ice. Garnish with maraschino cherry.

Spanish Main

2 oz. light rum
½ oz. dry vermouth
½ oz. sweet vermouth
1 dash bitters
1 maraschino cherry

Fill a cocktail shaker ½ full with ice. Pour in light rum, dry vermouth, and sweet vermouth, and add bitters. Give it a good shake, and strain into an old-fashioned glass ¾ full of ice. Garnish with maraschino cherry.

Spanish Town

2 oz. light rum
½ tsp. triple sec

Fill a cocktail shaker ½ full with ice. Pour in light rum and triple sec. Give it a good stir, and strain into a cocktail glass.

Spark in the Night

2 oz. dark rum
½ oz. coffee liqueur
1 tsp. lime juice

Fill a cocktail shaker ½ full with ice. Pour in dark rum, coffee liqueur, and lime juice. Give it a good shake, and strain into a cocktail glass.

Spirit in the Night

2 oz. light rum
¼ oz. cranberry liqueur
1 oz. grapefruit juice

Fill a cocktail shaker ½ full with ice. Pour in light rum, cranberry liqueur, and grapefruit juice. Give it a good stir, and strain into a cocktail glass.

Starseeker

2 oz. light rum
½ oz. orange juice
1 tsp. grenadine
1 oz. tonic water
1 orange slice

Pour light rum, orange juice, and grenadine into a highball glass. Give it a good stir, and top with tonic water. Garnish with orange slice.

Suffragette City

2 oz. white rum
½ oz. curaçao
1 tsp. grenadine
½ oz. lime juice

Fill a cocktail shaker ½ full with ice. Pour in white rum, curaçao, grenadine, and lime juice. Give it a good shake, and strain into a cocktail glass.

Summer Share

1 oz. light rum
1 oz. vodka
½ oz. tequila
1 oz. cranberry juice
1 oz. orange juice
1 oz. lemon-lime soda

Fill a cocktail shaker ½ full with ice. Pour in light rum, vodka, tequila, cranberry juice, and orange juice. Give it a good shake, and strain into a highball glass ¾ full of ice. Pour in lemon-lime soda.

Sundowner

2 oz. light rum
2 tsp. grenadine
½ oz. lemon juice
4 oz. tonic water

Fill a cocktail shaker ½ full with ice. Pour in light rum, grenadine, and lemon juice. Give it a good shake, and strain into a highball glass ¾ full of ice. Pour in tonic water. Give it a good stir.

Tahiti Club

2 oz. gold rum
½ tsp. maraschino liqueur
¼ oz. lime juice
¼ oz. lemon juice
½ oz. pineapple juice
1 maraschino cherry

Fill a cocktail shaker ½ full with ice. Pour in gold rum, maraschino liqueur, lime juice, lemon juice, and pineapple juice. Give it a good shake, and strain into a cocktail glass. Garnish with maraschino cherry.

Three-Miler Cocktail

1 oz. light rum
1 oz. brandy
1 tsp. grenadine
1 TB. lemon juice

Fill a cocktail shaker ½ full with ice. Pour in light rum, brandy, grenadine, and lemon juice. Give it a good shake, and strain into a cocktail glass.

Tidal Wave

½ oz. light rum
½ oz. vodka
½ oz. gin
½ oz. peach schnapps
¼ tsp. grenadine
2 oz. pineapple juice
2 oz. orange juice
1 TB. 151 proof rum
1 pineapple chunk
1 maraschino cherry

Fill a cocktail shaker ½ full with ice. Pour in light rum, vodka, gin, peach schnapps, grenadine, pineapple juice, and orange juice. Give it a good stir, and strain into a Collins glass ¾ full of ice. Float 151 proof rum on top, and garnish with pineapple chunk and maraschino cherry.

Tiger's Milk

1 oz. dark rum
1 oz. brandy
4 oz. milk
1 tsp. simple syrup

Fill a cocktail shaker ½ full with ice. Pour in dark rum, brandy, milk, and simple syrup. Give it a good shake, and strain into an old-fashioned glass ¾ full of ice.

Tobago

2 oz. light rum
½ oz. guava syrup
½ oz. lime juice
½ oz. simple syrup
1 tsp. pastis

Fill a cocktail shaker ½ full with ice. Pour in light rum, guava syrup, lime juice, simple syrup, and pastis. Give it a good shake, and strain into a cocktail glass.

Tom and Jerry

1 egg, separated
½ oz. simple syrup
1½ oz. light rum
1½ oz. brandy
2 oz. hot milk
1 tsp. ground nutmeg

Beat egg white until frothy, set aside, and then beat yolk. Add simple syrup to an Irish coffee mug, and mix in egg whites and yolk. Pour in light rum and brandy, and give it a good, vigorous stir. Pour in hot milk, and garnish with nutmeg.

Trade Winds

2 oz. añejo rum
½ oz. plum brandy
½ oz. orgeat syrup
½ oz. lime juice

Fill a cocktail shaker ½ full with ice. Pour in añejo rum, plum brandy, orgeat syrup, and lime juice. Give it a good shake, and strain into a wine glass.

Triad

1 oz. gold rum
½ oz. amaretto
½ oz. sweet vermouth
4 oz. ginger ale
1 lemon wedge

Fill a cocktail shaker ½ full with ice. Pour in gold rum, amaretto, and sweet vermouth. Give it a good shake, and strain into a highball glass ¾ full of ice. Pour in ginger ale and stir. Garnish with lemon wedge.

Trinidad Cocktail

2 oz. light rum
½ oz. lime juice
3 dashes bitters
4 oz. cola
1 lime wedge

Fill a cocktail shaker ½ full with ice. Pour in light rum and lime juice, and add bitters. Give it a good shake, and strain into a highball glass ¾ full of ice. Pour in cola and stir. Garnish with lime wedge.

Tropical Rainstorm

2 oz. dark rum
½ oz. cherry brandy
1 tsp. triple sec
½ oz. lemon juice

Fill a cocktail shaker ½ full with ice. Pour in dark rum, cherry brandy, triple sec, and lemon juice. Give it a good shake, and strain into a cocktail glass.

Tropical Teaser

1½ oz. dark rum
½ oz. almond liqueur
4 oz. grapefruit juice

Fill a cocktail shaker ½ full with ice. Pour in dark rum, almond liqueur, and grapefruit juice. Give it a good shake, and strain into a highball glass ¾ full of ice.

Twin Sisters

1 oz. light rum
1 oz. dark rum
1 TB. Rose's lime juice
4 oz. cola
1 lime wedge

Fill a cocktail shaker ½ full with ice. Pour in light rum, dark rum, and Rose's lime juice. Give it a good shake, and strain into a highball glass ¾ full of ice. Pour in cola and stir. Garnish with lime wedge.

Veteran

2½ oz. dark rum
½ oz. cherry brandy
1 maraschino cherry

Pour dark rum and cherry brandy into an old-fashioned glass full of ice. Give it a good stir. Garnish with maraschino cherry.

Walker's Revenge

1½ oz. dark rum
1½ oz. light rum
¼ oz. simple syrup
4 oz. unsweetened iced tea

Pour dark rum, light rum, and simple syrup into a highball glass ¾ full of ice. Pour in unsweetened iced tea, and give it a good stir.

White Jamaican

1½ oz. dark rum
¾ oz. coconut rum
¾ oz. white crème de cacao
4 oz. milk

Fill a cocktail shaker ½ full with ice. Pour in dark rum, coconut rum, white crème de cacao, and milk. Give it a good shake, and strain into a Collins glass ¾ full of ice.

White Lilly

1 oz. light rum
1 oz. gin
1 oz. triple sec
¼ tsp. pastis

Fill a cocktail shaker ½ full with ice. Pour in light rum, gin, triple sec, and pastis. Give it a good shake, and strain into a cocktail glass.

White Lion

1 tsp. superfine sugar
2 oz. white rum
½ tsp. grenadine
½ oz. lemon juice
2 dashes bitters

Fill a cocktail shaker ½ full with ice. Add superfine sugar; pour in white rum, grenadine, and lemon juice; and add bitters. Give it a good shake, and strain into a cocktail glass.

Whitney

2 oz. white rum
1 oz. rosé wine
1 TB. lemon juice
1 lemon twist

Pour white rum, rosé wine, and lemon juice into a wine glass. Give it a good stir. Garnish with lemon twist.

Wile E. Coyote

1 oz. light rum
1 oz. banana liqueur
1 oz. blackberry brandy
2 oz. pineapple juice
2 oz. cranberry juice
1 pineapple chunk

Pour light rum, banana liqueur, blackberry brandy, pineapple juice, and cranberry juice into a Collins glass ¾ full of ice. Give it a good stir. Garnish with pineapple chunk.

Xango

1½ oz. light rum
½ oz. triple sec
1 oz. grapefruit juice

Fill a cocktail shaker ½ full with ice. Pour in light rum, triple sec, and grapefruit juice. Give it a good shake, and strain into a cocktail glass.

XYZ

1½ oz. dark rum
½ oz. triple sec
1 oz. lemon juice
1 lemon twist

Fill a cocktail shaker ½ full with ice. Pour in dark rum, triple sec, and lemon juice. Give it a good shake, and strain into a cocktail glass. Garnish with lemon twist.

Yellow Bird

1 oz. light rum
½ oz. Galliano
½ oz. triple sec
1 oz. lemon juice
1 tsp. simple syrup
1 lemon twist

Fill a cocktail shaker ½ full with ice. Pour in light rum, Galliano, triple sec, lemon juice, and simple syrup. Give it a good shake, and strain into a cocktail glass. Garnish with lemon twist.

Yellow Strawberry

4 strawberries
2 tsp. simple syrup
1½ oz. light rum
½ oz. crème de bananes
3 oz. club soda

Muddle strawberries with simple syrup in an old-fashioned glass. Fill glass ¾ full with ice, and pour in light rum, crème de bananes, and club soda. Give it a good stir.

Zico

2 oz. white rum
1 oz. *cachaca*
2 oz. papaya nectar
½ oz. coconut cream
½ oz. lime juice

Fill a cocktail shaker ½ full with ice. Pour in white rum, cachaca, papaya nectar, coconut cream, and lime juice. Give a good shake, and strain into a Collins glass ¾ full of ice.

Liquor Lingo

Cachaca is an intense, sharp Brazilian liqueur made by distilling sugarcane juice, most well known as an ingredient in a caipirinha.

Zombie

1 oz. light rum
1 oz. dark rum
½ oz. 151 proof rum
½ oz. apricot brandy
1 tsp. grenadine
1 oz. pineapple juice
2 oz. orange juice
½ oz. lime juice
1 orange slice
1 maraschino cherry

Fill a cocktail shaker ½ full with ice. Pour in light rum, dark rum, 151 proof rum, apricot brandy, grenadine, pineapple juice, orange juice, and lime juice. Give it a good shake, and strain into a Collins glass ¾ full of ice. Garnish with orange slice and maraschino cherry.

Chapter 8

Tequila

One tequila, two tequila, three tequila, floor …
—George Carlin

Alamo Splash

2 oz. tequila
1 oz. orange juice
½ oz. pineapple juice
3 oz. lemon-lime soda

Fill a cocktail shaker ½ full with ice. Pour in tequila, orange juice, and pineapple juice. Give it a good shake, and strain into a highball glass ¾ full of ice. Pour in lemon-lime soda and stir.

Alleluia

1½ oz. tequila
1 tsp. blue curaçao
1 tsp. maraschino liqueur
½ oz. lemon juice
1 tsp. simple syrup
4 oz. tonic water
1 orange slice
1 maraschino cherry

Fill a cocktail shaker ½ full with ice. Pour in tequila, blue curaçao, maraschino liqueur, lemon juice, and simple syrup. Give it a good shake, and strain into a highball glass ¾ full of ice. Pour in tonic water, and garnish with orange slice and maraschino cherry.

Arizona Sunrise

2 oz. tequila
1 tsp. grenadine
½ oz. Rose's lime juice
4 oz. orange juice
1 orange slice
1 maraschino cherry

Fill a cocktail shaker ½ full with ice.
Pour in tequila, grenadine, Rose's lime
juice, and orange juice. Give it a good
shake, and strain into a highball glass
¾ full of ice. Garnish with orange slice
and maraschino cherry.

Big Red Hooter

1½ oz. tequila
¼ oz. almond liqueur
1 oz. grenadine
3 oz. pineapple juice
1 maraschino cherry

Fill a cocktail shaker ½ full with ice.
Pour in tequila, almond liqueur, grenadine, and pineapple juice. Give it a
good shake, and strain into a highball
glass ¾ full of ice. Garnish with
maraschino cherry.

Black Mexican

1 oz. tequila
1 oz. *black Sambuca*

Fill a cocktail shaker ½ full with ice.
Pour in tequila and black Sambuca.
Give it a good stir, and strain into an
old-fashioned glass full of ice.

Liquor Lingo

Black Sambuca is an anise-flavored liqueur. It's slightly more robust
than its mellower sibling, white Sambuca.

Blackberry Tequila

2 oz. tequila
1 oz. crème de cassis
½ oz. lemon juice
1 lemon twist

Fill a cocktail shaker ½ full with ice.
Pour in tequila, crème de cassis, and
lemon juice. Give it a good shake, and
strain into a cocktail glass. Garnish
with lemon twist.

Blackjack Margarita

2 oz. tequila
½ oz. triple sec
½ oz. raspberry liqueur
2 oz. lime juice
1 lime wedge

Fill a cocktail shaker ½ full with ice.
Pour in tequila, triple sec, raspberry
liqueur, and lime juice. Give it a good
shake, and strain into an old-fashioned
glass ¾ full of ice. Garnish with lime
wedge.

Bloody Maria

2 oz. tequila
¼ oz. lemon juice
4 oz. tomato juice
1 dash Tabasco sauce
1 dash Worcestershire sauce
⅛ tsp. celery salt
⅛ tsp. salt
⅛ tsp. pepper
1 celery stalk

Fill a cocktail shaker ½ full with ice. Pour in tequila, lemon juice, tomato juice, Tabasco sauce, Worcestershire sauce, celery salt, salt, and pepper. Give it a good shake, and strain into a highball glass ¾ full of ice. Garnish with celery stalk.

Blue Diablo

2 oz. tequila
2 tsp. blue curaçao
½ oz. lemon juice
1 TB. Rose's lime juice
1 lemon wedge

Fill a cocktail shaker ½ full with ice. Pour in tequila, blue curaçao, lemon juice, and Rose's lime juice. Give it a good shake, and strain into a highball glass ¾ full of ice. Garnish with lemon wedge.

Blue Margarita

2 oz. tequila
½ oz. triple sec
½ oz. blue curaçao
2 oz. lime juice
1 lime wedge

Fill a cocktail shaker ½ full with ice. Pour in tequila, triple sec, blue curaçao, and lime juice. Give it a good shake, and strain into an old-fashioned glass ¾ full of ice. Garnish with lime wedge.

Blue Shark

1½ oz. tequila
1 oz. vodka
½ oz. blue curaçao

Fill a cocktail shaker ½ full with ice. Pour in tequila, vodka, and blue curaçao. Give it a good shake, and strain into a cocktail glass.

Blue Tahoe

2 oz. tequila
1 oz. blue curaçao
1 oz. lime juice
3 oz. champagne
1 maraschino cherry

Fill a cocktail shaker ½ full with ice. Pour in tequila, blue curaçao, and lime juice. Give it a good shake, and strain into a highball glass ½ full of ice. Pour in champagne, and garnish with maraschino cherry.

Brave Albino Bull

2 oz. tequila
1 oz. coffee liqueur
1 oz. milk

Fill a cocktail shaker ½ full with ice. Pour in tequila, coffee liqueur, and milk. Give it a good stir, and strain into an old-fashioned glass ¾ full of ice.

Cocktail Conversation

In this book, I use general liqueur names as often as possible. Often, a recipe will call for a specific alcohol or liqueur like, in the case of coffee liqueur, Kahlúa or Tia Maria. Should you run out and buy Tia Maria if you have Kahlúa at home? I say no. Use what you've got. Of course, if you have the proper recommended brand, absolutely use it. Differences in flavor profiles and aroma will make a drink taste and smell different. But if you're just hankering to make a Brave Albino Bull and don't have Tia Maria, use whatever coffee liqueur you have on hand.

Brave Bull

2 oz. tequila
1 oz. coffee liqueur

Fill a cocktail shaker ½ full with ice. Pour in tequila and coffee liqueur. Give it a good stir, and strain into an old-fashioned glass ¾ full of ice.

Butcherblock

1½ oz. tequila
1½ oz. coffee liqueur
½ oz. light cream
2 tsp. shaved chocolate

Fill a cocktail shaker ½ full with ice. Pour in tequila, coffee liqueur, and light cream. Give it a good stir, and strain into an old-fashioned glass ¾ full of ice. Garnish with shaved chocolate.

Cactus Banger

2 oz. tequila
½ oz. *Galliano*
4 oz. orange juice
1 maraschino cherry

Fill a cocktail shaker ½ full with ice. Pour in tequila, Galliano, and orange juice. Give it a good stir, and strain into a highball glass ¾ full of ice. Garnish with maraschino cherry.

Liquor Lingo

Galliano is a sweet, herbaceous Italian liqueur made from anise, licorice, vanilla, flowers, spices, and herbs. It's yellow in color.

Cactus Cream

2 oz. tequila
4 oz. cream soda

Fill a highball glass ¾ full with ice. Pour in tequila and cream soda. Give it a good stir.

California Dream

2 oz. tequila
1 oz. sweet vermouth
½ oz. dry vermouth
1 maraschino cherry

Fill a cocktail shaker ½ full with ice. Pour in tequila, sweet vermouth, and dry vermouth. Give it a good stir, and strain into a cocktail glass. Garnish with maraschino cherry.

Campesina

½ lime, cut into 4 pieces
2 tsp. simple syrup
2½ oz. tequila
1 oz. club soda

Muddle lime wedges with simple syrup in an old-fashioned glass. Fill glass ¾ full with crushed ice, and add tequila. Pour in club soda, and give it a good stir.

Cazuela

2½ oz. tequila
1 tsp. grenadine
1 oz. orange juice
1 oz. grapefruit juice
1 oz. lemon juice
1 orange slice
1 lemon slice
1 maraschino cherry

Fill a cocktail shaker ½ full with ice. Pour in tequila, grenadine, orange juice, grapefruit juice, and lemon juice. Give it a good shake, and strain into a Collins glass ¾ full of ice. Garnish with orange slice, lemon slice, and maraschino cherry.

Chapala

2 oz. tequila
¼ oz. triple sec
1 tsp. grenadine
1 oz. orange juice
1 oz. lemon juice
1 orange slice
1 maraschino cherry

Fill a cocktail shaker ½ full with ice. Pour in tequila, triple sec, grenadine, orange juice, and lemon juice. Give it a good shake, and strain into an old-fashioned glass ¾ full of ice. Garnish with orange slice and maraschino cherry.

Charro

2½ oz. tequila
1 oz. evaporated milk
1 oz. cold espresso coffee

Fill a cocktail shaker ½ full with ice. Pour in tequila, evaporated milk, and coffee. Give it a good shake, and strain into an old-fashioned glass ¾ full of ice.

Cinco de Mayo

2½ oz. tequila
1 oz. grenadine
1 oz. Rose's lime juice
1 lime slice

Fill a cocktail shaker ½ full with ice. Pour in tequila, grenadine, and Rose's lime juice. Give it a good shake, and strain into an old-fashioned glass ¾ full of ice. Garnish with lime slice.

Cocktail Conversation

You probably notice big, brightly colored "Cinco de Mayo" signs outside your favorite Mexican restaurant on the 5th of May each year, but Cinco de Mayo isn't simply an excuse for a festive day. It is actually the day Mexican freedom fighters defeated French troops at the battle of Puebla in 1862 and finally gained their independence from imperial invaders. I'll drink to that.

Colorado Skies

1½ oz. tequila
1 oz. blue curaçao
4 oz. grapefruit juice

Fill a cocktail shaker ½ full with ice. Pour in tequila, blue curaçao, and grapefruit juice. Give it a good shake, and strain into a highball glass ¾ full of ice.

Compadre

2 oz. tequila
½ tsp. maraschino liqueur
1 tsp. grenadine
2 dashes orange bitters
1 maraschino cherry

Fill a cocktail shaker ½ full with ice. Pour in tequila, maraschino liqueur, and grenadine, and add orange bitters. Give it a good stir, and strain into a cocktail glass. Garnish with maraschino cherry.

Conquita

1½ oz. tequila
1½ oz. grapefruit juice
1 tsp. lemon juice
1 lemon slice

Fill a cocktail shaker ½ full with ice. Pour in tequila, grapefruit juice, and lemon juice. Give it a good shake, and strain into an old-fashioned glass ¾ full of ice. Garnish with lemon slice.

Cosmoquila

1½ oz. tequila
1 oz. triple sec
1 oz. cranberry juice
½ tsp. lime juice
1 lime slice

Fill a cocktail shaker ½ full with ice. Pour in tequila, triple sec, cranberry juice, and lime juice. Give it a good shake, and strain into a cocktail glass. Garnish with lime slice.

Cowboy Killer

1 oz. tequila
1 oz. Irish cream
½ oz. butterscotch schnapps
½ oz. light cream
1 maraschino cherry

Fill a cocktail shaker ½ full with ice. Pour in tequila, Irish cream, butterscotch schnapps, and light cream. Give it a good shake, and strain into a brandy snifter ½ full of ice. Garnish with maraschino cherry.

Doctor Dawson

2 oz. tequila
½ oz. lemon juice
2 tsp. simple syrup
1 dash bitters
1 egg
3 oz. club soda
1 lemon wedge

Fill a cocktail shaker ½ full with ice. Pour in tequila, lemon juice, and simple syrup, and add bitters and egg. Give it a good, vigorous shake, and strain into a highball glass ¾ full of ice. Pour in club soda. Garnish with lemon wedge.

Dorado

1 TB. honey
2 oz. tequila
1 oz. lemon juice
1 lemon slice

Fill a cocktail shaker ½ full with ice. Pour in honey, tequila, and lemon juice. Give it a good, vigorous shake, and strain into a cocktail glass. Garnish with lemon slice.

Doralto

2 oz. tequila
½ oz. lemon juice
1 tsp. simple syrup
1 dash bitters
4 oz. tonic water
1 lemon wedge

Fill a cocktail shaker ½ full with ice. Pour in tequila, lemon juice, and simple syrup, and add bitters. Give it a good shake, and strain into a highball glass ¾ full of ice. Pour in tonic water, and garnish with lemon wedge.

Durango

2 oz. tequila
2 oz. grapefruit juice
2 tsp. orgeat syrup
1 oz. water
1 mint sprig

Fill a cocktail shaker ½ full with ice. Pour in tequila, grapefruit juice, and orgeat syrup. Give it a good, vigorous shake, and strain into an old-fashioned glass ¾ full of ice. Pour in water, and garnish with mint sprig.

El Cid

2 oz. tequila
1 oz. lime juice
½ oz. orgeat syrup
3 oz. tonic water
1 lime wedge

Fill a cocktail shaker ½ full with ice. Pour in tequila, lime juice, and orgeat syrup. Give it a good shake, and strain into a Collins glass ¾ full of ice. Pour in tonic water, and garnish with lime wedge.

El Diablo

2 oz. tequila
¾ oz. crème de cassis
¼ oz. lime juice
3 oz. ginger ale
1 lime wedge

Fill a highball glass ¾ full with ice. Pour in tequila, crème de cassis, and lime juice. Give it a good stir. Pour in ginger ale, and garnish with lime wedge.

Electric Margarita

2 oz. tequila
¾ oz. blue curaçao
1 oz. *Rose's lime juice*
1 lime slice

Fill a cocktail shaker ½ full with ice. Pour in tequila, blue curaçao, and Rose's lime juice. Give it a good shake, and strain into a cocktail glass. Garnish with lime slice.

> **Liquor Lingo**
>
> **Rose's lime juice** is a nonalcoholic, sweetened lime juice that's really more like a syrup. It's very easy to find in about any supermarket in the nation. Whatever you do, *do not* substitute Rose's lime juice for fresh lime juice, and vice versa, when a recipe calls for it specifically.

Freddy Fudpucker

2 oz. tequila
4 oz. orange juice
½ oz. Galliano

Fill a highball glass ¾ full with ice. Pour in tequila and orange juice. Give it a good stir. Gently drip Galliano on top.

Frogster

1½ oz. tequila
1½ oz. blue curaçao
4 oz. orange juice

Fill a cocktail shaker ½ full with ice. Pour in tequila, blue curaçao, and orange juice. Give it a good shake, and strain into a highball glass ¾ full of ice.

Gates of Hell

1½ oz. tequila
¼ oz. lemon juice
¼ oz. lime juice
2 tsp. cherry brandy

Fill a cocktail shaker ½ full with ice. Pour in tequila, lemon juice, and lime juice. Give it a good shake, and strain into an old-fashioned glass ¾ full of ice. Gently drip cherry brandy on top.

Gentle Ben

1½ oz. tequila
¾ oz. vodka
¾ oz. gin
1 tsp. sloe gin
3 oz. orange juice
1 orange slice

Fill a cocktail shaker ½ full with ice. Pour in tequila, vodka, gin, sloe gin, and orange juice. Give it a good shake, and strain into a highball glass ¾ full of ice. Garnish with orange slice.

Gentle Bull

2 oz. tequila
1 oz. coffee liqueur
¼ oz. heavy cream

Fill a cocktail shaker ½ full with ice. Pour in tequila, coffee liqueur, and heavy cream. Give it a good shake, and strain into an old-fashioned glass ¾ full of ice.

Gold Margarita

2 oz. gold tequila
½ oz. curaçao
2 oz. lime juice
1 lime wedge

Fill a cocktail shaker ½ full with ice. Pour in tequila, curaçao, and lime juice. Give it a good shake, and strain into an old-fashioned glass ¾ full of ice. Garnish with lime wedge.

Grateful Dead

½ oz. tequila
½ oz. rum
½ oz. vodka
½ oz. raspberry liqueur
½ oz. triple sec
1 oz. sour mix

Fill a cocktail shaker ½ full with ice. Pour in tequila, rum, vodka, raspberry liqueur, triple sec, and sour mix. Give it a good shake, and strain into a highball glass ¾ full of ice.

Heavy G

2 oz. tequila
2 oz. triple sec
2 oz. lime juice
2 oz. lemon-lime soda

Fill a cocktail shaker ½ full with ice. Pour in tequila, triple sec, and lime juice. Give it a good stir, and strain into a Collins glass ¾ full of ice. Pour in lemon-lime soda.

Hot Pants

2 oz. tequila
¾ oz. peppermint schnapps
1 tsp. grenadine
1 tsp. simple syrup
½ oz. grapefruit juice

Fill a cocktail shaker ½ full with ice. Pour in tequila, peppermint schnapps, grenadine, simple syrup, and grapefruit juice. Give it a good shake, and strain into an old-fashioned glass ¾ full of ice.

Iguana

1 oz. tequila
1 oz. vodka
¾ oz. coffee liqueur
1 oz. sour mix
1 lime slice

Fill a cocktail shaker ½ full with ice. Pour in tequila, vodka, coffee liqueur, and sour mix. Give it a good shake, and strain into a cocktail glass. Garnish with lime slice.

Joumbaba

2 oz. tequila
1 oz. grapefruit juice
4 oz. tonic water

Fill a highball glass ¾ full with ice. Pour in tequila, grapefruit juice, and tonic water. Give it a good stir.

Jubilee

1 oz. tequila
½ oz. vodka
½ oz. gin
½ oz. blue curaçao
1 oz. lemon juice
1 tsp. simple syrup
4 oz. club soda
1 maraschino cherry

Fill a cocktail shaker ½ full with ice. Pour in tequila, vodka, gin, blue curaçao, lemon juice, and simple syrup. Give it a good shake, and strain into a highball glass ¾ full of ice. Pour in club soda, and garnish with maraschino cherry.

Jumping Bean

1½ oz. tequila
½ oz. white Sambuca
3 espresso beans

Fill a cocktail shaker ½ full with ice. Pour in tequila and white Sambuca. Give it a good stir, and strain into a brandy snifter. Drop in espresso beans.

Lake George Iced Tea

½ oz. gold tequila
½ oz. light rum
½ oz. vodka
½ oz. gin
½ oz. triple sec
1 oz. pineapple juice
1 TB. lemon juice
4 oz. cola

Fill a cocktail shaker ½ full with ice. Pour in tequila, light rum, vodka, gin, triple sec, pineapple juice, and lemon juice. Give it a good shake, and strain into a highball glass ¾ full of ice. Pour in cola.

Lolita

1 TB. honey
2 oz. tequila
1 oz. lime juice
3 dashes bitters
1 maraschino cherry

Fill a cocktail shaker ½ full with ice. Pour in honey, tequila, and lime juice, and add bitters. Give it a good shake, and strain into a cocktail glass. Garnish with maraschino cherry.

Malibu Wave

2 oz. tequila
½ oz. blue curaçao
1 oz. triple sec
1 oz. sour mix
1 lime slice

Fill a cocktail shaker ½ full with ice. Pour in tequila, blue curaçao, triple sec, and sour mix. Give it a good shake, and strain into a cocktail glass. Garnish with lime slice.

Mango Margarita

2 oz. tequila
½ oz. Grand Marnier
1 oz. mango nectar
2 oz. lime juice
1 lime wedge

Fill a cocktail shaker ½ full with ice. Pour in tequila, Grand Marnier, mango nectar, and lime juice. Give it a good shake, and strain into an old-fashioned glass ¾ full of ice. Garnish with lime wedge.

Mango Sauza Margarita

The lovely, golden-walled Tocqueville in New York's Union Square is a savory spot where I always find a mixing and mingling of flavors that keep me coming back for more—cocktails included. Here is their citrusy-sweet take on a mango margarita.

3 oz. Sauza tequila
1 oz. *Cointreau*
½ oz. lemon juice
½ oz. lime juice
2 oz. mango purée or mango juice
1 TB. simple syrup
1 lime wedge

Fill a cocktail shaker ½ full with ice. Pour in Sauza tequila, Cointreau, lemon juice, lime juice, mango purée, and simple syrup. Give it a good shake, and strain into an old-fashioned glass ¾ full of ice. Garnish with lime wedge.

Liquor Lingo

Cointreau is a refined, brandy-based orange liqueur that takes a regular margarita to a higher level.

Margarita

2 oz. tequila
½ oz. triple sec
2 oz. lime juice
1 lime wedge

Fill a cocktail shaker ½ full with ice. Pour in tequila, triple sec, and lime juice. Give it a good shake, and strain into an old-fashioned glass ¾ full of ice. Garnish with lime wedge.

Spills

As you run through certain aisles of your supermarket, you will undoubtedly spot frozen and bottled versions of margarita mix. Although it's tempting to take advantage of these shortcuts ... don't! It'll take you the same amount of time to open and scoop out the frozen stuff as it will to cut open and squeeze a lime (and the latter is usually cheaper, too!). Fresh juice is always the way to go—you will absolutely taste the difference.

Maria Theresa

2 oz. tequila
1 TB. cranberry juice
½ oz. lime juice
1 tsp. simple syrup
1 lime slice

Fill a cocktail shaker ½ full with ice. Pour in tequila, cranberry juice, lime juice, and simple syrup. Give it a good shake, and strain into a cocktail glass. Garnish with lime slice.

Massacre

2 tsp. tequila
1 tsp. *Campari*
4 oz. ginger ale
1 lime wedge

Fill a highball glass ¾ full with ice. Pour in tequila, Campari, and ginger ale. Give it a good stir, and garnish with lime wedge.

Liquor Lingo

Campari, a.k.a. Campari bitters, is an herbal Italian aperitif that contains 24 percent alcohol and is often used as an ingredient in various classic cocktails such as the Negroni (see Chapter 6) or the Americano (see Chapter 12).

Matador

2 oz. tequila
¼ oz. lime juice
3 oz. pineapple juice

Fill a cocktail shaker ½ full with ice. Pour in tequila, lime juice, and pineapple juice. Give it a good shake, and strain into a cocktail glass.

Mexican Coffee

1½ oz. tequila
1 oz. coffee liqueur
2 oz. hot espresso coffee
¼ cup whipped cream
1 tsp. shaved nutmeg

Pour tequila and coffee liqueur into an Irish coffee glass. Pour in hot espresso coffee, and top with whipped cream. Garnish with shaved nutmeg.

Mexicana

2 oz. tequila
1 oz. pineapple juice
½ oz. lime juice
1 tsp. grenadine
1 lime slice

Fill a cocktail shaker ½ full with ice. Pour in tequila, pineapple juice, lime juice, and grenadine. Give it a good shake, and strain into a cocktail glass. Garnish with lime slice.

Mexicola

2 oz. tequila
2 TB. lime juice
4 oz. cola
1 lime wedge

Fill a highball glass ¾ full with ice. Pour in tequila, lime juice, and cola. Give it a good stir. Garnish with lime wedge.

Pacific Sunshine

1½ oz. tequila
1 oz. blue curaçao
1 oz. sour mix
1 lime slice

Fill a cocktail shaker ½ full with ice. Pour in tequila, blue curaçao, and sour mix. Give it a good shake, and strain into a cocktail glass. Garnish with lime slice.

Panther

2 oz. tequila
¾ oz. sour mix
1 oz. grapefruit juice
1 lime slice

Fill a cocktail shaker ½ full with ice. Pour in tequila, sour mix, and grapefruit juice. Give it a good shake, and strain into an old-fashioned glass full of ice. Garnish with lime slice.

Panther Sweat

1½ oz. tequila
½ oz. banana liqueur
½ oz. triple sec
4 oz. grapefruit juice
1 lime slice

Fill a cocktail shaker ½ full with ice. Pour in tequila, banana liqueur, triple sec, and grapefruit juice. Give it a good shake, and strain into a highball glass ¾ full of ice. Garnish with lime slice.

Peach Margarita

2 oz. tequila
½ oz. Grand Marnier
1 oz. peach nectar
2 oz. lime juice
1 lime wedge

Fill a cocktail shaker ½ full with ice. Pour in tequila, Grand Marnier, peach nectar, and lime juice. Give it a good shake, and strain into an old-fashioned glass ¾ full of ice. Garnish with lime wedge.

Piñata

1½ oz. tequila
½ oz. banana liqueur
1 oz. lime juice

Fill a cocktail shaker ½ full with ice. Pour in tequila, banana liqueur, and lime juice. Give it a good shake, and strain into an old-fashioned glass ¾ full of ice.

Piper

2 oz. tequila
½ oz. dark *crème de cacao*
¼ oz. lemon juice
2 oz. cold espresso coffee

Pour tequila, dark crème de cacao, lemon juice, and cold espresso coffee into an Irish coffee glass ¾ full of ice. Give it a good stir.

Liquor Lingo

Crème de cacao is a chocolate-flavored liqueur that comes in both dark and white (clear) varieties.

Prado

2 oz. tequila
¾ oz. cherry liqueur
1 tsp. grenadine
1 oz. lime juice
1 egg white
1 maraschino cherry

Fill a cocktail shaker ½ full with ice. Pour in tequila, cherry liqueur, grenadine, lime juice, and egg white. Give it a good, vigorous shake, and strain into a highball glass ¾ full of ice. Garnish with maraschino cherry.

Red-Headed Mexican

2 oz. tequila
1 TB. cranberry juice
4 oz. lemon-lime soda
1 lemon twist

Fill an old-fashioned glass ¾ full with ice. Pour in tequila, cranberry juice, and lemon-lime soda. Give it a good stir. Garnish with lemon twist.

Rosita

1½ oz. tequila
1 oz. Campari
½ oz. dry vermouth
½ oz. sweet vermouth
1 dash bitters
1 lemon twist

Fill an old-fashioned glass ¾ full with ice. Pour in tequila, Campari, dry vermouth, and sweet vermouth, and add bitters. Give it a good stir, and garnish with lemon twist.

Santa Fe

1½ oz. tequila
½ oz. triple sec
4 oz. lemon-lime soda
1 lime wedge

Fill a highball glass ¾ full with ice. Pour in tequila, triple sec, and lemon-lime soda. Give it a good stir, and garnish with lime wedge.

Shady Lady

2 oz. tequila
1 oz. melon liqueur
5 oz. grapefruit juice
1 maraschino cherry

Fill a cocktail shaker ½ full with ice. Pour in tequila, melon liqueur, and grapefruit juice. Give it a good stir, and strain into a highball glass ¾ full of ice. Garnish with maraschino cherry.

Shaker

2 oz. tequila
1 tsp. grenadine
½ oz. lemon juice
3 oz. pineapple juice

Fill a cocktail shaker ½ full with ice. Pour in tequila, grenadine, lemon juice, and pineapple juice. Give it a good stir, and strain into a cocktail glass.

Silk Stockings

2 oz. tequila
1 oz. white crème de cacao
1 tsp. *Chambord*
½ oz. heavy cream

Fill a cocktail shaker ½ full with ice. Pour in tequila, white crème de cacao, Chambord, and heavy cream. Give it a good shake, and strain into a cocktail glass.

Liquor Lingo

Chambord is a brandy-based raspberry-flavored liqueur made from black raspberries, honey, and herbs.

Sloe Tequila

1½ oz. tequila
1 oz. sloe gin
¾ oz. lime juice
1 oz. simple syrup

Fill a cocktail shaker ½ full with ice. Pour in tequila, sloe gin, lime juice, and simple syrup. Give it a good shake, and strain into a cocktail glass.

Spanish Moss

1½ oz. tequila
1 oz. coffee liqueur
½ tsp. green crème de menthe

Fill a cocktail shaker ½ full with ice. Pour in tequila, coffee liqueur, and green crème de menthe. Give it a good shake, and strain into an old-fashioned glass ¾ full of ice.

Strawberry Margarita

2 oz. tequila
½ oz. Grand Marnier
1 oz. strawberry liqueur
2 oz. lime juice
1 strawberry

Fill a cocktail shaker ½ full with ice. Pour in tequila, Grand Marnier, strawberry liqueur, and lime juice. Give it a good shake, and strain into an old-fashioned glass ¾ full of ice. Garnish with strawberry.

Tequila Canyon

1½ oz. tequila
¼ oz. triple sec
4 oz. cranberry juice
¼ oz. pineapple juice
¼ oz. orange juice
1 orange slice

Fill a cocktail shaker ½ full with ice. Pour in tequila, triple sec, cranberry juice, pineapple juice, and orange juice. Give it a good shake, and strain into a highball glass ¾ full of ice. Garnish with orange slice.

Tequila Collins

2½ oz. tequila
1 oz. lemon juice
1 tsp. simple syrup
4 oz. club soda
1 orange slice
1 maraschino cherry

Fill a cocktail shaker ½ full with ice. Pour in tequila, lemon juice, and simple syrup. Give it a good shake, and strain into a Collins glass ¾ full of ice. Pour in club soda, and garnish with orange slice and maraschino cherry.

Tequila Cooler

2 oz. light tequila
4 oz. lemon-lime soda
1 lemon wedge

Fill a highball glass ¾ full with ice. Pour in tequila and lemon-lime soda. Give it a good stir, and garnish with lemon wedge.

Tequila Daisy

2 oz. tequila
½ tsp. grenadine
1 oz. lemon juice
½ tsp. simple syrup
1 orange slice
1 maraschino cherry

Fill a cocktail shaker ½ full with ice. Pour in tequila, grenadine, lemon juice, and simple syrup. Give it a good shake, and strain into an old-fashioned glass ¾ full of ice. Garnish with orange slice and maraschino cherry.

Tequila Fix

2 oz. tequila
1 oz. lemon juice
1 tsp. simple syrup
1 lemon slice
1 maraschino cherry

Fill a cocktail shaker ½ full with ice. Pour in tequila, lemon juice, and simple syrup. Give it a good shake, and strain into a highball glass full of ice. Garnish with lemon slice and maraschino cherry.

Tequila Ghost

2 oz. tequila
1 oz. pastis
½ oz. lemon juice
1 lemon twist

Fill a cocktail shaker ½ full with ice. Pour in tequila, pastis, and lemon juice. Give it a good shake, and strain into a cocktail glass. Garnish with lemon twist.

Tequila Gimlet

2½ oz. tequila
½ oz. lime juice
½ Rose's lime juice
1 lime slice

Fill a cocktail shaker ½ full with ice. Pour in tequila, lime juice, and Rose's lime juice. Give it a good stir, and strain into a cocktail glass. Garnish with lime slice.

Tequila Manhattan

3 oz. tequila
1 oz. sweet vermouth
2 dashes bitters
1 maraschino cherry

Fill a cocktail shaker ½ full with ice. Pour in tequila and sweet vermouth, and add bitters. Give it a good stir, and strain into a cocktail glass. Garnish with maraschino cherry.

Tequila Martini

3 oz. tequila
¼ tsp. dry vermouth
1 lemon twist

Fill a cocktail shaker ½ full with ice. Pour in tequila and dry vermouth. Give it a good stir, and strain into a cocktail glass. Garnish with lemon twist.

Tequila Mockingbird

2 oz. tequila
2 tsp. white crème de menthe
1 oz. lemon juice

Fill a cocktail shaker ½ full with ice. Pour in tequila, white crème de menthe, and lemon juice. Give it a good shake, and strain into a cocktail glass.

Tequila Pink

3 oz. tequila
¼ tsp. dry vermouth
¼ tsp. grenadine

Fill a cocktail shaker ½ full with ice. Pour in tequila, dry vermouth, and grenadine. Give it a good stir, and strain into a cocktail glass.

Tequila Sour

2 oz. tequila
1 oz. lemon juice
1 oz. simple syrup
1 orange slice
1 maraschino cherry

Fill a cocktail shaker ½ full with ice. Pour in tequila, lemon juice, and simple syrup. Give it a good shake, and strain into a highball glass ¾ full of ice. Garnish with orange slice and maraschino cherry.

Tequila Stinger

2 oz. tequila
1 oz. white crème de menthe

Fill a cocktail shaker ½ full with ice. Pour in tequila and white crème de menthe. Give it a good stir, and strain into a cocktail glass.

Tequila Suave

2 oz. tequila
2 tsp. white crème de cacao
1 tsp. grenadine
1 oz. lemon juice
1 dash bitters
1 maraschino cherry

Fill a cocktail shaker ½ full with ice. Pour in tequila, white crème de cacao, grenadine, and lemon juice, and add bitters. Give it a good shake, and strain into a cocktail glass. Garnish with maraschino cherry.

Tequila Sunrise

1½ oz. tequila
4 oz. orange juice
1 TB. grenadine

Fill a highball glass ¾ full with ice. Pour in tequila and orange juice. Give it a good stir, and drip grenadine into center of cocktail.

Tequila Sunset

2 oz. tequila
5 oz. orange juice
½ oz. blackberry brandy

Fill a highball glass ¾ full with ice. Pour in tequila and orange juice. Give it a good stir, and gently drip blackberry brandy on top.

Tequini

2 oz. tequila
1 TB. dry vermouth
1 lemon twist

Fill a cocktail shaker ½ full with ice. Pour in tequila and dry vermouth. Give it a good stir, and strain into a cocktail glass. Garnish with lemon twist.

Tequonic

2 oz. tequila
½ oz. lemon juice
3 oz. tonic water

Fill an old-fashioned glass ¾ full with ice. Pour in tequila, lemon juice, and tonic water. Give it a good stir.

Tijuana Sunrise

1½ oz. tequila
½ oz. Campari
3 oz. orange juice
1 TB. lime juice
1 orange slice

Fill a cocktail shaker ½ full with ice. Pour in tequila, Campari, orange juice, and lime juice. Give it a good shake, and strain into an old-fashioned glass ¾ full of ice. Garnish with orange slice.

Toreador

2 oz. tequila
1 oz. dark crème de cacao
¼ oz. heavy cream
2 TB. whipped cream
1 tsp. cocoa powder

Fill a cocktail shaker ½ full with ice. Pour in tequila, dark crème de cacao, and heavy cream. Give it a good stir, and strain into a cocktail glass. Dollop whipped cream on top, and garnish with cocoa powder.

Viva Villa

2 oz. tequila
1 oz. lime juice
2 tsp. lemon juice
¼ oz. simple syrup
1 lemon twist

Fill a cocktail shaker ½ full with ice. Pour in tequila, lime juice, lemon juice, and simple syrup. Give it a good shake, and strain into a cocktail glass. Garnish with lemon twist.

Waborita

2 oz. tequila
2 oz. triple sec
2 oz. lime juice
1 lime slice

Fill a cocktail shaker ½ full with ice. Pour in tequila, triple sec, and lime juice. Give it a good shake, and strain into a cocktail glass. Garnish with lime slice.

Wild Thing

2 oz. tequila
½ oz. lime juice
1 oz. cranberry juice
1 oz. club soda
1 lime wedge

Fill an old-fashioned glass with ice. Pour in tequila, lime juice, cranberry juice, and club soda. Give it a good stir, and garnish with lime wedge.

Xylophone

1½ oz. tequila
½ oz. white crème de cacao
½ oz. light cream
½ oz. simple syrup

Fill a cocktail shaker ½ full with ice. Pour in tequila, white crème de cacao, light cream, and simple syrup. Give it a good shake, and strain into a cocktail glass.

Chapter 9

Vodka

Passing the vodka bottle. And playing guitar.
—Keith Richards, on how to keep in shape

Alfie Cocktail

2 oz. lemon vodka
1 tsp. triple sec
1 TB. pineapple juice
1 lemon twist

Fill a cocktail shaker ½ full with ice. Pour in lemon vodka, triple sec, and pineapple juice. Give it a good shake, and strain into a cocktail glass. Garnish with lemon twist.

Algae

1 oz. vodka
½ oz. melon liqueur
¼ oz. blue curaçao
¼ oz. raspberry liqueur
2 oz. sour mix
3 oz. lemon-lime soda

Fill a cocktail shaker ½ full with ice. Pour in vodka, melon liqueur, blue curaçao, raspberry liqueur, and sour mix. Give it a good shake, and strain into a highball glass ¾ full of ice. Pour in lemon-lime soda.

Anti-Freeze

1½ oz. vodka
½ oz. peppermint schnapps
½ oz. blue curaçao

Fill a cocktail shaker ½ full with ice. Pour in vodka, peppermint schnapps, and blue curaçao. Give it a good shake, and strain into an old-fashioned glass full of ice.

Apple Judy

1 oz. vodka
½ oz. Grand Marnier
3 oz. apple juice

Fill a cocktail shaker ½ full with ice. Pour in vodka, Grand Marnier, and apple juice. Give it a good shake, and strain into a cocktail glass.

Appletini

2 oz. vodka
1 oz. apple schnapps
1 oz. apple juice

Fill a cocktail shaker ½ full with ice. Pour in vodka, apple schnapps, and apple juice. Give it a good shake, and strain into a cocktail glass.

Apricot Respite

2 oz. vodka
2 oz. apricot nectar
2 oz. tonic water

Fill a highball glass ¾ full with ice. Pour in vodka, apricot nectar, and tonic water. Give it a good stir.

April Rain

2 oz. vodka
½ oz. Rose's lime juice
½ oz. vermouth
1 lime slice

Fill a cocktail shaker ½ full with ice. Pour in vodka, Rose's lime juice, and vermouth. Give it a good stir, and strain into a cocktail glass. Garnish with lime slice.

Aqueduct

2 oz. vodka
¼ oz. curaçao
¼ oz. apricot liqueur
1 tsp. lemon juice
1 tsp. lime juice
1 lemon twist

Fill a cocktail shaker ½ full with ice. Pour in vodka, curaçao, apricot liqueur, lemon juice, and lime juice. Give it a good shake, and strain into a cocktail glass. Garnish with lemon twist.

Auburn Cocktail

1½ oz. vodka
½ oz. Galliano
¼ oz. crème de cassis
1 oz. orange juice

Fill a cocktail shaker ½ full with ice. Pour in vodka, Galliano, crème de cassis, and orange juice. Give it a good shake, and strain into a cocktail glass.

Bare Cheeks

2 oz. vodka
2 tsp. grenadine
¼ oz. lemon juice
1 oz. apple juice
1 lemon twist

Fill a cocktail shaker ½ full with ice. Pour in vodka, grenadine, lemon juice, and apple juice. Give it a good shake, and strain into a cocktail glass. Garnish with lemon twist.

Bay Breeze

2 oz. vodka
3 oz. pineapple juice
1 oz. cranberry juice

Fill a highball glass ¾ full with ice. Pour in vodka, pineapple juice, and cranberry juice. Give it a good stir.

Bellini Martini

2 oz. vodka
1 oz. peach schnapps
1 oz. peach nectar
1 TB. lemon juice
1 lemon twist

Fill a cocktail shaker ½ full with ice. Pour in vodka, peach schnapps, peach nectar, and lemon juice. Give it a good shake, and strain into a cocktail glass. Garnish with lemon twist.

Belmont Stakes

2 oz. vodka
2 oz. gold rum
½ oz. strawberry liqueur
1 tsp. grenadine
½ oz. lime juice
1 orange slice

Fill a cocktail shaker ½ full with ice. Pour in vodka, gold rum, strawberry liqueur, grenadine, and lime juice. Give it a good shake, and strain into a cocktail glass. Garnish with orange slice.

Big Daddy

2 oz. vodka
2 oz. water
1 lemon twist

Fill an old-fashioned glass with ice. Pour in vodka and water. Give it a good stir, and garnish with lemon twist.

Bird of Paradise

2 oz. vodka
1 tsp. grenadine
1 oz. orange juice
1 TB. lemon juice
1 orange slice

Fill a cocktail shaker ½ full with ice. Pour in vodka, grenadine, orange juice, and lemon juice. Give it a good shake, and strain into a cocktail glass. Garnish with orange slice.

Black Eye

2 oz. vodka
½ oz. blackberry brandy

Fill a cocktail shaker ½ full with ice. Pour in vodka and blackberry brandy. Give it a good stir, and strain into a cocktail glass.

Black Magic

2 oz. vodka
¾ oz. coffee liqueur
½ tsp. lemon juice

Fill a cocktail shaker ½ full with ice. Pour in vodka, coffee liqueur, and lemon juice. Give it a good shake, and strain into an old-fashioned glass ¾ full of ice.

Black Russian

2 oz. vodka
¾ oz. coffee liqueur

Fill a cocktail shaker ½ full with ice. Pour in vodka and coffee liqueur. Give it a good shake, and pour into an old-fashioned glass ¾ full of ice.

Blind Melon

1½ oz. vodka
1 oz. melon liqueur
1 oz. triple sec

Fill a cocktail shaker ½ full with ice. Pour in vodka, melon liqueur, and triple sec. Give it a good shake, and strain into a cocktail glass.

Bloody Bull

2 oz. vodka
3 oz. tomato juice
2 oz. beef bouillon
½ oz. lemon juice
½ tsp. Tabasco sauce
⅛ tsp. black pepper
1 lemon wedge

Fill a cocktail shaker ½ full with ice. Pour in vodka, tomato juice, beef bouillon, lemon juice, Tabasco sauce, and black pepper. Give it a good shake, and strain into a highball glass ¾ full of ice. Garnish with lemon wedge.

Bloody Mary

2 oz. vodka
4 oz. tomato juice
½ oz. lemon juice
¼ tsp. Worcestershire sauce
½ tsp. Tabasco sauce
½ tsp. horseradish
⅛ tsp. salt
⅛ tsp. black pepper
1 celery stalk
1 lemon wedge

Fill a cocktail shaker ½ full with ice. Pour in vodka, tomato juice, lemon juice, Worcestershire sauce, Tabasco sauce, horseradish, salt, and black pepper. Give it a good shake, and strain into a highball glass ¾ full of ice. Garnish with celery stalk and lemon wedge.

Blue Glacier

3 oz. vodka
1 TB. blue curaçao
1 lemon twist

Fill a cocktail shaker ½ full with ice. Pour in vodka and blue curaçao. Give it a good stir, and strain into a cocktail glass. Garnish with lemon twist.

Blue Lagoon

2 oz. vodka
½ oz. blue curaçao
4 oz. lemonade
1 maraschino cherry

Fill a cocktail shaker ½ full with ice. Pour in vodka, blue curaçao, and lemonade. Give it a good stir, and strain into a highball glass ¾ full of ice. Garnish with maraschino cherry.

Blue Meanie

2 oz. vodka
1 oz. blue curaçao
1 oz. sour mix

Fill a cocktail shaker ½ full with ice. Pour in vodka, blue curaçao, and sour mix. Give it a good shake, and strain into a cocktail glass.

Blue Monday

2 oz. vodka
½ oz. blue curaçao
½ oz. triple sec

Fill a cocktail shaker ½ full with ice. Pour in vodka, blue curaçao, and triple sec. Give it a good stir, and strain into a cocktail glass.

Bluebeard

2 oz. vodka
½ oz. blueberry schnapps

Fill a cocktail shaker ½ full with ice. Pour in vodka and blueberry schnapps. Give it a good stir, and strain into a cocktail glass.

Blushing Bride

2 oz. vodka
1 oz. cranberry juice
1 oz. orange juice
2 oz. lemon-lime soda
1 maraschino cherry

Fill a highball glass ¾ full with ice. Pour in vodka, cranberry juice, orange juice, and lemon-lime soda. Give it a good stir, and garnish with maraschino cherry.

Bolshoi Punch

2 oz. vodka
½ oz. light rum
¼ oz. crème de cassis
¼ oz. lemon juice
2 tsp. simple syrup

Fill a cocktail shaker ½ full with ice. Pour in vodka, light rum, crème de cassis, lemon juice, and simple syrup. Give it a good shake, and strain into an old-fashioned glass ¾ full of ice.

Bootlegger Tea

1 oz. vodka
1 oz. light rum
1 oz. triple sec
1 tsp. grenadine
1 oz. sour mix
3 oz. lemon-lime soda

Fill a cocktail shaker ½ full with ice. Pour in vodka, light rum, triple sec, grenadine, and sour mix. Give it a good shake, and strain into a Collins glass ¾ full of ice. Pour in lemon-lime soda.

Brain Eraser

1 oz. vodka
½ oz. coffee liqueur
½ oz. amaretto
3 oz. club soda

Fill an old-fashioned glass ¾ full with ice. Pour in vodka, followed by coffee liqueur, followed by amaretto, and finally club soda.

Brazen Hussy

1½ oz. vodka
1 oz. triple sec
½ oz. lemon juice
1 lemon twist

Fill a cocktail shaker ½ full with ice. Pour in vodka, triple sec, and lemon juice. Give it a good shake, and strain into a cocktail glass. Garnish with lemon twist.

Broken Heart

1½ oz. vodka
1 oz. Chambord
1 tsp. grenadine
2 oz. orange juice

Fill a cocktail shaker ½ full with ice. Pour in vodka, Chambord, grenadine, and orange juice. Give it a good shake, and strain into a cocktail glass.

Brooklyn Vanilla Egg Cream

An egg cream is, for sure, a New York City phenomenon rarely seen outside the five boroughs. It's a delicious mix of vanilla (or chocolate) syrup, milk, and seltzer water sprayed in at the end to give it a big, frothy top that resembles whipped-up egg whites (hence the name). My dear and talented friend Sylva Popaz came up with this kicked-up version during her bartending days. Remember to shake it really well to get that same frothy-top effect!

1 oz. vodka
1 oz. vanilla Häagen-Dazs cream
  liqueur (or white crème de cacao)
¼ oz. milk
6 oz. club soda

Fill a cocktail shaker ½ full with ice. Pour in vodka, vanilla Häagen-Dazs cream liqueur, milk, and club soda. Give it a good, vigorous shake, and strain into a Collins glass.

Brown Hen

3 oz. vodka
2 dashes bitters

Fill a cocktail shaker ½ full with ice. Pour in vodka, and add bitters. Give it a good stir, and strain into a cocktail glass.

Bull Shot

2 oz. vodka
4 oz. beef bouillon
½ tsp. Tabasco sauce
⅛ tsp. black pepper
1 lemon wedge

Fill a cocktail shaker ½ full with ice. Pour in vodka, beef bouillon, Tabasco sauce, and black pepper. Give it a good shake, and strain into a highball glass ¾ full of ice. Garnish with lemon wedge.

Bullfrog

2 oz. vodka
½ oz. lemon juice
½ oz. lime juice
1 tsp. simple syrup
1 lime twist

Fill a cocktail shaker ½ full with ice. Pour in vodka, lemon juice, lime juice, and simple syrup. Give it a good stir, and strain into a cocktail glass. Garnish with lemon twist.

Caipiroska

1 lime, cut into 8 wedges
2 tsp. sugar
3 oz. vodka

Muddle lime wedges with sugar in an old-fashioned glass. Fill the glass with ice, and pour in vodka.

Cajun Martini

3 oz. vodka
¼ tsp. vermouth
1 pickled okra

Fill a cocktail shaker ½ full with ice. Pour in vodka and vermouth. Give it a good stir, and strain into a cocktail glass. Garnish with pickled okra.

Cape Codder

2 oz. vodka
4 oz. cranberry juice
1 tsp. lime juice
1 lime wedge

Fill a highball glass ¾ full with ice. Pour in vodka, cranberry juice, and lime juice. Give it a good stir, and garnish with lime wedge.

Cappuccino Cocktail

1 oz. vodka
1 oz. coffee brandy
1 oz. light cream

Fill a cocktail shaker ½ full with ice. Pour in vodka, coffee brandy, and light cream. Give it a good shake, and strain into a cocktail glass.

Cherry Bomb

2 oz. vodka
1 oz. crème de cacao
½ oz. grenadine
1 maraschino cherry

Fill a cocktail shaker ½ full with ice. Pour in vodka, crème de cacao, and grenadine. Give it a good shake, and strain into an old-fashioned glass ¾ full of ice. Garnish with maraschino cherry.

Cherry Martini

2 oz. vodka
½ oz. maraschino liqueur
1 maraschino cherry

Fill a cocktail shaker ½ full with ice. Pour in vodka and maraschino liqueur. Give it a good stir, and strain into a cocktail glass. Garnish with maraschino cherry.

Cielo

1½ oz. vodka
½ oz. crème de cassis
2 TB. lime juice
2 dashes bitters
4 oz. ginger ale

Fill a highball glass ¾ full with ice. Pour in vodka, crème de cassis, and lime juice, and add bitters. Give it a good stir, and pour in ginger ale.

Citrus Cooler

2 oz. vodka
1 oz. triple sec
1 oz. lime juice
5 oz. lemonade
1 lemon wedge

Fill a highball glass ¾ full with ice. Pour in vodka, triple sec, lime juice, and lemonade. Give it a good stir. Garnish with lemon wedge.

Climax

½ oz. vodka
½ oz. amaretto
½ oz. crème de bananes
½ oz. triple sec
½ oz. crème de cacao
1 oz. light cream

Fill a cocktail shaker ½ full with ice. Pour in vodka, amaretto, crème de bananes, triple sec, crème de cacao, and light cream. Give it a good shake, and strain into a cocktail glass.

Coffee Cooler

1 scoop coffee ice cream
1½ oz. vodka
1 oz. coffee liqueur
¼ oz. heavy cream
3 oz. cold coffee
1 tsp. simple syrup

Add coffee ice cream to an old-fashioned glass. Fill a cocktail shaker ½ full with ice. Pour in vodka, coffee liqueur, heavy cream, cold coffee, and simple syrup. Give it a good shake, and strain over ice cream in the old-fashioned glass.

Colorado Bulldog

1 oz. vodka
1 oz. coffee liqueur
½ oz. milk
1 oz. cola

Fill a cocktail shaker ½ full with ice. Pour in vodka, coffee liqueur, and milk. Give it a good shake, and strain into an old-fashioned glass ¾ full of ice. Pour in cola.

Cool Breeze

2½ oz. vodka
1 oz. pink grapefruit juice
1 oz. pineapple juice
2 oz. cranberry juice
2 oz. ginger ale

Fill a Collins glass ¾ full with ice. Pour in vodka, pink grapefruit juice, pineapple juice, cranberry juice, and ginger ale. Give it a good stir.

Copperhead

2 oz. vodka
4 oz. ginger ale

Fill a highball glass ¾ full with ice. Pour in vodka and ginger ale. Give it a good stir.

Cosmopolitan

2 oz. vodka
½ oz. triple sec
¼ oz. lime juice
½ oz. cranberry juice
1 lime twist

Fill a cocktail shaker ½ full with ice. Pour in vodka, triple sec, lime juice, and cranberry juice. Give it a good shake, and strain into a cocktail glass. Garnish with lime twist.

Crash Landing

½ tsp. sugar
2 oz. vodka
2 tsp. grenadine
¼ oz. lemon juice
¼ oz. lime juice
1 lemon twist

Fill a cocktail shaker ½ full with ice. Add sugar and then pour in vodka, grenadine, lemon juice, and lime juice. Give it a good shake, and strain into a cocktail glass. Garnish with lemon twist.

Creamsicle

2 oz. vanilla vodka
3 oz. orange juice
2 oz. milk

Fill a cocktail shaker ½ full with ice. Pour in vanilla vodka, orange juice, and milk. Give it a good shake, and strain into a highball glass ¾ full of ice.

Crisp Apple

2 oz. vodka
1 TB. peppermint schnapps
4 oz. apple juice

Fill a highball glass ¾ full with ice. Pour in vodka, peppermint schnapps, and apple juice. Give it a good stir.

Czarina

1½ oz. vodka
½ oz. apricot brandy
¼ oz. dry vermouth
1 dash bitters

Fill a cocktail shaker ½ full with ice. Pour in vodka, apricot brandy, and dry vermouth, and add bitters. Give it a good stir, and strain into a cocktail glass.

Dark Eyes

2 oz. vodka
½ oz. blackberry brandy
2 tsp. lime juice

Fill a cocktail shaker ½ full with ice. Pour in vodka, blackberry brandy, and lime juice. Give it a good shake, and strain into a cocktail glass.

Deep Blue

1½ oz. vodka
½ oz. blue curaçao
2 oz. champagne

Fill a cocktail shaker ½ full with ice. Pour in vodka and blue curaçao. Give it a good stir, and strain into a champagne flute. Pour in champagne.

Desert Sunrise

2 oz. vodka
2 oz. cranberry juice
2 oz. pineapple juice
1 tsp. grenadine

Fill a cocktail shaker ½ full with ice. Pour in vodka, cranberry juice, pineapple juice, and grenadine. Give it a good shake, and strain into a highball glass ¾ full of ice.

Dirty Bastard

1½ oz. vodka
½ oz. blackberry brandy
4 oz. cranberry juice
1 TB. lime juice
1 lime wedge

Fill a cocktail shaker ½ full with ice. Pour in vodka, blackberry brandy, cranberry juice, and lime juice. Give it a good stir, and strain into a highball glass ¾ full of ice. Garnish with lime wedge.

Earthquake II

1½ oz. vodka
1½ oz. gin
½ oz. white crème de menthe

Fill a cocktail shaker ½ full with ice. Pour in vodka, gin, and white crème de menthe. Give it a good shake, and strain into a brandy snifter ¾ full of crushed ice.

Eiffel Tower

1½ oz. vodka
1½ oz. cognac
½ oz. anisette
½ oz. triple sec
1 orange twist

Fill a cocktail shaker ½ full with ice. Pour in vodka, cognac, anisette, and triple sec. Give it a good shake, and strain into a cocktail glass. Garnish with orange twist.

'57 Chevy

1 oz. vodka
½ oz. apricot liqueur
½ oz. Southern Comfort
5 oz. pineapple juice

Fill a cocktail shaker ½ full with ice. Pour in vodka, apricot liqueur, Southern Comfort, and pineapple juice. Give it a good shake, and strain into a highball glass ¾ full of ice.

'57 Chevy with a White License Plate

1½ oz. vodka
1½ oz. white crème de menthe

Fill a cocktail shaker ½ full with ice. Pour in vodka and white crème de menthe. Give it a good stir, and strain into an old-fashioned glass full of ice.

Fire and Ice

3 oz. pepper vodka
¼ tsp. dry vermouth

Fill a cocktail shaker ½ full with ice. Pour in pepper vodka and dry vermouth. Give it a good stir, and strain into a cocktail glass.

Firefly

2 oz. vodka
4 oz. grapefruit juice
1 tsp. grenadine

Fill a cocktail shaker ½ full with ice. Pour in vodka and grapefruit juice. Give it a good shake, and strain into a highball glass ¾ full of ice. Drip grenadine into center of cocktail.

Firehammer

1½ oz. vodka
½ oz. amaretto
½ oz. triple sec
½ oz. lemon juice

Fill a cocktail shaker ½ full with ice. Pour in vodka, amaretto, triple sec, and lemon juice. Give it a good shake, and strain into a cocktail glass.

Fish Lips

1½ oz. vodka
½ oz. kirschwasser
½ oz. triple sec
1 oz. grapefruit juice

Fill a cocktail shaker ½ full with ice.
Pour in vodka, kirschwasser, triple sec,
and grapefruit juice. Give it a good
shake, and strain into a cocktail glass.

Flying Grasshopper

2 oz. vodka
½ oz. green crème de menthe
1 oz. white crème de cacao
1 mint sprig

Fill a cocktail shaker ½ full with
ice. Pour in vodka, green crème de
menthe, and white crème de cacao.
Give it a good shake, and strain into a
cocktail glass. Garnish with mint sprig.

Foggy Afternoon

1½ oz. vodka
½ oz. triple sec
½ oz. apricot brandy
1 tsp. crème de bananes
¼ oz. lemon juice
1 maraschino cherry

Fill a cocktail shaker ½ full with ice.
Pour in vodka, triple sec, apricot
brandy, crème de bananes, and lemon
juice. Give it a good shake, and strain
into a cocktail glass. Garnish with
maraschino cherry.

Foggy Morning

2½ oz. vodka
¼ tsp. vermouth
¼ oz. lemon juice
1 tsp. peach nectar
1 lemon twist

Fill a cocktail shaker ½ full with ice.
Pour in vodka, vermouth, lemon juice,
and peach nectar. Give it a good shake,
and strain into a cocktail glass. Garnish with lemon twist.

Frisky Witch

1½ oz. vodka
1½ oz. black Sambuca

Fill a cocktail shaker ½ full with ice.
Pour in vodka and black Sambuca.
Give it a good stir, and strain into an
old-fashioned glass ¾ full of ice.

Fuzzy Martini

2½ oz. vodka
½ oz. peach schnapps
1 tsp. lemon juice
1 peach slice

Fill a cocktail shaker ½ full with ice. Pour in vodka, peach schnapps, and lemon juice. Give it a good stir, and strain into a cocktail glass. Garnish with peach slice.

Fuzzy Monkey

1 oz. vodka
1 oz. peach schnapps
½ oz. crème de bananes
4 oz. orange juice

Fill a highball glass ¾ full with ice. Pour in vodka, peach schnapps, crème de bananes, and orange juice. Give it a good stir.

Fuzzy Navel

1 oz. vodka
1 oz. peach schnapps
5 oz. orange juice

Fill a highball glass ¾ full with ice. Pour in vodka, peach schnapps, and orange juice. Give it a good stir.

Gables Collins

1½ oz. vodka
1 oz. crème de noyaux
1 TB. lemon juice
¼ oz. pineapple juice
4 oz. club soda
1 pineapple chunk

Fill a cocktail shaker ½ full with ice. Pour in vodka, crème de noyaux, lemon juice, and pineapple juice. Give it a good shake, and strain into a Collins glass ¾ full of ice. Pour in club soda, and garnish with pineapple chunk.

Gangbuster Punch

2 oz. vodka
1 oz. peach schnapps
2 oz. cranberry juice
3 oz. lemon-lime soda

Fill a cocktail shaker ½ full with ice. Pour in vodka, peach schnapps, and cranberry juice. Give it a good shake, and strain into a Collins glass ¾ full of ice. Pour in lemon-lime soda.

Giraffe

1½ oz. vodka
1 oz. melon liqueur
4 oz. pineapple juice
½ oz. cranberry juice

Fill a cocktail shaker ½ full with ice. Pour in vodka, melon liqueur, and pineapple juice. Give it a good shake, and strain into a Collins glass ¾ full of ice. Drip cranberry juice on top.

Glacier Mint

2 oz. vodka
1 oz. lemon vodka
1 TB. green crème de menthe

Fill a cocktail shaker ½ full with ice. Pour in vodka, lemon vodka, and green crème de menthe. Give it a good stir, and strain into an old-fashioned glass ¾ full of ice.

Godchild

2 oz. vodka
1 oz. amaretto
¼ oz. heavy cream

Fill a cocktail shaker ½ full with ice. Pour in vodka, amaretto, and heavy cream. Give it a good shake, and strain into a champagne flute.

Godmother

2 oz. vodka
1 oz. amaretto

Fill a cocktail shaker ½ full with ice. Pour in vodka and amaretto. Give it a good stir, and strain into an old-fashioned glass full of ice.

Gorilla Milk

1½ oz. vodka
1 oz. dark crème de cacao
2 oz. milk

Fill a cocktail shaker ½ full with ice. Pour in vodka, dark crème de cacao, and milk. Give it a good shake, and strain into an old-fashioned glass ¾ full of ice.

Grape Crush Cocktail

1½ oz. vodka
½ oz. Chambord
1 oz. sour mix
4 oz. lemon-lime soda

Fill a cocktail shaker ½ full with ice. Pour in vodka, Chambord, and sour mix. Give it a good shake, and strain into a Collins glass ¾ full of ice. Pour in lemon-lime soda, and give it a good stir.

Grape Quencher

1½ oz. vodka
1 oz. triple sec
1 oz. Rose's lime juice
4 oz. white grape juice

Fill a cocktail shaker ½ full with ice. Pour in vodka, triple sec, and Rose's lime juice. Give it a good shake, and strain into a Collins glass ¾ full of ice. Pour in white grape juice, and give it a good stir.

Green Fantasy

1½ oz. vodka
1 oz. melon liqueur
¼ oz. dry vermouth
1 lemon twist

Fill a cocktail shaker ½ full with ice. Pour in vodka, melon liqueur, and dry vermouth. Give it a good stir, and strain into a cocktail glass. Garnish with lemon twist.

Green Island

1 oz. vodka
½ oz. green curaçao
1 oz. pineapple juice
1 oz. lime juice
1 tsp. simple syrup
1 lime slice

Fill a cocktail shaker ½ full with ice. Pour in vodka, green curaçao, pineapple juice, lime juice, and simple syrup. Give it a good shake, and strain into a cocktail glass. Garnish with lime slice.

Greyhound

2 oz. vodka
5 oz. grapefruit juice

Fill a highball glass ½ full with ice. Pour in vodka and grapefruit juice. Give it a good stir.

Hamlet

1½ oz. vodka
½ oz. Campari
2 oz. orange juice

Fill a cocktail shaker ½ full with ice. Pour in vodka, Campari, and orange juice. Give it a good shake, and strain into a cocktail glass.

Harlem Vodka Cocktail

2 oz. vodka
¼ oz. maraschino liqueur
1 oz. pineapple juice
2 pineapple chunks

Fill a cocktail shaker ½ full with ice. Pour in vodka, maraschino liqueur, and pineapple juice. Give it a good shake, and strain into a cocktail glass. Garnish with pineapple chunks.

Harvey Wallbanger

1½ oz. vodka
4 oz. orange juice
½ oz. Galliano

Fill a highball glass ¾ full with ice. Pour in vodka and orange juice. Give it a good stir. Drip Galliano on top.

Cocktail Conversation

Who's Harvey? A few stories exist, but two seem to come up over and over. The first is pure surfer lore: apparently, a wave-rider named Harvey liked to add Galliano to his drink of choice, the screwdriver, and had a penchant for walking into walls. Others say the drink was created by a mixologist named Bill Doner, who came up with it while tending bar at The Office in Newport Beach.

Headlights

2 oz. vodka
½ oz. yellow Chartreuse
1 TB. lemon juice

Fill a cocktail shaker ½ full with ice. Pour in vodka, yellow Chartreuse, and lemon juice. Give it a good shake, and strain into a cocktail glass.

Holy Water

1½ oz. vodka
½ oz. triple sec
3 oz. tonic water
1 tsp. grenadine

Fill an old-fashioned glass ¾ full with ice. Pour in vodka and triple sec. Give it a good stir, and pour in tonic water. Drip grenadine in center of cocktail.

Horny Toad

2 oz. vodka
½ oz. triple sec
4 oz. lemonade

Fill an old-fashioned glass ¾ full with ice. Pour in vodka, triple sec, and lemonade. Give it a good stir.

Idonis

1½ oz. vodka
½ oz. apricot brandy
1 oz. pineapple juice

Fill a cocktail shaker ½ full with ice. Pour in vodka, apricot brandy, and pineapple juice. Give it a good shake, and strain into a cocktail glass.

Italian Ice

1 oz. vodka
1 oz. blue curaçao
1 oz. Chambord
1 oz. sour mix
4 oz. lemon-lime soda

Fill a cocktail shaker ½ full with ice. Pour in vodka, blue curaçao, Chambord, and sour mix. Give it a good shake, and strain into a Collins glass ¾ full of crushed ice. Pour in lemon-lime soda, and give it a good stir.

Jackath

1½ oz. vodka
½ oz. brandy
1 tsp. crème de cassis
1 tsp. triple sec
2 dashes orange bitters

Fill a cocktail shaker ½ full with ice. Pour in vodka, brandy, crème de cassis, and triple sec, and add orange bitters. Give it a good shake, and strain into a cocktail glass.

Jackie O

Created by mixologist-with-the-most Lolly Mason of Boston's much-lauded Upstairs at the Square, this classic cocktail pays homage to one of Massachusetts's most famous and beloved residents. Lolly's cocktail TV series, *Lolly's Remedies*, has been named a must-watch by both *Boston* magazine and *The Boston Herald*, and the generous mistress of mixology contributed this favorite of hers for you to make at home.

2 tsp. cherry juice
2 tsp. sugar
1 oz. orange vodka
½ oz. citron vodka
½ oz. crème de cassis
2 tsp. lemon juice
1 oz. cranberry juice
2 oz. apricot nectar
1 splash champagne
1 lime slice
1 orange slice

Dip the rim of a cocktail glass in cherry juice. Sprinkle sugar in a small dish, and place the glass upside down in the dish so the rim is coated with sugar. Fill a cocktail shaker ½ full with ice. Pour in orange vodka, citron vodka, crème de cassis, lemon juice, cranberry juice, and apricot nectar. Give it a good shake, and strain into a cocktail glass. Add splash of champagne, and garnish with lime and orange slices.

Jane's Addiction

2 oz. vodka
½ oz. crème de noyaux
1 tsp. apricot brandy
2 oz. orange juice
1 lemon twist

Fill a cocktail shaker ½ full with ice. Pour in vodka, crème de noyaux, apricot brandy, and orange juice. Give it a good shake, and strain into a cocktail glass. Garnish with lemon twist.

Joy Jumper

2 oz. vodka
2 tsp. kummel
1 tsp. lime juice
1 tsp. lemon juice
½ tsp. simple syrup
1 lemon twist

Fill a cocktail shaker ½ full with ice. Pour in vodka, kummel, lime juice, lemon juice, and simple syrup. Give it a good shake, and strain into a cocktail glass. Garnish with lemon twist.

Jungle Jim

1½ oz. vodka	Fill a cocktail shaker ½ full with ice.
½ oz. crème de bananes	Pour in vodka, crème de bananes, and
2 oz. milk	milk. Give it a good shake, and strain
	into a cocktail glass.

Kamikaze Cocktail

2 oz. vodka	Fill a cocktail shaker ½ full with ice.
1 oz. triple sec	Pour in vodka, triple sec, and Rose's
½ oz. Rose's lime juice	lime juice. Give it a good shake, and
	strain into a cocktail glass.

Kangaroo Cocktail

2 oz. vodka	Fill a cocktail shaker ½ full with ice.
¾ oz. dry vermouth	Pour in vodka and dry vermouth. Give
	it a good stir, and strain into a cocktail
	glass.

Karma Chameleon

2 oz. vodka	Fill a cocktail shaker ½ full with ice.
1 oz. peach schnapps	Pour in vodka, peach schnapps, and
1 tsp. grenadine	grenadine. Give it a good shake, and
5 oz. lemon-lime soda	strain into a Collins glass ¾ full of ice.
1 lime slice	Pour in lemon-lime soda. Give it a
1 maraschino cherry	good stir, and garnish with lime slice
	and maraschino cherry.

Karoff

1½ oz. vodka	Fill a highball glass ¾ full with ice.
1 oz. cranberry juice	Pour in vodka, cranberry juice, and
3 oz. club soda	club soda. Give it a good stir, and
1 lime wedge	garnish with lime wedge.

Kashmir

2 oz. vodka	Fill a cocktail shaker ½ full with ice.
1 oz. white crème de cacao	Pour in vodka, white crème de cacao,
1 tsp. grenadine	grenadine, and lemon juice. Give it a
1 TB. lemon juice	good shake, and strain into a cocktail
	glass.

Ketelina

This refreshing, exotic imbibable comes from the equally refreshing and exotic Montage Resort Spa in Laguna Beach.

2 oz. Ketel One vodka
1 oz. Alizé Red Passion
½ oz. pineapple juice
1 lemon twist

Fill a cocktail shaker ½ full with ice. Pour in the Ketel One vodka, Alizé Red Passion, and pineapple juice. Give it a good shake, and strain into a chilled cocktail glass. Garnish with lemon twist.

Killer Kool-Aid

1 oz. vodka
½ oz. Cherry Heering
½ oz. peach schnapps
1 TB. lemon juice
4 oz. orange juice

Fill a highball glass ¾ full with ice. Pour in vodka, Cherry Heering, peach schnapps, lemon juice, and orange juice. Give it a good stir.

The Knitting Factory

This drink is the Nolita House owners' tribute to their space, which was the original location for New York City's famous Knitting Factory.

1½ oz. Stoli Razberi vodka
½ oz. triple sec
½ oz. framboise
1 dash lime juice
1 tsp. cranberry juice
1 lime twist

Fill a cocktail shaker ½ full with ice. Pour Stoli Razberi vodka, triple sec, framboise, lime juice, and cranberry juice. Give it a good shake, and strain into a chilled martini glass. Garnish with lime twist.

Koi Yellow Martini

In LA, to be seen at Koi is … well, to be seen at one of the hottest, chicest spots in all of Tinseltown. But just because you're not a big name of the big screen doesn't mean you can't drink like one. Here, Koi contributed their "yellow" martini for starry-eyed sipping.

1 lemon wedge
2 tsp. sugar
3 oz. raspberry vodka
2 TB. lemon juice
½ oz. simple syrup
3 raspberries

Gently rub the rim of a cocktail glass with lemon wedge. Sprinkle sugar in a small dish, and place the glass upside down in the dish so the rim is coated with sugar. Fill a cocktail shaker ½ full with ice. Pour in raspberry vodka, lemon juice, and simple syrup. Give it a good shake, and strain into a cocktail glass. Garnish with raspberries.

Kremlin Cocktail

1½ oz. vodka
1 oz. white crème de cacao
1 oz. light cream

Fill a cocktail shaker ½ full with ice. Pour in vodka, white crème de cacao, and light cream. Give it a good shake, and strain into an old-fashioned glass full of ice.

La Carre

1½ oz. vodka
2 tsp. *kummel*
2 tsp. dry vermouth
1 lemon twist

Fill a cocktail shaker ½ full with ice. Pour in vodka, kummel, and dry vermouth. Give it a good stir, and strain into a cocktail glass. Garnish with lemon twist.

Liquor Lingo

Kummel is a sweet, caraway-flavored liqueur.

Latham's Rule

1½ oz. vodka
½ oz. Grand Marnier
2 oz. orange juice
2 dashes orange bitters

Fill a cocktail shaker ½ full with ice. Pour in vodka, Grand Marnier, and orange juice, and add orange bitters. Give it a good shake, and strain into an old-fashioned glass ¾ full of ice.

Laughing at the Waves

2 oz. vodka
½ oz. Campari
½ oz. dry vermouth
1 lemon twist

Fill a cocktail shaker ½ full with ice. Pour in vodka, Campari, and dry vermouth. Give it a good stir, and strain into a cocktail glass. Garnish with lime twist.

Lava Lamp Martini

2 tsp. honey
3 oz. lemon vodka
1 tsp. grenadine
1 lemon twist

Fill a cocktail shaker ½ full with ice. Pour in honey, lemon vodka, and grenadine. Give it a good shake, and strain into a cocktail glass. Garnish with lemon twist.

Limelon

2 oz. vodka
1 oz. melon liqueur
3 oz. lime juice
1 oz. simple syrup
1 lime slice

Fill a cocktail shaker ½ full with ice. Pour in vodka, melon liqueur, lime juice, and simple syrup. Give it a good shake, and strain into a highball glass ¾ full of ice. Garnish with lime slice.

Liquid Gold

2 oz. vodka
½ oz. Galliano
1 tsp. lemon juice
1 lemon slice

Fill a cocktail shaker ½ full with ice. Pour in vodka, Galliano, and lemon juice. Give it a good shake, and strain into an old-fashioned glass ¾ full of ice. Garnish with lemon slice.

Madras

1½ oz. vodka
3 oz. orange juice
1 oz. cranberry juice
1 orange slice

Fill a highball glass ¾ full with ice. Pour in vodka, orange juice, and cranberry juice. Give it a good stir. Garnish with orange slice.

Major Tom

2 oz. vodka
½ oz. triple sec
½ oz. kirschwasser
1 oz. grapefruit juice
1 orange twist

Fill a cocktail shaker ½ full with ice. Pour in vodka, triple sec, kirschwasser, and grapefruit juice. Give it a good shake, and strain into a cocktail glass. Garnish with orange twist.

Mama Mia

2 oz. vodka
½ oz. amaretto
½ oz. light cream

Fill a cocktail shaker ½ full with ice. Pour in vodka, amaretto, and light cream. Give it a good shake, and strain into a cocktail glass.

Mama's Martini

2½ oz. vanilla vodka
1 TB. apricot brandy
1 tsp. lemon juice
3 dashes orange bitters

Fill a cocktail shaker ½ full with ice. Pour in vanilla vodka, apricot brandy, and lemon juice, and add orange bitters. Give it a good stir, and strain into a cocktail glass.

Mazrick

2 oz. vodka
½ oz. triple sec
½ oz. amaretto
2 tsp. Galliano
1½ oz. pineapple juice
1½ oz. orange juice
2 dashes bitters

Fill a cocktail shaker ½ full with ice. Pour in vodka, triple sec, amaretto, Galliano, pineapple juice, and orange juice, and add bitters. Give it a good shake, and strain into a highball glass ¾ full of ice.

Melon Ball Cocktail

1½ oz. vodka
1 oz. melon liqueur
4 oz. orange juice
1 TB. pineapple juice

Fill a cocktail shaker ½ full with ice. Pour in vodka, melon liqueur, orange juice, and pineapple juice. Give it a good shake, and strain into a highball glass ¾ full of ice.

Montauk Sue's Chocolate Martini

Susan Holmes has known my family so long, we sometimes refer to her as the fifth Zavatto sister. Sue is a Renaissance woman if I've ever met one; making indulgent cocktails such as this is just one of her many talents.

4 drops chocolate syrup
2 oz. vodka
1 oz. Godiva chocolate liqueur
½ oz. white crème de cacao
1 oz. light cream

Put 1 drop chocolate syrup inside a cocktail glass at each quarter-turn. Fill a cocktail shaker ½ full with ice. Pour in vodka, Godiva chocolate liqueur, white crème de cacao, and light cream. Give it a good shake, and strain into the cocktail glass.

Morning Glory

2½ oz. vodka
½ oz. dark crème de cacao
1 oz. light cream
1 tsp. grated nutmeg

Fill a cocktail shaker ½ full with ice. Pour in vodka, dark crème de cacao, and light cream. Give it a good shake, and strain into the cocktail glass. Garnish with grated nutmeg.

Moscow Mule

2 oz. vodka
1 oz. lime juice
4 oz. ginger beer
1 lime wedge

Fill a highball glass ¾ full with ice. Pour in vodka, lime juice, and ginger beer. Give it a good stir, and garnish with lime wedge.

Mudslide

2 oz. vodka
½ oz. Kahlúa
½ oz. Irish cream
1 oz. light cream

Fill a cocktail shaker ½ full with ice. Pour in vodka, Kahlúa, Irish cream, and light cream. Give it a good shake, and strain into an old-fashioned glass ¾ full of ice.

Mule

1½ oz. vodka
3 oz. ginger beer
1 lime wedge

Fill an old-fashioned glass ¾ full with ice. Pour in vodka and ginger beer. Give it a good stir, and garnish with lime wedge.

Ninotchka Cocktail

2 oz. vodka
½ oz. crème de cacao
½ oz. lemon juice

Fill a cocktail shaker ½ full with ice. Pour in vodka, crème de cacao, and lemon juice. Give it a good shake, and strain into an old-fashioned glass full of ice.

Nudge

1½ oz. vodka
½ oz. coffee liqueur
½ oz. crème de cacao
3 oz. hot coffee

Fill an Irish coffee glass with vodka, coffee liqueur, and crème de cacao. Pour in hot coffee, and give it a good stir.

Nutty Belgian

1 oz. vodka
1 oz. *Frangelico*
1 oz. chocolate liqueur

Fill a cocktail shaker ½ full with ice. Pour in vodka, Frangelico, and chocolate liqueur. Give it a good shake, and strain into an old-fashioned glass full of ice.

On the Town

2 oz. vodka
1 oz. Campari
2 oz. orange juice
1 egg white

Fill a cocktail shaker ½ full with ice. Pour in vodka, Campari, orange juice, and egg white. Give it a good, vigorous shake, and strain into an old-fashioned glass ¾ full of ice.

Orange Mule

1½ oz. vodka
1 oz. triple sec
4 oz. ginger ale
1 orange slice

Fill a highball glass ¾ full with ice. Pour in vodka, triple sec, and ginger ale. Give it a good stir, and garnish with orange slice.

Orgasm

2 oz. vodka
½ oz. amaretto
½ oz. coffee liqueur
1 oz. light cream

Fill a cocktail shaker ½ full with ice. Pour in vodka, amaretto, coffee liqueur, and light cream. Give it a good shake, and strain into an old-fashioned glass ¾ full of ice.

Paisano

2 oz. vodka
¾ oz. Frangelico
2 oz. milk

Fill a cocktail shaker ½ full with ice. Pour in vodka, Frangelico, and milk. Give it a good shake, and strain into an old-fashioned glass ¾ full of ice.

Patty's Polish Apple

My friend Patty Fiorenza is one of the most adventurous people I've ever known. She's lived in a tiny Alaskan village where the only way in or out is via plane or snowmobile, she's taught English in Poland, had a stint in rural Georgia, traveled to Iceland, and backpacked all over Eastern Europe. But she always comes back with good stories—and, at times, even a good drink or two. While she was living in Poland, she discovered a simple vodka-based (of course!), drink frequently downed at wedding celebrations. Here's my slightly altered version.

2 oz. vodka (Polish, preferably!)
1 oz. apple schnapps
4 oz. apple juice
1 green apple slice

Fill a mixing glass ½ full with ice. Pour in vodka, apple schnapps, and apple juice. Give it a good shake, and pour into a highball glass ½ full of ice. Garnish with green apple slice.

Peace of Mind

2 oz. vodka
1 oz. kummel
1 lemon twist

Fill a cocktail shaker ½ full with ice. Pour in vodka and kummel. Give it a good stir. Strain into a cocktail glass, and garnish with lemon twist.

Peach Buck

2 oz. vodka
½ oz. peach schnapps
1 oz. lemon juice
2 oz. ginger ale

Fill a cocktail shaker ½ full with ice. Pour in vodka, peach schnapps, and lemon juice. Give it a good shake, and strain into a highball glass ¾ full of ice. Pour in ginger ale, and give it a good stir.

Pearl Harbor

1½ oz. vodka
½ oz. melon liqueur
3 oz. orange juice
2 oz. pineapple juice
1 pineapple wedge

Fill a cocktail shaker ½ full with ice. Pour in vodka, melon liqueur, orange juice, and pineapple juice. Give it a good shake, and strain into a highball glass ¾ full of ice. Garnish with pineapple wedge.

Petit Zinc

2 oz. vodka
½ oz. triple sec
½ oz. sweet vermouth
1 oz. orange juice
1 orange slice

Fill a cocktail shaker ½ full with ice. Pour in vodka, triple sec, sweet vermouth, and orange juice. Give it a good shake, and strain into a cocktail glass. Garnish with orange slice.

Pink Elephant

Tocqueville restaurant in New York has found the answer to seeing pink elephants: drinking them. Try this zingy vodka cocktail as the main event at your next soirée.

3 oz. citrus vodka
1½ oz. grape juice
1½ oz. lemon juice

Fill a cocktail shaker ½ full with ice. Pour in citrus vodka, grape juice, and lemon juice. Give it a good shake, and strain into an old-fashioned glass ½ full of ice. Garnish with lemon wedge.

Pink Lemonade

1½ oz. vodka
¼ oz. cranberry juice
¼ oz. lemon juice
2 oz. sour mix
2 oz. lemon-lime soda
1 lemon slice

Fill a cocktail shaker ½ full with ice. Pour in vodka, cranberry juice, lemon juice, and sour mix. Give it a good shake, and strain into a highball glass ¾ full of ice. Pour in lemon-lime soda, and garnish with lemon slice.

Polynesian Cocktail

1 lime wedge
2 tsp. sugar
2 oz. vodka
½ oz. cherry brandy
¼ oz. lime juice

Gently rub the rim of a cocktail glass with lime wedge. Sprinkle sugar in a small dish, and place the glass upside down in the dish so the rim is coated with sugar. Fill a cocktail shaker ½ full with ice. Pour in vodka, cherry brandy, and lime juice. Give it a good shake, and strain into a cocktail glass.

Le Pop Rocks Martini

Remember Pop Rocks? My sister Janet introduced me to them when I was kid. After one packet, I was hooked on the tiny meteor shower that would occur in my mouth every time I put some on my tongue. Paul Muszynski at Bistro 110 in Chicago created this whimsical cocktail for all you grown-ups who like to feel like a carefree kid every now and again.

1 lemon wedge
1 pkg. Pop Rocks
1 oz. Skyy berry vodka
1 oz. Skyy citrus vodka
1 oz. Mango Fruja liqueur
1 TB. cranberry juice
1 TB. sour mix

Gently rub the rim of a cocktail glass with lemon wedge. Sprinkle Pop Rocks in a small dish, and place the glass upside down in the dish so the rim is coated with candy. Fill a cocktail shaker ½ full with ice. Pour in Skyy berry vodka, Skyy citrus vodka, Mango Fruja liqueur, cranberry juice, and sour mix. Give it a good shake, and strain into a cocktail glass.

Purple Haze Cocktail

2 oz. vodka
½ oz. Chambord
½ oz. lemon juice

Fill a cocktail shaker ½ full with ice. Pour in vodka, Chambord, and lemon juice. Give it a good shake, and strain into a cocktail glass.

Purple Passion

1½ oz. vodka
½ oz. triple sec
1 oz. grape juice
¼ oz. cranberry juice

Fill a cocktail shaker ½ full with ice. Pour in vodka, triple sec, grape juice, and cranberry juice. Give it a good shake, and strain into a cocktail glass.

Queen Bee

2 oz. vodka
½ oz. coffee brandy
½ oz. cream sherry

Fill a cocktail shaker ½ full with ice. Pour in vodka, coffee brandy, and cream sherry. Give it a good shake, and strain into a cocktail glass.

Razzleberry

2 oz. vodka
1 oz. DeKuyper Razzmatazz
5 oz. lemon-lime soda

Fill a Collins glass ¾ full with ice. Pour in vodka, DeKuyper Razzmatazz, and lemon-lime soda. Give it a good stir.

Red Apple

1½ oz. vodka
1 oz. apple juice
1 tsp. grenadine
1 TB. lemon juice

Fill a cocktail shaker ½ full with ice. Pour in vodka, apple juice, grenadine, and lemon juice. Give it a good shake, and strain into a cocktail glass.

Robin's Nest

1½ oz. vodka
½ oz. white crème de cacao
1 oz. cranberry juice

Fill a cocktail shaker ½ full with ice. Pour in vodka, white crème de cacao, and cranberry juice. Give it a good shake, and strain into a cocktail glass.

Roll Me Over

2 oz. vodka
1 oz. vanilla schnapps
1 oz. cranberry juice
1 TB. lemon juice

Fill a cocktail shaker ½ full with ice. Pour in vodka, vanilla schnapps, cranberry juice, and lemon juice. Give it a good shake, and strain into a cocktail glass.

Russian Bear

2 oz. vodka
1 oz. dark crème de cacao
½ oz. heavy cream

Fill a cocktail shaker ½ full with ice. Pour in vodka, dark crème de cacao, and heavy cream. Give it a good shake, and strain into a cocktail glass.

Russian Brunch

1 oz. vodka
2 oz. orange juice
1 oz. champagne

Pour vodka, orange juice, and then champagne into a champagne flute.

Russian Candy

2 oz. vodka
½ oz. peach schnapps
1 tsp. grenadine

Fill a cocktail shaker ½ full with ice. Pour in vodka and peach schnapps. Give it a good shake, and strain into a cocktail glass. Drip grenadine into center of cocktail.

Russian Cocktail

1 oz. vodka
1 oz. gin
1 oz. white crème de cacao

Fill a cocktail shaker ½ full with ice. Pour in vodka, gin, and white crème de cacao. Give it a good stir, and strain into a cocktail glass.

Russian Coffee

1 tsp. sugar
1 oz. vodka
½ oz. coffee liqueur
1 TB. amaretto
4 oz. hot coffee
2 TB. whipped cream

Add sugar to an Irish coffee mug. Pour in vodka, coffee liqueur, amaretto, and hot coffee. Give it a good stir, and top with whipped cream.

Russian Iceberg

2 oz. vodka
½ oz. peppermint schnapps

Fill a cocktail shaker ½ full with ice. Pour in vodka and peppermint schnapps. Give it a good shake, and strain into an old-fashioned glass full of ice.

Russian Quaalude

1 oz. vodka
½ oz. Irish cream
½ oz. Frangelico
½ oz. coffee liqueur
½ oz. heavy cream

Pour vodka into an old-fashioned glass. Gently add Irish cream, followed by Frangelico, followed by coffee liqueur, and finally heavy cream.

Russian Rose

3 oz. vodka	Fill a cocktail shaker ½ full with ice.
1 TB. grenadine	Pour in vodka and grenadine, and add
2 dashes orange bitters	orange bitters. Give it a good shake,
	and strain into a cocktail glass.

Russian Sunset

2 oz. vodka	Fill a cocktail shaker ½ full with ice.
1 oz. triple sec	Pour in vodka, triple sec, grenadine,
1 tsp. grenadine	and sour mix. Give it a good shake,
1 oz. sour mix	and strain into a cocktail glass.

Salty Dog

1 lemon wedge	Gently rub the rim of a cocktail glass
2 tsp. salt	with lemon wedge. Sprinkle salt in a
2 oz. vodka	small dish, and place the glass upside
5 oz. grapefruit juice	down in the dish so the rim is coated
	with salt. Fill the glass ¾ full with ice.
	Pour in vodka and grapefruit juice.
	Give it a good stir.

Sarah

2 oz. vodka	Fill a cocktail shaker ½ full with ice.
½ oz. cherry brandy	Pour in vodka, cherry brandy, Cam-
½ oz. Campari	pari, dry vermouth, and crème de
½ oz. dry vermouth	bananes. Give it a good shake, and
1 tsp. crème de bananes	strain into a cocktail glass.

Screaming Banana Banshee

1½ oz. vodka	Fill a cocktail shaker ½ full with ice.
½ oz. crème de bananes	Pour in vodka, crème de bananes,
½ oz. white crème de cacao	white crème de cacao, and light cream.
½ oz. light cream	Give it a good shake, and strain into
1 maraschino cherry	a cocktail glass. Garnish with mara-
	schino cherry.

Screwdriver

2 oz. vodka	Fill a highball glass ¾ full with ice.
5 oz. orange juice	Pour in vodka and orange juice. Give
	it a good stir.

Sea Breeze

2 oz. vodka
2 oz. grapefruit juice
3 oz. cranberry juice
1 lime wedge

Fill a highball glass ¾ full with ice. Pour in vodka, grapefruit juice, and cranberry juice. Give it a good stir, and garnish with lime wedge.

Seaside Bloody Mary

3 oz. vodka
2 oz. tomato juice
2 oz. clam juice
¼ tsp. Worcestershire sauce
¼ tsp. Tabasco sauce
⅛ tsp. black pepper

Fill a cocktail shaker ½ full with ice. Pour in vodka, tomato juice, clam juice, Worcestershire sauce, Tabasco sauce, and black pepper. Give it a good shake. Strain into a highball glass ¾ full of ice.

Sex on the Beach

1½ oz. vodka
½ oz. peach schnapps
2 oz. orange juice
2 oz. cranberry juice
¼ oz. pineapple juice

Fill a cocktail shaker ½ full with ice. Pour in vodka, peach schnapps, orange juice, cranberry juice, and pineapple juice. Give it a good shake, and strain into a highball glass ¾ full of ice.

Shogun

2 oz. vodka
1 TB. grenadine
1 oz. orange juice
1 orange twist

Fill a cocktail shaker ½ full with ice. Pour in vodka, grenadine, and orange juice. Give it a good shake, and strain into a cocktail glass. Garnish with orange twist.

Silver Sunset

1 oz. vodka
½ oz. apricot brandy
½ oz. Campari
1½ oz. orange juice
½ oz. lemon juice
1 egg white
1 orange slice
1 maraschino cherry

Fill a cocktail shaker ½ full with ice. Pour in vodka, apricot brandy, Campari, orange juice, lemon juice, and egg white. Give it a good, vigorous shake, and strain into a cocktail glass. Garnish with orange slice and maraschino cherry.

Smoked Martini

2½ oz. vodka
1 TB. Scotch whisky
1 lemon twist

Fill a cocktail shaker ½ full with ice. Pour in vodka and Scotch whisky. Give it a good stir, and strain into a cocktail glass. Garnish with lemon twist.

Sour Appletini

2 oz. citrus vodka
½ oz. sour apple schnapps
½ oz. triple sec
1 oz. lime juice
1 green apple slice

Fill a cocktail shaker ½ full with ice. Pour in vodka, sour apple schnapps, triple sec, and lime juice. Give it a good shake, and strain into a cocktail glass. Garnish with green apple slice.

Southampton Stinger

2½ oz. vodka
½ oz. Galliano
½ oz. apricot brandy
2 pieces candied ginger

Fill a cocktail shaker ½ full with ice. Pour in vodka, Galliano, and apricot brandy. Give it a good shake, and strain into a cocktail glass. Garnish with candied ginger.

Southside

4 mint sprigs
½ oz. simple syrup
2½ oz. vodka
½ oz. lemon juice

Muddle 3 mint sprigs with simple syrup in a cocktail shaker. Add ice, and pour in vodka and lemon juice. Give it a good shake, and strain into a cocktail glass. Garnish with remaining mint sprig.

Soviet Cocktail

2½ oz. vodka
½ oz. dry sherry
1 TB. dry vermouth
1 lemon twist

Fill a cocktail shaker ½ full with ice. Pour in vodka, dry sherry, and dry vermouth. Give it a good shake, and strain into a cocktail glass. Garnish with lemon twist.

Stuffy in a Suit

1½ oz. vodka
½ oz. Lillet
½ oz. triple sec
1 egg white
1 dash orange bitters
1 orange slice

Fill a cocktail shaker ½ full with ice. Pour in vodka, Lillet, triple sec, and egg white, and add orange bitters. Give it a good, vigorous shake, and strain into a cocktail glass. Garnish with orange slice.

Tawny Russian

2 oz. vodka
1 oz. amaretto

Fill an old-fashioned glass with ice. Pour in vodka and amaretto. Give it a good stir.

Temptress

2 oz. citrus vodka
1 TB. grenadine
4 oz. ginger ale

Fill a highball glass ¾ full with ice. Pour in vodka, grenadine, and ginger ale. Give it a good stir.

Tovarich

2 oz. vodka
½ oz. kummel
2 TB. lime juice

Fill a cocktail shaker ½ full with ice. Pour in vodka, kummel, and lime juice. Give it a good shake, and strain into a cocktail glass.

Vodka and Bitter Lemon

½ tsp. superfine sugar
2 oz. vodka
½ oz. lemon juice
4 oz. tonic water

Fill a cocktail shaker ½ full with ice. Add superfine sugar and then pour in vodka and lemon juice. Give it a good shake, and strain into a highball glass ¾ full of ice. Pour in tonic water.

Vodka and Tonic

2 oz. vodka
4 oz. tonic
1 lemon wedge

Fill a highball glass ¾ full with ice. Pour in vodka and tonic. Give it a good stir, and garnish with lemon wedge.

Vodka Cobbler

1 tsp. superfine sugar
3 oz. club soda
2 oz. vodka
1 lemon slice
1 orange slice
1 maraschino cherry

Add superfine sugar in an old-fashioned glass and add club soda to dissolve sugar. Fill the glass ¾ full with crushed ice. Pour in vodka, and give it a good stir. Garnish with lemon slice, orange slice, and maraschino cherry.

Vodka Collins

2½ oz. vodka
1 oz. lemon juice
1 tsp. simple syrup
4 oz. club soda
1 orange slice
1 maraschino cherry

Fill a cocktail shaker ½ full with ice. Pour in vodka, lemon juice, and simple syrup. Give it a good shake, and strain into a Collins glass ¾ full of ice. Pour in club soda, and garnish with orange slice and maraschino cherry.

Vodka Cooler

2 oz. vodka
4 oz. lemon-lime soda
1 lemon wedge

Fill a highball glass ¾ full with ice. Pour in vodka and lemon-lime soda. Give it a good stir, and garnish with lemon wedge.

Vodka Daisy

2 oz. vodka
½ tsp. grenadine
1 oz. lemon juice
1 oz. simple syrup
1 orange slice
1 maraschino cherry

Fill a cocktail shaker ½ full with ice. Pour in vodka, grenadine, lemon juice, and simple syrup. Give it a good shake, and strain into an old-fashioned glass ¾ full of ice. Garnish with orange slice and maraschino cherry.

Vodka Fix

2 oz. vodka
¾ oz. lemon juice
1 oz. simple syrup
1 lemon slice
1 maraschino cherry

Fill a cocktail shaker ½ full with ice. Pour in vodka, lemon juice, and simple syrup. Give it a good shake, and strain into a highball glass full of ice. Garnish with lemon slice and maraschino cherry.

Vodka Gibson

3 oz. vodka
1 tsp. dry vermouth
1 cocktail onion

Fill a cocktail shaker ½ full with ice. Pour in vodka and dry vermouth. Give it a good stir, and strain into a cocktail glass. Garnish with cocktail onion.

Vodka Gimlet

2 oz. vodka
¼ oz. Rose's lime juice
1 lime wedge

Fill a cocktail shaker ½ full with ice. Pour in vodka and Rose's lime juice. Give it a good shake, and strain into an old-fashioned glass full of ice. Garnish with lime wedge.

Vodka Grand Marnier Cocktail

2 oz. vodka
½ oz. Grand Marnier
½ oz. lime juice
1 orange twist

Fill a cocktail shaker ½ full with ice. Pour in vodka, Grand Marnier, and lime juice. Give it a good shake, and strain into a cocktail glass. Garnish with orange twist.

Vodka Grasshopper

1½ oz. vodka
1 oz. green crème de menthe
1 oz. white crème de cacao

Fill a cocktail shaker ½ full with ice. Pour in vodka, green crème de menthe, and white crème de cacao. Give it a good shake, and strain into a cocktail glass.

Vodka Martini

3 oz. vodka
1 tsp. vermouth
1 cocktail olive

Fill a cocktail shaker ½ full with ice. Pour in vodka and vermouth. Give it a good stir, and strain into a cocktail glass. Garnish with cocktail olive.

 Cocktail Conversation

For a perfectly cold vodka martini, store your vodka in the freezer. It won't freeze.

Vodka Sling

2 oz. vodka
¾ oz. lemon juice
1 oz. simple syrup
1 lemon twist

Fill a cocktail shaker ½ full with ice. Pour in vodka, lemon juice, and simple syrup. Give it a good shake, and strain into an old-fashioned glass full of ice. Garnish with lemon twist.

Vodka Smash

5 mint sprigs
1 tsp. superfine sugar
1 oz. club soda
2 oz. vodka
1 lemon twist

Muddle 4 mint sprigs, superfine sugar, and club soda in an old-fashioned glass. Fill the glass ¾ full with ice, and pour in vodka. Give it a good stir, and garnish with remaining mint sprig and lemon twist.

Vodka Sonic

2 oz. vodka
2 oz. club soda
2 oz. tonic water
1 lime wedge

Fill a highball glass ½ full with ice. Pour in vodka, club soda, and tonic water. Give it a good stir, and garnish with lime wedge.

Vodka Sour

2 oz. vodka
¾ oz. lemon juice
1 oz. simple syrup
1 orange slice
1 maraschino cherry

Fill a cocktail shaker ½ full with ice. Pour in vodka, lemon juice, and simple syrup. Give it a good shake, and strain into a highball glass ¾ full of ice. Garnish with orange slice and maraschino cherry.

Vodka Stinger

2 oz. vodka
1 oz. white crème de menthe

Fill a cocktail shaker ½ full with ice. Pour in vodka and white crème de menthe. Give it a good stir, and strain into a cocktail glass.

Vodka Swizzle

2 oz. vodka
¾ oz. lime juice
1 oz. simple syrup
1 dash bitters
3 oz. club soda

Fill a cocktail shaker ½ full with ice. Pour in vodka, lime juice, and simple syrup, and add bitters. Give it a good shake, and strain into a highball glass ¾ full of ice. Pour in club soda.

Volga Boatman

2½ oz. vodka
1 TB. kirschwasser
1 oz. orange juice

Fill a cocktail shaker ½ full with ice. Pour in vodka, kirschwasser, and orange juice. Give it a good stir, and strain into a cocktail glass.

Voodoo Doll

2½ oz. vodka
¼ oz. Chambord
1 TB. cranberry juice
1 TB. orange juice

Fill a cocktail shaker ½ full with ice. Pour in vodka, Chambord, cranberry juice, and orange juice. Give it a good shake, and strain into a cocktail glass.

Warsaw

2 oz. vodka
¼ oz. dry vermouth
½ oz. blackberry brandy
1 TB. lemon juice

Fill a cocktail shaker ½ full with ice. Pour in vodka, dry vermouth, blackberry brandy, and lemon juice. Give it a good shake, and strain into a cocktail glass.

Watermelon Martini

2 oz. vodka
½ oz. watermelon schnapps
½ oz. triple sec
1 oz. lime juice
1 watermelon slice

Fill a cocktail shaker ½ full with ice. Pour in vodka, watermelon schnapps, triple sec, and lime juice. Give it a good shake, and strain into a cocktail glass. Garnish with watermelon slice.

Whistling Gypsy Cocktail

2 oz. vodka
½ oz. coffee liqueur
1 oz. Irish cream

Fill a cocktail shaker ½ full with ice. Pour in vodka, coffee liqueur, and Irish cream. Give it a good shake, and strain into an old-fashioned glass full of ice.

White Russian

2 oz. vodka
¾ oz. coffee liqueur
1 oz. milk

Fill a cocktail shaker ½ full with ice. Pour in vodka, coffee liqueur, and milk. Give it a good shake, and pour into an old-fashioned glass ¾ full of ice.

White Spider

2½ oz. vodka
½ oz. white crème de menthe

Fill a cocktail shaker ½ full with ice. Pour in vodka and white crème de menthe. Give it a good shake, and pour into an old-fashioned glass full of ice.

Windex

2½ oz. vodka
½ oz. triple sec
½ oz. blue curaçao
1 lemon twist

Fill a cocktail shaker ½ full with ice. Pour in vodka, triple sec, and blue curaçao. Give it a good shake, and strain into a cocktail glass. Garnish with lemon twist.

Woo Woo Cocktail

2 oz. vodka
½ oz. peach schnapps
1 oz. cranberry juice

Fill a cocktail shaker ½ full with ice. Pour in vodka, peach schnapps, and cranberry juice. Give it a good shake, and strain into a cocktail glass.

Yellow Birdie

1½ oz. vodka
½ oz. crème de bananes
4 oz. lemon-lime soda

Fill a highball glass ¾ full with ice. Pour in vodka, crème de bananes, and lemon-lime soda. Give it a good stir.

Yellow Fever

1½ oz. vodka
½ oz. Galliano
½ oz. lemon juice
3 oz. pineapple juice

Fill a cocktail shaker ½ full with ice. Pour in vodka, Galliano, lemon juice, and pineapple juice. Give it a good shake, and pour into a highball glass ¾ full of ice.

Zipper Head

2 oz. vodka
1 oz. Chambord
5 oz. club soda

Fill a highball glass ¾ full with ice. Pour in vodka, Chambord, and club soda. Give it a good stir.

Chapter 10

Whisky

Oh, the whiskey makes you sweeter than you are …
—Amy Allison

Aberdeen Sour

2 oz. Scotch whisky
½ oz. triple sec
1 oz. orange juice
1 oz. lemon juice
1 maraschino cherry

Fill a cocktail shaker ½ full with ice. Pour in Scotch whisky, triple sec, orange juice, and lemon juice. Give it a good shake, and strain into an old-fashioned glass ¾ full of ice. Garnish with maraschino cherry.

Affinity

1½ oz. Scotch whisky
1 oz. dry vermouth
1 oz. sweet vermouth
2 dashes orange bitters
1 lemon twist
1 maraschino cherry

Fill a cocktail shaker ½ full with ice. Pour in Scotch whisky, dry vermouth, and sweet vermouth, and add orange bitters. Give it a good stir, and strain into a cocktail glass. Garnish with lemon twist and maraschino cherry.

Algonquin

2 oz. blended whisky
½ oz. dry vermouth
1 oz. pineapple juice

Fill a cocktail shaker ½ full with ice. Pour in blended whisky, vermouth, and pineapple juice. Give it a good shake, and strain into a cocktail glass.

> **Cocktail Conversation**
>
> Although it's nothing like it was back in the Dorothy Parker Roundtable days, the Algonquin Hotel and (in)famous bar does indeed still exist in New York City.

Aquarious

2 oz. blended whisky
1 oz. cherry brandy
1 oz. cranberry juice

Fill a cocktail shaker ½ full with ice. Pour in blended whisky, cherry brandy, and cranberry juice. Give it a good shake, and strain into an old-fashioned glass ¾ full of ice.

Banff Cocktail

2 oz. Canadian whisky
1 oz. Grand Marnier
1 oz. kirschwasser
1 dash bitters
1 lemon twist

Fill a cocktail shaker ½ full with ice. Pour in Canadian whisky, Grand Marnier, and kirschwasser, and add bitters. Give it a good shake, and strain into a cocktail glass. Garnish with lemon twist.

Bay Horse

2 oz. blended whisky
1 oz. pastis
1 oz. dark crème de cacao
½ oz. heavy cream
½ tsp. grated nutmeg

Fill a cocktail shaker ½ full with ice. Pour in blended whisky, pastis, dark crème de cacao, and heavy cream. Give it a good shake, and strain into an old-fashioned glass ¾ full of ice. Garnish with grated nutmeg.

Black Hawk

2½ oz. blended whisky
1½ oz. sloe gin
1 maraschino cherry

Fill a cocktail shaker ½ full with ice. Pour in blended whisky and sloe gin. Give it a good shake, and strain into a cocktail glass. Garnish with maraschino cherry.

Blimey

2 oz. Scotch whisky
1 oz. lime juice
½ oz. simple syrup

Fill a cocktail shaker ½ full with ice.
Pour in Scotch whisky, lime juice, and
simple syrup. Give it a good shake,
and strain into a cocktail glass.

Blinder

2 oz. Scotch whisky
1 tsp. grenadine
5 oz. grapefruit juice

Fill a cocktail shaker ½ full with ice.
Pour in Scotch whisky, grenadine, and
grapefruit juice. Give it a good shake,
and strain into a highball glass ¾ full
of ice.

Blinker

1½ oz. rye whisky
1 tsp. grenadine
1 oz. grapefruit juice

Fill a cocktail shaker ½ full with ice.
Pour in rye whisky, grenadine, and
grapefruit juice. Give it a good shake,
and strain into a cocktail glass.

Blood and Sand

1 oz. Scotch whisky
½ oz. sweet vermouth
½ oz. cherry brandy
¾ oz. orange juice

Fill a cocktail shaker ½ full with ice.
Pour in Scotch whisky, sweet vermouth, cherry brandy, and orange
juice. Give it a good shake, and strain
into a cocktail glass.

Cablegram

½ tsp. superfine sugar
2 oz. blended whisky
¼ oz. lemon juice
4 oz. ginger ale
1 lemon wedge

Fill a cocktail shaker ½ full with ice.
Add superfine sugar and then pour in
blended whisky and lemon juice. Give
it a good shake, and strain into a highball glass ¾ full of ice. Pour in ginger
ale. Give it a good stir, and garnish
with lemon wedge.

Spills _____

You might be tempted to substitute one kind of whisky for another if you want to mix a particular cocktail that calls for, say, Irish whiskey but only have Scotch. Although the last thing I want to do is put the quabash on your creativity, you should probably avoid this kind of substitution. Different whiskies can have very different flavor profiles, and a cocktail that calls for a particular type is better off made as instructed.

California Lemonade

2 oz. rye whisky
1 oz. lemon juice
1 tsp. simple syrup
4 oz. club soda
1 lemon slice

Fill a cocktail shaker ½ full with ice. Pour in rye whisky, lemon juice, and simple syrup. Give it a good shake, and strain into a highball glass ¾ full of ice. Pour in club soda. Give it a good stir, and garnish with lemon slice.

Canadian Cherry

2 oz. Canadian whisky
1 oz. cherry brandy
1 TB. lemon juice
1 TB. orange juice
1 orange twist

Fill a cocktail shaker ½ full with ice. Pour in Canadian whisky, cherry brandy, lemon juice, and orange juice. Give it a good shake, and strain into a cocktail glass. Garnish with orange twist.

Canadian Cocktail

½ tsp. superfine sugar
2 oz. Canadian whisky
1 oz. triple sec
1 dash bitters

Fill a cocktail shaker ½ full with ice. Add superfine sugar, pour in Canadian whisky and triple sec, and add bitters. Give it a good shake, and strain into a cocktail glass.

Canadian Pineapple

2 oz. Canadian whisky
1 tsp. maraschino liqueur
1 oz. pineapple juice
1 TB. lemon juice
1 pineapple wedge

Fill a cocktail shaker ½ full with ice. Pour in Canadian whisky, maraschino liqueur, pineapple juice, and lemon juice. Give it a good shake, and strain into a cocktail glass. Garnish with pineapple wedge.

Cat and Fiddle

2 oz. Canadian whisky
1 oz. triple sec
1 tsp. pastis
1 tsp. Dubonnet Blonde
1 lemon twist

Fill a cocktail shaker ½ full with ice. Pour in Canadian whisky, triple sec, pastis, and Dubonnet Blonde. Give it a good shake, and strain into a cocktail glass. Garnish with lemon twist.

Celtic Mix

1½ oz. Scotch whisky
1½ oz. Irish whiskey
1 TB. lemon juice
2 dashes bitters

Fill a cocktail shaker ½ full with ice. Pour in Scotch whisky, Irish whiskey, and lemon juice, and add bitters. Give it a good shake, and strain into a cocktail glass.

Commodore

2 oz. Canadian whisky
1 oz. lime juice
1 tsp. simple syrup
1 dash bitters
1 lime twist

Fill a cocktail shaker ½ full with ice. Pour in Canadian whisky, lime juice, and simple syrup, and add bitters. Give it a good shake, and strain into a cocktail glass. Garnish with lime twist.

Dandy

1 oz. rye whisky
1 oz. Dubonnet Rouge
1 tsp. triple sec
2 dashes bitters
1 lemon twist
1 orange twist

Fill a cocktail shaker ½ full with ice. Pour in rye whisky, Dubonnet Rouge, and triple sec, and add bitters. Give it a good shake, and strain into a cocktail glass. Garnish with lemon twist and orange twist.

De Rigueur

2 oz. rye whisky
1 oz. grapefruit juice
1 TB. honey

Fill a cocktail shaker ½ full with ice. Pour in rye whisky and grapefruit juice, and add in honey. Give it a good shake, and strain into a cocktail glass.

Dinah

2 oz. rye whisky
½ oz. lemon juice
½ oz. simple syrup
2 mint sprigs

Fill a cocktail shaker ½ full with ice. Pour in rye whisky, lemon juice, and simple syrup. Give it a good shake, and strain into a cocktail glass. Garnish with mint sprigs.

Double Standard Sour

1 oz. rye whisky
1 oz. gin
1 tsp. grenadine
¾ oz. lemon juice
1 oz. simple syrup
1 orange slice
1 maraschino cherry

Fill a cocktail shaker ½ full with ice. Pour in rye whisky, gin, grenadine, lemon juice, and simple syrup. Give it a good shake, and strain into a Delmonico glass. Garnish with orange slice and maraschino cherry.

Dry Manhattan

2 oz. blended whisky
¾ oz. dry vermouth
2 dashes bitters
1 lemon twist

Fill a cocktail shaker ½ full with ice. Pour in blended whisky and dry vermouth, and add bitters. Give it a good stir, and strain into a cocktail glass. Garnish with lemon twist.

Dubonnet Manhattan

2 oz. rye whisky
1 oz. Dubonnet Rouge
2 dashes bitters
1 maraschino cherry

Fill a cocktail shaker ½ full with ice. Pour in rye whisky and Dubonnet Rouge, and add bitters. Give it a good stir, and strain into a cocktail glass. Garnish with maraschino cherry.

Evan's Cocktail

2½ oz. rye whisky
½ oz. apricot brandy
½ oz. triple sec

Fill a cocktail shaker ½ full with ice. Pour in rye whisky, apricot brandy, and triple sec. Give it a good stir, and strain into a cocktail glass.

Everybody's Irish

2½ oz. Irish whiskey
½ oz. green crème de menthe
½ oz. green Chartreuse

Fill a cocktail shaker ½ full with ice. Pour in Irish whiskey, green crème de menthe, and green Chartreuse. Give it a good shake, and strain into a cocktail glass.

Fancy Whisky

2 oz. rye whisky
½ oz. orange curaçao
2 dashes bitters
1 lemon twist

Fill a cocktail shaker ½ full with ice. Pour in rye whisky and orange curaçao, and add bitters. Give it a good shake, and strain into a cocktail glass. Garnish with lemon twist.

Frisco Sour

½ tsp. superfine sugar
2 oz. blended whisky
½ oz. Benedictine
½ oz. lemon juice
½ oz. lime juice
1 lemon wedge

Fill a cocktail shaker ½ full with ice. Add superfine sugar and then pour in blended whisky, Benedictine, lemon juice, and lime juice. Give it a good shake, and strain into a Delmonico glass. Garnish with lemon wedge.

Gloom Lifter

½ tsp. superfine sugar
2 oz. Irish whiskey
¼ oz. brandy
1 tsp. grenadine
1 oz. lemon juice
1 egg white

Fill a cocktail shaker ½ full with ice. Add superfine sugar and then pour in Irish whiskey, brandy, grenadine, lemon juice, and egg white. Give it a good, vigorous shake, and strain into a cocktail glass.

Godfather

2 oz. Scotch whisky
½ oz. amaretto

Fill a cocktail shaker ½ full with ice. Pour in Scotch whisky and amaretto. Give it a good stir, and strain into a cocktail glass.

Highland Fling

2 oz. Scotch whisky
½ oz. sweet vermouth
2 dashes orange bitters
1 maraschino cherry

Fill a cocktail shaker ½ full with ice. Pour in Scotch whisky and sweet vermouth, and add orange bitters. Give it a good stir, strain into a cocktail glass, and garnish with maraschino cherry.

Horse's Neck

2 oz. rye whisky
6 oz. ginger ale
1 lemon twist

Fill a Collins glass ¾ full with ice. Pour in rye whisky and ginger ale. Give it a good stir, and garnish with lemon twist.

Horsecar

1½ oz. rye whisky
¾ oz. dry vermouth
¾ oz. sweet vermouth
1 dash bitters
1 maraschino cherry

Fill a cocktail shaker ½ full with ice. Pour in rye whisky, dry vermouth, and sweet vermouth, and add bitters. Give it a good stir, and strain into a cocktail glass. Garnish with maraschino cherry.

Horseshoe

2 oz. Scotch whisky
1 oz. dry vermouth
1 oz. sweet vermouth
5 oz. club soda
1 lemon twist

Fill a Collins glass ¾ full with ice. Pour in Scotch whisky, dry vermouth, sweet vermouth, and club soda. Give it a good stir, and garnish with lemon twist.

Hot Brick

½ TB. butter
1 tsp. sugar
½ tsp. cinnamon
1½ oz. rye whisky
3 oz. hot water

Add butter, sugar, and cinnamon to an Irish coffee glass. Pour in rye whisky and hot water.

Hot Deck

2 oz. rye whisky
½ oz. sweet vermouth
½ tsp. ginger extract

Fill a cocktail shaker ½ full with ice. Pour in rye whisky, sweet vermouth, and ginger extract. Give it a good shake, and strain into a cocktail glass.

Imperial Fizz

½ tsp. superfine sugar
2 oz. blended whisky
1 oz. lemon juice
4 oz. club soda
1 lemon wedge

Fill a cocktail shaker ½ full with ice. Add superfine sugar and then pour in blended whisky and lemon juice. Give it a good shake, and strain into a high-ball glass ¾ full of ice. Pour in club soda, and garnish with lemon wedge.

Ink Street

½ tsp. superfine sugar
1½ oz. rye whisky
½ oz. lemon juice
½ oz. lime juice

Fill a cocktail shaker ½ full with ice. Add superfine sugar and then pour in rye whisky, lemon juice, and lime juice. Give it a good shake, and strain into a cocktail glass.

Irish Canadian

2 oz. Canadian whisky
1 oz. *Irish Mist*

Fill a cocktail shaker ½ full with ice. Pour in Canadian whisky and Irish Mist. Give it a good stir, and strain into a cocktail glass.

Liquor Lingo

Irish Mist is an Irish whiskey–based liqueur made with honey and herbs.

Japanese Fizz

2 oz. blended whisky
½ oz. port
¾ oz. lemon juice
1 oz. simple syrup

Fill a cocktail shaker ½ full with ice. Pour in blended whisky, port, lemon juice, and simple syrup. Give it a good shake, and strain into a highball glass ½ full of ice.

Jersey Gentleman

2 oz. blended whisky
½ oz. pastis
1 oz. pineapple juice

Fill a cocktail shaker ½ full with ice. Pour in blended whisky, pastis, and pineapple juice. Give it a good shake, and strain into a cocktail glass.

John Collins

2 oz. blended whisky
¾ oz. lemon juice
1 oz. simple syrup
4 oz. club soda
1 orange slice
1 maraschino cherry

Fill a cocktail shaker ½ full with ice. Pour in blended whisky, lemon juice, and simple syrup. Give it a good shake, and strain into a Collins glass ½ full of ice. Pour in club soda, and garnish with orange slice and maraschino cherry.

La Belle Quebec

1 oz. Canadian whisky
½ oz. cherry brandy
½ oz. brandy
¾ oz. lemon juice
1 oz. simple syrup

Fill a cocktail shaker ½ full with ice. Pour in Canadian whisky, cherry brandy, brandy, lemon juice, and simple syrup. Give it a good shake, and strain into a cocktail glass.

L.A. Cocktail

2 oz. blended whisky
1 TB. sweet vermouth
½ oz. lemon juice
½ oz. simple syrup
1 egg
1 maraschino cherry

Fill a cocktail shaker ½ full with ice. Pour in blended whisky, sweet vermouth, lemon juice, simple syrup, and egg. Give it a good, vigorous shake, and strain into a Delmonico glass. Garnish with maraschino cherry.

Lady Luv

2 oz. blended whisky
½ oz. dark rum
½ oz. añejo rum
1 TB. dark crème de cacao

Fill a cocktail shaker ½ full with ice. Pour in blended whisky, dark rum, añejo rum, and dark crème de cacao. Give it a good shake, and strain into a cocktail glass.

Lawhill

1½ oz. rye whisky
½ oz. dry vermouth
¼ oz. pastis
¼ oz. maraschino liqueur
½ oz. orange juice
1 dash bitters

Fill a cocktail shaker ½ full with ice. Pour in rye whisky, dry vermouth, pastis, maraschino liqueur, and orange juice, and add bitters. Give it a good shake, and strain into a cocktail glass.

Linstead

2 oz. Scotch whisky
1½ oz. pineapple juice
1 dash bitters

Fill a cocktail shaker ½ full with ice. Pour in Scotch whisky and pineapple juice, and add bitters. Give it a good shake, and strain into a cocktail glass.

Loch Lomond

2½ oz. Scotch whisky
1 tsp. sugar
3 dashes bitters

Fill a cocktail shaker ½ full with ice. Pour in Scotch whisky and sugar, and add bitters. Give it a good stir, and strain into a cocktail glass.

Madame Rene

2 oz. rye whisky
½ oz. añejo rum
1 oz. orange juice
1 dash bitters

Fill a cocktail shaker ½ full with ice. Pour in rye whisky, añejo rum, and orange juice, and add bitters. Give it a good shake, and strain into a cocktail glass.

Manhasset

2 oz. blended whisky
2 tsp. sweet vermouth
2 tsp. dry vermouth
½ oz. lemon juice
¾ oz. simple syrup

Fill a cocktail shaker ½ full with ice. Pour in blended whisky, sweet vermouth, dry vermouth, lemon juice, and simple syrup. Give it a good shake, and strain into a cocktail glass.

Manhattan

2 oz. blended whisky
1 oz. sweet vermouth
2 dashes Angostura bitters
1 maraschino cherry

Fill cocktail shaker with ice. Pour in blended whisky and sweet vermouth, and add Angostura bitters. Give it a good stir, and strain into a cocktail glass (unless, of course, you'd prefer it on the rocks—this is perfectly acceptable Manhattan behavior). Garnish with maraschino cherry.

Maple Leaf

2 oz. Canadian whisky
½ oz. maple syrup
½ oz. lemon juice

Fill a cocktail shaker ½ full with ice. Pour in Canadian whisky, maple syrup, and lemon juice. Give it a good shake, and strain into a cocktail glass.

Miami Beach

1 oz. Scotch whisky
1 oz. dry vermouth
1 oz. grapefruit juice

Fill a cocktail shaker ½ full with ice. Pour in Scotch whisky, dry vermouth, and grapefruit juice. Give it a good shake, and strain into a cocktail glass.

Milk Punch

2 oz. blended whisky
½ oz. dark rum
1 TB. simple syrup
4 oz. milk
1 tsp. grated nutmeg

Fill a cocktail shaker ½ full with ice. Pour in blended whisky, dark rum, simple syrup, and milk. Give it a good shake, and strain into highball glass ½ full of ice. Garnish with nutmeg.

Millionaire

1½ oz. rye whisky
½ oz. orange curaçao
1 tsp. pastis
1 tsp. grenadine
1 egg white

Fill a cocktail shaker ½ full with ice. Pour in rye whisky, orange curaçao, pastis, grenadine, and egg white. Give it a good, vigorous shake, and strain into a cocktail glass.

Modern Cocktail

2 oz. Scotch whisky
½ oz. dark rum
½ oz. pastis
¼ oz. lemon juice
2 dashes orange bitters
1 maraschino cherry

Fill a cocktail shaker ½ full with ice. Pour in Scotch whisky, dark rum, pastis, and lemon juice, and add orange bitters. Give it a good shake, and strain into a cocktail glass. Garnish with maraschino cherry.

Morning, Teacher

1 tsp. superfine sugar
1½ oz. blended whisky
½ oz. brandy
¼ oz. pastis
¼ oz. orange curaçao
1 dash bitters
4 oz. club soda

Fill a cocktail shaker ½ full with ice. Add superfine sugar; pour in blended whisky, brandy, pastis, and orange curaçao; and add bitters. Give it a good shake, and strain into a highball glass ½ full of ice. Pour in club soda.

New York Cocktail

2 oz. blended whisky
1 tsp. grenadine
¾ oz. lemon juice
1 oz. simple syrup
1 lemon twist

Fill a cocktail shaker ½ full with ice. Pour in blended whisky, grenadine, lemon juice, and simple syrup. Give it a good shake, and strain into a cocktail glass. Garnish with lemon twist.

Old Nick

2 oz. blended whisky
1 oz. *Drambuie*
½ oz. orange juice
1 TB. lemon juice
2 dashes bitters
1 maraschino cherry

Fill a cocktail shaker ½ full with ice. Pour in blended whisky, Drambuie, orange juice, and lemon juice, and add bitters. Give it a good shake, and strain into a cocktail glass. Garnish with maraschino cherry.

Liquor Lingo

Drambuie is a Scotch whisky blended with honey, herbs, and spices.

Old-Fashioned

The Old-Fashioned was invented at the Pendennis Club in Louisville, Kentucky, in the 1920s.

1 tsp. sugar
2 dashes bitters
3 oz. club soda
2 orange slices
2 maraschino cherries
2 oz. blended whisky

Muddle sugar, bitters, a splash of club soda, 1 orange slice, and 1 maraschino cherry in an old-fashioned glass. Remove orange rind. Fill the glass ¾ full with ice. Pour in blended whisky and remaining club soda, and garnish with remaining orange slice and maraschino cherry.

Opening Cocktail

2 oz. rye whisky
¼ oz. sweet vermouth
¼ oz. grenadine
1 lemon twist

Fill a cocktail shaker ½ full with ice. Pour in rye whisky, sweet vermouth, and grenadine. Give it a good stir, and strain into a cocktail glass. Garnish with lemon twist.

Park Paradise

2 oz. Canadian whisky
½ oz. sweet vermouth
1 tsp. maraschino liqueur
1 dash bitters

Fill a cocktail shaker ½ full with ice. Pour in Canadian whisky, sweet vermouth, and maraschino liqueur, and add bitters. Give it a good stir, and strain into a cocktail glass.

Perfect Manhattan

2¼ oz. blended whisky
½ oz. sweet vermouth
½ oz. dry vermouth
2 dashes bitters
1 lemon twist

Fill a cocktail shaker ½ full with ice. Pour in blended whisky, sweet vermouth, and dry vermouth, and add bitters. Give it a good stir, and strain into a cocktail glass. Garnish with lemon twist.

Pink Almond

1 oz. blended whisky
½ oz. kirschwasser
½ oz. crème de noyaux
½ oz. orgeat syrup
1 tsp. grenadine
½ oz. lemon juice
1 lemon twist

Fill a cocktail shaker ½ full with ice. Pour in blended whisky, kirschwasser, crème de noyaux, orgeat syrup, grenadine, and lemon juice. Give it a good shake, and strain into a cocktail glass. Garnish with lemon twist.

Poor Tim

2 oz. rye whisky
½ oz. dry vermouth
¼ oz. Chambord

Fill a cocktail shaker ½ full with ice. Pour in rye whisky, dry vermouth, and Chambord. Give it a good stir, and strain into a cocktail glass.

Preakness

2 oz. rye whisky
½ oz. Benedictine
½ oz. sweet vermouth
2 tsp. brandy
2 dashes bitters
1 lemon twist

Fill a cocktail shaker ½ full with ice. Pour in rye whisky, Benedictine, sweet vermouth, and brandy, and add bitters. Give it a good stir, and strain into a cocktail glass. Garnish with lemon twist.

Prince Edward

2 oz. Scotch whisky
½ oz. Lillet
¼ oz. Drambuie
1 orange slice

Fill a cocktail shaker ½ full with ice. Pour in Scotch whisky, Lillet, and Drambuie. Give it a good stir, and strain into a cocktail glass. Garnish with orange slice.

Purgavie

2 oz. Canadian whisky
1 oz. Amer Picon
2 oz. orange juice
3 oz. club soda
2 dashes orange bitters

Fill a highball glass ¾ full with ice. Pour in Canadian whisky, Amer Picon, orange juice, and club soda, and add orange bitters. Give it a good stir.

Quebec

2 oz. Canadian whisky
½ oz. dry vermouth
¼ oz. Amer Picon
¼ oz. maraschino liqueur

Fill a cocktail shaker ½ full with ice. Pour in Canadian whisky, dry vermouth, Amer Picon, and maraschino liqueur. Give it a good stir, and strain into a cocktail glass.

Rattlesnake

2 oz. blended whisky
¼ oz. pastis
½ oz. lemon juice
¾ oz. simple syrup
1 egg white

Fill a cocktail shaker ½ full with ice. Pour in blended whisky, pastis, lemon juice, simple syrup, and egg white. Give it a good, vigorous shake, and strain into a cocktail glass.

Rob Roy

2½ oz. Scotch whisky
1 oz. sweet vermouth
1 dash orange bitters
1 maraschino cherry

Fill a cocktail shaker ½ full with ice. Pour in Scotch whisky and sweet vermouth, and add orange bitters. Give it a good stir, and strain into a cocktail glass. Garnish with maraschino cherry.

Robert Burns

2 oz. Scotch whisky
½ oz. sweet vermouth
¼ oz. pastis
1 dash orange bitters
1 lemon twist

Fill a cocktail shaker ½ full with ice. Pour in Scotch whisky, sweet vermouth, and pastis, and add orange bitters. Give it a good stir, and strain into a cocktail glass. Garnish with lemon twist.

Rusty Nail

2 oz. Scotch whisky
1 oz. Drambuie
1 lemon twist

Fill a cocktail shaker ½ full with ice. Pour in Scotch whisky and Drambuie. Give it a good stir, and strain into a cocktail glass. Garnish with lemon twist.

Sandy Collins

2 oz. Scotch whisky
¾ oz. lemon juice
1 oz. simple syrup
4 oz. club soda
1 orange slice
1 maraschino cherry

Fill a cocktail shaker ½ full with ice. Pour in Scotch whisky, lemon juice, and simple syrup. Give it a good shake, and strain into a Collins glass ½ full of ice. Pour in club soda, and garnish with orange slice and maraschino cherry.

Seven and Seven

2 oz. Seagram's 7 whiskey
5 oz. 7 UP
1 lemon twist

Fill a highball glass ¾ full with ice. Pour in Seagram's 7 whiskey and 7 UP. Give it a good stir, and garnish with lemon twist.

Sherman Cocktail

2 oz. rye whisky
½ oz. dark rum
½ oz. tawny port
1 dash orange bitters
1 dash bitters

Fill a cocktail shaker ½ full with ice. Pour in rye whisky, dark rum, and tawny port, and add orange bitters and bitters. Give it a good stir, and strain into a cocktail glass.

Socrates

2 oz. Canadian whisky
¾ oz. apricot brandy
1 tsp. triple sec
1 dash bitters

Fill a cocktail shaker ½ full with ice. Pour in Canadian whisky, apricot brandy, and triple sec, and add bitters. Give it a good stir, and strain into a cocktail glass.

Soul Kiss

1 oz. rye whisky
1 oz. dry vermouth
½ oz. Dubonnet Rouge
½ oz. orange juice

Fill a cocktail shaker ½ full with ice. Pour in rye whisky, dry vermouth, Dubonnet Rouge, and orange juice. Give it a good shake, and strain into a cocktail glass.

St. Lawrence

1½ oz. Canadian whisky
½ oz. dry vermouth
½ oz. Grand Marnier
1 dash bitters

Fill a cocktail shaker ½ full with ice. Pour in Canadian whisky, dry vermouth, and Grand Marnier, and add bitters. Give it a good shake, and strain into a cocktail glass.

 Cocktail Conversation

If you've ever been to visit the lands of our fair northern neighbor—specifically Quebec—you'd know that the St. Lawrence is a major river that runs through Quebec City.

Stiletto

2 oz. rye whisky
½ oz. amaretto
½ oz. lemon juice
1 tsp. lime juice

Fill a cocktail shaker ½ full with ice. Pour in rye whisky, amaretto, lemon juice, and lime juice. Give it a good shake, and strain into an old-fashioned glass full of ice.

Stony Brook

2 oz. blended whisky
¾ oz. triple sec
¼ oz. orgeat syrup
1 egg white
1 orange twist

Fill a cocktail shaker ½ full with ice. Pour in blended whisky, triple sec, orgeat syrup, and egg white. Give it a good, vigorous shake, and strain into an old-fashioned glass full of ice. Garnish with orange twist.

Strongarm

2 oz. rye whisky
½ oz. triple sec
½ oz. lemon juice
1 maraschino cherry

Fill a cocktail shaker ½ full with ice. Pour in rye whisky, triple sec, and lemon juice. Give it a good shake, and strain into a cocktail glass. Garnish with maraschino cherry.

Tammany Hall

This take on a Manhattan comes from my dear friend and drinkin' buddy, Phil
Kitchel. He says: "It's a more refined Manhattan, the name notwithstanding.
Irish whiskey is cleaner and sweeter, so you don't need as much vermouth, and
you can serve it straight up because it's so smooth. Its beauty is its color in a
cocktail glass: auburn at the top, red cherry on the bottom."

½ oz. sweet vermouth
2½ oz. Irish whiskey
2 to 3 drops Angostura bitters
1 maraschino cherry

Fill cocktail shaker with ice. Pour in
sweet vermouth and Irish whiskey.
Give it a good shake, and strain into a
cocktail glass. Add Angostura bitters
drops, and garnish with maraschino
cherry.

Temptation

2 oz. rye whisky
¼ oz. orange curaçao
¼ oz. pastis
¼ oz. Dubonnet Rouge
1 lemon peel

Fill a cocktail shaker ½ full with ice.
Pour in rye whisky, orange curaço,
pastis, and Dubonnet Rouge. Give it a
good shake, and strain into a cocktail
glass. Garnish with lemon peel.

Thunderclap

2 oz. rye whisky
1 oz. gin
1 oz. brandy

Fill a cocktail shaker ½ full with ice.
Pour in rye whisky, gin, and brandy.
Give it a good stir, and strain into a
cocktail glass.

Tipperary

1½ oz. Irish whiskey
1 oz. green Chartreuse
1 oz. sweet vermouth

Fill a cocktail shaker ½ full with ice.
Pour in Irish whiskey, green Chartreuse, and sweet vermouth. Give it a
good shake, and strain into a cocktail
glass.

T.L.C.

2 oz. rye whisky
¾ oz. triple sec
1 tsp. Dubonnet Blonde
1 tsp. *Ricard*
1 dash bitters
1 lemon twist
1 maraschino cherry

Fill a cocktail shaker ½ full with ice.
Pour in rye whisky, triple sec,
Dubonnet Blonde, and Ricard, and
add bitters. Give it a good shake, and
strain into a cocktail glass. Garnish
with lemon twist and maraschino
cherry.

Liquor Lingo

Ricard is a French anise-flavored liqueur with notes of citrus and a touch of sweetness.

T.N.T.

2 oz. blended whisky
1 oz. anisette

Fill a cocktail shaker ½ full with ice. Pour in blended whisky and anisette. Give it a good shake, and strain into a cocktail glass.

Trois Rivieres

2 oz. Canadian whisky
¾ oz. Dubonnet Rouge
½ oz. triple sec
1 orange twist

Fill a cocktail shaker ½ full with ice. Pour in Canadian whisky, Dubonnet Rouge, and triple sec. Give it a good shake, and strain into a cocktail glass. Garnish with orange twist.

Turtle

2¼ oz. Canadian whisky
¾ oz. Benedictine

Fill a cocktail shaker ½ full with ice. Pour in Canadian whisky and Benedictine. Give it a good stir, and strain into a cocktail glass.

Twin Hills

2 oz. blended whisky
½ oz. Benedictine
¼ oz. lemon juice
¼ oz. lime juice
½ oz. simple syrup
1 lemon slice
1 lime slice

Fill a cocktail shaker ½ full with ice. Pour in blended whisky, Benedictine, lemon juice, lime juice, and simple syrup. Give it a good shake, and strain into a cocktail glass. Garnish with lemon slice and lime slice.

Whisky Blue Monday

2 oz. whisky
1 oz. blueberry brandy
¼ oz. brandy

Fill a cocktail shaker ½ full with ice. Pour in whisky, blueberry brandy, and brandy. Give it a good stir, and strain into a cocktail glass.

Whisky Cobbler

1 tsp. superfine sugar
3 oz. club soda
2½ oz. blended whisky
1 lemon slice
1 orange slice
1 maraschino cherry

In an old-fashioned soda glass, add superfine sugar and pour in club soda. Fill the glass ¾ full with crushed ice. Pour in whisky, and give it a good stir. Garnish with lemon slice, orange slice, and maraschino cherry.

Whisky Collins

2½ oz. blended whisky
1 oz. lemon juice
1¼ oz. simple syrup
4 oz. club soda
1 orange slice
1 maraschino cherry

Fill a cocktail shaker ½ full with ice. Pour in blended whisky, lemon juice, and simple syrup. Give it a good shake, and strain into a Collins glass ¾ full of ice. Pour in club soda, and garnish with orange slice and maraschino cherry.

Whisky Cooler

2 oz. blended whisky
4 oz. lemon-lime soda
1 lemon wedge

Fill a highball glass ¾ full with ice. Pour in blended whisky and lemon-lime soda. Give it a good stir, and garnish with lemon wedge.

Whisky Daisy

2 oz. blended whisky
½ tsp. grenadine
1 oz. lemon juice
1 oz. simple syrup
1 orange slice
1 maraschino cherry

Fill a cocktail shaker ½ full with ice. Pour in blended whisky, grenadine, lemon juice, and simple syrup. Give it a good shake, and strain into an old-fashioned glass ¾ full of ice. Garnish with orange slice and maraschino cherry.

Whisky Fix

2 oz. blended whisky
¾ oz. lemon juice
1 oz. simple syrup
1 lemon slice
1 maraschino cherry

Fill a cocktail shaker ½ full with ice. Pour in blended whisky, lemon juice, and simple syrup. Give it a good shake, and strain into a highball glass full of ice. Garnish with lemon slice and maraschino cherry.

Whisky Highball

2 oz. blended whisky
4 oz. ginger ale
1 lime wedge

Fill a highball glass with ice. Pour in blended whisky and ginger ale. Garnish with lime wedge.

Whisky Sangaree

2 oz. blended whisky
1 tsp. simple syrup
2 oz. club soda
½ oz. tawny port
1 lemon twist
½ tsp. grated nutmeg

Fill an old-fashioned glass ¾ full with ice. Pour in blended whisky and simple syrup. Pour in club soda, and float tawny port on top. Garnish with lemon twist and grated nutmeg.

Whisky Sling

2 oz. blended whisky
¾ oz. lemon juice
1 oz. simple syrup
1 lemon twist

Fill a cocktail shaker ½ full with ice. Pour in blended whisky, lemon juice, and simple syrup. Give it a good shake, and strain into an old-fashioned glass full of ice. Garnish with lemon twist.

Whisky Smash

5 mint sprigs
1 tsp. superfine sugar
1 oz. club soda
2 oz. blended whisky
1 lemon twist

Muddle 4 mint sprigs, superfine sugar, and club soda in an old-fashioned glass. Fill the glass ¾ full with ice, and pour in blended whisky. Give it a good stir, and garnish with remaining mint sprig and lemon twist.

Whisky Sour

2 oz. blended whisky
¾ oz. lemon juice
1 oz. simple syrup
1 orange slice
1 maraschino cherry

Fill a cocktail shaker ½ full with ice. Pour in blended whisky, lemon juice, and simple syrup. Give it a good shake, and strain into a highball glass ¾ full of ice. Garnish with orange slice and maraschino cherry.

Whisky Swizzle

2 oz. blended whisky
1 oz. lime juice
1 oz. simple syrup
1 dash bitters
3 oz. club soda

Fill a cocktail shaker ½ full with ice. Pour in blended whisky, lime juice, and simple syrup, and add bitters. Give it a good shake, and strain into a highball glass ¾ full of ice. Pour in club soda.

Wild-Eyed Rose

2 oz. Irish whiskey
½ oz. grenadine
½ oz. fresh lime juice

Fill a cocktail shaker ½ full with ice. Pour in Irish whiskey, grenadine, and fresh lime juice. Give it a good shake, and strain into a cocktail glass.

Chapter  11

Brandy

Claret is the liquor for boys; port for men; but he who
aspires to be a hero must drink brandy.

—Samuel Johnson

Alabama

1½ oz. brandy
½ oz. orange curaçao
¾ oz. lime juice
1 oz. simple syrup
1 orange twist

Fill a cocktail shaker ½ full
with ice. Pour in brandy, orange
curaçao, lime juice, and simple
syrup. Give it a good shake, and
strain into a cocktail glass. Garnish
with orange twist.

Ambrosia

1 oz. brandy
1 oz. applejack brandy
½ oz. triple sec
½ oz. lemon juice
3 oz. champagne

Fill a cocktail shaker ½ full with
ice. Pour in brandy, applejack
brandy, triple sec, and lemon juice.
Give it a good shake, and strain
into a highball glass full of ice.
Pour in champagne.

American Beauty

1 oz. brandy
½ oz. dry vermouth
¼ tsp. white crème de menthe
1 tsp. grenadine
1 oz. orange juice
½ oz. ruby port

Fill a cocktail shaker ½ full with ice. Pour in brandy, dry vermouth, white crème de menthe, grenadine, and orange juice. Give it a good shake, and strain into a cocktail glass. Carefully drip port on top.

Angel's Wing

½ oz. dark crème de cacao
½ oz. brandy
½ oz. heavy cream

In a pousse-café glass, add dark crème de cacao, followed by brandy, and finally heavy cream.

Ante

2 oz. calvados
1 oz. Dubonnet Rouge
½ oz. triple sec
2 dashes bitters

Fill a cocktail shaker ½ full with ice. Pour in calvados, Dubonnet Rouge, and triple sec, and add bitters. Give it a good stir, and strain into a cocktail glass.

Apple Brandy Cocktail

2 oz. *apple brandy*
¼ oz. grenadine
½ oz. lemon juice

Fill a cocktail shaker ½ full with ice. Pour in apple brandy, grenadine, and lemon juice. Give it a good shake, and strain into a cocktail glass.

Liquor Lingo

Apple brandy is the aged, distilled product of fermented apple cider. Popular examples are applejack brandy (from the United States) and calvados (from France).

Apricot Fizz

2 oz. apricot brandy
½ oz. lime juice
½ oz. lemon juice
1 oz. simple syrup

Fill a cocktail shaker ½ full with ice. Pour in apricot brandy, lime juice, lemon juice, and simple syrup. Give it a good shake, and pour into a Delmonico glass.

Apricot Sour

2 oz. apricot brandy
¾ oz. lemon juice
1 oz. simple syrup

Fill a cocktail shaker ½ full with ice. Pour in apricot brandy, lemon juice, and simple syrup. Give it a good shake, and pour into a sour glass full of ice.

Asphalt

2 oz. brandy
4 oz. cola
1 lemon wedge

Fill a highball glass ¾ full with ice. Pour in brandy and cola. Give it a good stir, and garnish with lemon wedge.

B&B

½ oz. brandy
½ oz. Benedictine

In a cordial glass, add brandy and then Benedictine.

Baby Doll

1 lemon wedge
2 tsp. sugar
2 oz. cognac
1½ oz. Grand Marnier
1 TB. lemon juice

Gently rub the rim of a cocktail glass with lemon wedge. Sprinkle sugar in a small dish, and place the glass upside down in the dish so the rim is coated with sugar. Fill a cocktail shaker ½ full with ice. Pour in cognac, Grand Marnier, and lemon juice. Give it a good stir, and strain into the cocktail glass.

Baltimore Bracer

1¼ oz. brandy
1¼ oz. anisette
1 egg white

Fill a cocktail shaker ½ full with ice. Pour in brandy, anisette, and egg white. Give it a good, vigorous shake, and strain into a cocktail glass.

Bengal

1½ oz. brandy
½ oz. triple sec
½ oz. maraschino liqueur
1 oz. pineapple juice
2 dashes bitters

Fill a cocktail shaker ½ full with ice. Pour in brandy, triple sec, maraschino liqueur, and pineapple juice, and add bitters. Give it a good shake, and strain into a cocktail glass.

Betsy Ross

1½ oz. brandy
1½ oz. tawny port
¼ oz. orange curaçao
1 dash bitters

Fill a cocktail shaker ½ full with ice. Pour in brandy, tawny port, and orange curaçao, and add bitters. Give it a good shake, and strain into a cocktail glass.

Between the Sheets

1½ oz. brandy
½ oz. rum
½ oz. triple sec
½ oz. lemon juice

Fill a cocktail shaker ½ full with ice. Pour in brandy, rum, triple sec, and lemon juice. Give it a good shake, and strain into a cocktail glass.

Black Baltimore

1½ oz. brandy
1 oz. black Sambuca
1 egg white

Fill a cocktail shaker ½ full with ice. Pour in brandy, black Sambuca, and egg white. Give it a good, vigorous shake, and strain into a cocktail glass.

Black Pagoda

2 oz. brandy
1 oz. sweet vermouth
1 oz. dry vermouth
½ oz. triple sec

Fill a cocktail shaker ½ full with ice. Pour in brandy, sweet vermouth, dry vermouth, and triple sec. Give it a good shake, and strain into a cocktail glass.

Bob Dandy

1½ oz. brandy
1½ oz. Dubonnet Blonde
1 lemon twist

Fill a cocktail shaker ½ full with ice. Pour in brandy and Dubonnet Blonde. Give it a good stir, and strain into a cocktail glass. Garnish with lemon twist.

Bombay

1½ oz. brandy
½ oz. dry vermouth
½ oz. sweet vermouth
1 tsp. orange curaçao
1 tsp. pastis

Fill a cocktail shaker ½ full with ice. Pour in brandy, dry vermouth, sweet vermouth, orange curaçao, and pastis. Give it a good shake, and strain into a cocktail glass.

Booster

2 oz. brandy
½ oz. orange curaçao
1 egg white

Fill a cocktail shaker ½ full with ice. Pour in brandy, orange curaçao, and egg white. Give it a good, vigorous shake, and strain into a cocktail glass.

Bosom Caresser

2 oz. brandy
1½ oz. Madeira
¾ oz. triple sec

Fill a cocktail shaker ½ full with ice. Pour in brandy, Madeira, and triple sec. Give it a good shake, and strain into a cocktail glass.

Brandied Egg Sour

1½ oz. brandy
½ oz. triple sec
½ oz. lemon juice
¾ oz. simple syrup
1 egg

Fill a cocktail shaker ½ full with ice. Pour in brandy, triple sec, lemon juice, simple syrup, and egg. Give it a good, vigorous shake, and strain into a cocktail glass.

Brandy Blazer

1 tsp. sugar
2½ oz. hot water
2½ oz. brandy
1 lemon twist

In an Irish coffee glass, add sugar and then pour in hot water to dissolve sugar. Pour in brandy, and give it a good stir. Garnish with lemon twist.

Brandy Cobbler

1 tsp. superfine sugar
3 oz. club soda
2 oz. brandy
1 lemon slice
1 orange slice
1 maraschino cherry

In an old-fashioned glass, add superfine sugar and then pour in club soda to dissolve sugar. Fill the glass ¾ full with crushed ice. Pour in brandy, and give it a good stir. Garnish with lemon slice, orange slice, and maraschino cherry.

Brandy Cocktail

2½ oz. brandy
1 tsp. sugar
2 dashes bitters
1 lemon twist

Fill a cocktail shaker ½ full with ice. Pour in brandy, and sugar, and add bitters. Give it a good stir, and strain into a cocktail glass. Garnish with lemon twist.

Brandy Collins

2½ oz. brandy
1 oz. lemon juice
1 tsp. simple syrup
4 oz. club soda
1 orange slice
1 maraschino cherry

Fill a cocktail shaker ½ full with ice. Pour in brandy, lemon juice, and simple syrup. Give it a good shake, and strain into a Collins glass ¾ full of ice. Pour in club soda, and garnish with orange slice and maraschino cherry.

Brandy Cooler

2 oz. brandy
4 oz. lemon-lime soda
1 lemon wedge

Fill a highball glass ¾ full with ice. Pour in brandy and lemon-lime soda. Give it a good stir, and garnish with lemon wedge.

Brandy Daisy

2 oz. brandy
½ tsp. grenadine
1 oz. lemon juice
1 oz. simple syrup
1 orange slice
1 maraschino cherry

Fill a cocktail shaker ½ full with ice. Pour in brandy, grenadine, lemon juice, and simple syrup. Give it a good shake, and strain into an old-fashioned glass ¾ full of ice. Garnish with orange slice and maraschino cherry.

Brandy Fix

2 oz. brandy
¾ oz. lemon juice
1 oz. simple syrup
1 lemon slice
1 maraschino cherry

Fill a cocktail shaker ½ full with ice. Pour in brandy, lemon juice, and simple syrup. Give it a good shake, and strain into a highball glass full of ice. Garnish with lemon slice and maraschino cherry.

Brandy Gump

1½ oz. brandy
¼ oz. grenadine
1 oz. lemon juice

Fill a cocktail shaker ½ full with ice. Pour in brandy, grenadine, and lemon juice. Give it a good shake, and strain into a cocktail glass.

Brandy Highball

2 oz. brandy
4 oz. ginger ale
1 lime wedge

Fill a highball glass with ice. Pour in brandy and ginger ale. Garnish with lime wedge.

Brandy Manhattan

2 oz. brandy
1 oz. sweet vermouth
2 dashes Angostura bitters
1 maraschino cherry

Fill a cocktail shaker ½ full with ice.
Pour in brandy and sweet vermouth,
and add Angostura bitters. Give it a
good stir, and strain into a cocktail
glass. Garnish with maraschino cherry.

Brandy Milk Punch

2 oz. brandy
½ oz. dark rum
1 TB. simple syrup
4 oz. milk
1 tsp. grated nutmeg

Fill a cocktail shaker ½ full with ice.
Pour in brandy, dark rum, milk, and
simple syrup. Give it a good shake,
and strain into a highball glass ½ full
of ice. Garnish with grated nutmeg.

Brandy Old-Fashioned

1 tsp. sugar
2 dashes bitters
3 oz. club soda
2 orange slices
2 maraschino cherries
2 oz. brandy

Muddle sugar, bitters, splash of club
soda, 1 orange slice, and 1 maraschino
cherry in an old-fashioned glass. Remove orange rind. Fill the glass ¾ full
with ice. Pour in brandy and remaining club soda, and garnish with re
maining orange slice and maraschino
cherry.

Brandy Sangaree

2 oz. brandy
1 tsp. simple syrup
2 oz. club soda
½ oz. tawny port
1 lemon twist
½ tsp. grated nutmeg

Fill an old-fashioned glass ¾ full with
ice. Pour in brandy and simple syrup.
Pour in club soda, and float tawny port
on top. Garnish with lemon twist and
grated nutmeg.

Brandy Sling

2 oz. brandy
¾ oz. lemon juice
1 oz. simple syrup
1 lemon twist

Fill a cocktail shaker ½ full with ice.
Pour in brandy, lemon juice, and simple syrup. Give it a good shake, and
strain into an old-fashioned glass full
of ice. Garnish with lemon twist.

Brandy Smash

5 mint sprigs
1 tsp. superfine sugar
1 oz. club soda
2 oz. brandy
1 lemon twist

Muddle 4 mint sprigs, superfine sugar, and club soda in an old-fashioned glass. Fill the glass ¾ full with ice, and pour in brandy. Give it a good stir, and garnish with remaining mint sprig and lemon twist.

Brandy Sour

2 oz. brandy
¾ oz. lemon juice
1 oz. simple syrup
1 orange slice
1 maraschino cherry

Fill a cocktail shaker ½ full with ice. Pour in brandy, lemon juice, and simple syrup. Give it a good shake, and strain into a highball glass ¾ full of ice. Garnish with orange slice and maraschino cherry.

Brandy Swizzle

2 oz. brandy
1 oz. lime juice
1 oz. simple syrup
1 dash bitters
3 oz. club soda

Fill a cocktail shaker ½ full with ice. Pour in brandy, lime juice, and simple syrup, and add bitters. Give it a good shake, and strain into a highball glass ¾ full of ice. Pour in club soda.

Cadiz

1 oz. blackberry brandy
1 oz. dry sherry
½ oz. triple sec
½ oz. heavy cream

Fill a cocktail shaker ½ full with ice. Pour in blackberry brandy, dry sherry, triple sec, and heavy cream. Give it a good shake, and strain into a cocktail glass.

Caledonia

1 oz. cognac
1 oz. dark crème de cacao
1 oz. milk
1 dash bitters
1 egg yolk
½ tsp. cinnamon

Fill a cocktail shaker ½ full with ice. Pour in cognac, dark crème de cacao, and milk, and add bitters and egg yolk. Give it a good, vigorous shake, and strain into a cocktail glass. Dust with cinnamon.

Champs Elysées

1 oz. brandy
½ oz. yellow Chartreuse
1 oz. lemon juice
1 oz. simple syrup
1 dash bitters

Fill a cocktail shaker ½ full with ice. Pour in brandy, yellow Chartreuse, lemon juice, and simple syrup, and add bitters. Give it a good shake, and strain into a cocktail glass.

Charles Cocktail

2 oz. brandy
1½ oz. sweet vermouth
2 dashes bitters

Fill a cocktail shaker ½ full with ice. Pour in brandy and sweet vermouth, and add bitters. Give it a good shake, and strain into a cocktail glass.

Cherry Blossom

1½ oz. cherry brandy
1 oz. brandy
¼ oz. orange curaçao
¼ oz. grenadine
½ oz. lemon juice

Fill a cocktail shaker ½ full with ice. Pour in cherry brandy, brandy, orange curaçao, grenadine, and lemon juice. Give it a good shake, and strain into a cocktail glass.

Chicago

2 oz. brandy
¼ oz. orange curaçao
1 dash bitters

Fill a cocktail shaker ½ full with ice. Pour in brandy and orange curaçao, and add bitters. Give it a good stir, and strain into a cocktail glass.

City Slicker

2 oz. brandy
1 oz. triple sec
1 tsp. pastis
1 TB. lemon juice

Fill a cocktail shaker ½ full with ice. Pour in brandy, triple sec, pastis, and lemon juice. Give it a good shake, and strain into a cocktail glass.

Classic

2 oz. brandy
½ oz. triple sec
¼ oz. maraschino liqueur
½ oz. lemon juice

Fill a cocktail shaker ½ full with ice. Pour in brandy, triple sec, maraschino liqueur, and lemon juice. Give it a good shake, and strain into a cocktail glass.

Cold Deck

1½ oz. brandy
¾ oz. sweet vermouth
¾ oz. white crème de menthe

Fill a cocktail shaker ½ full with ice. Pour in brandy, sweet vermouth, and white crème de menthe. Give it a good shake, and strain into a cocktail glass.

Corpse Reviver

1½ oz. brandy
¾ oz. apple brandy
¾ oz. sweet vermouth

Fill a cocktail shaker ½ full with ice. Pour in brandy, apple brandy, and sweet vermouth. Give it a good stir, and strain into a cocktail glass.

Dad's Brandy Alexander

This cocktail is one dear to my heart. My family had several lovely holiday traditions that made them special for us—our own unique little Zavatto Holiday Season. One I have always loved and have recently resurrected in my own home is the traditional Mike Zavatto Christmas Brandy Alexander. It's creamy and decadent, and the nutmeg gives it that special flavor that always makes me think about the holiday season.

2 oz. brandy
1 oz. dark crème de cacao
1 oz. light cream
1 tsp. grated nutmeg

Fill a cocktail shaker ½ full with ice. Pour in brandy, dark crème de cacao, and light cream. Give it a good shake, and strain into a cocktail glass. Garnish with grated nutmeg.

Dance With a Dream

2½ oz. brandy
½ oz. triple sec
1 tsp. anisette

Fill a cocktail shaker ½ full with ice. Pour in brandy, triple sec, and anisette. Give it a good shake, and strain into a cocktail glass.

Deauville Cocktail

1 oz. brandy
1 oz. apple brandy
¾ oz. triple sec
½ oz. lemon juice
1 maraschino cherry

Fill a cocktail shaker ½ full with ice. Pour in brandy, apple brandy, triple sec, and lemon juice. Give it a good shake, and strain into a cocktail glass. Garnish with maraschino cherry.

Depth Bomb

1½ oz. brandy
1½ oz. apple brandy
¼ oz. grenadine
¼ oz. lemon juice

Fill a cocktail shaker ½ full with ice. Pour in brandy, apple brandy, grenadine, and lemon juice. Give it a good shake, and strain into a cocktail glass.

Dirty Mother

1½ oz. brandy
1½ oz. Kahlùa

Fill an old-fashioned glass with ice. Pour in brandy and Kahlùa. Give it a good stir.

Dirty White Mother

1 oz. brandy
1 oz. Kahlùa
1 oz. light cream

Fill an old-fashioned glass with ice. Pour in brandy and Kahlùa. Give it a good stir. Float light cream on top.

East India Cocktail

2 oz. brandy
½ oz. triple sec
½ oz. pineapple juice
2 dashes bitters

Fill a cocktail shaker ½ full with ice. Pour in brandy, triple sec, and pineapple juice, and add bitters. Give it a good shake, and strain into a cocktail glass.

Fancy Brandy

2¼ oz. brandy
¼ oz. maraschino liqueur
1 dash orange bitters
1 dash bitters

Fill a cocktail shaker ½ full with ice. Pour in brandy and maraschino liqueur, and add orange bitters and bitters. Give it a good shake, and strain into a cocktail glass.

Fantasio

1½ oz. brandy
¾ oz. dry vermouth
¼ oz. maraschino liqueur
¼ oz. white crème de menthe

Fill a cocktail shaker ½ full with ice. Pour in brandy, dry vermouth, maraschino liqueur, and white crème de menthe. Give it a good shake, and strain into a cocktail glass.

French Connection

2 oz. cognac
1 oz. amaretto

Fill an old-fashioned glass with ice. Pour in cognac and amaretto. Give it a good stir.

Froupe

1½ oz. brandy
1½ oz. sweet vermouth
¼ oz. Benedictine

Fill a cocktail shaker ½ full with ice. Pour in brandy, sweet vermouth, and Benedictine. Give it a good shake, and strain into a cocktail glass.

Gazette

1½ oz. brandy
1 oz. sweet vermouth
1 tsp. lemon juice

Fill a cocktail shaker ½ full with ice. Pour in brandy, sweet vermouth, and lemon juice. Give it a good shake, and strain into a cocktail glass.

Harvard

2 oz. brandy
1 oz. sweet vermouth
¼ oz. grenadine
½ oz. lemon juice
1 dash bitters

Fill a cocktail shaker ½ full with ice. Pour in brandy, sweet vermouth, grenadine, and lemon juice, and add bitters. Give it a good shake, and strain into a cocktail glass.

Italian Stinger

1¾ oz. brandy
1 oz. Galliano

Fill a cocktail shaker ½ full with ice. Pour in brandy and Galliano. Give it a good shake, and strain into an old-fashioned glass full of ice.

Jack Rose

2 oz. applejack brandy
½ oz. grenadine
1 oz. lemon juice

Fill a cocktail shaker ½ full with ice. Pour in applejack brandy, grenadine, and lemon juice. Give it a good shake, and strain into a cocktail glass.

Janet Howard Cocktail

2½ oz. brandy
¼ oz. orgeat syrup
1 dash bitters

Fill a cocktail shaker ½ full with ice.
Pour in brandy and orgeat syrup, and
add bitters. Give it a good shake, and
strain into a cocktail glass.

Japanese

2 oz. brandy
¼ oz. orgeat syrup
¼ oz. lime juice
1 dash bitters
1 lime twist

Fill a cocktail shaker ½ full with ice.
Pour in brandy, orgeat syrup, and lime
juice, and add bitters. Give it a good
shake, and strain into a cocktail glass.
Garnish with lime twist.

King's Cognac Peg

1½ oz. cognac
4 oz. champagne

Add a few ice cubes to a wine glass.
Pour in cognac and champagne.

Kiss the Boys Good-Bye

1 oz. brandy
1 oz. sloe gin
1 oz. lemon juice
½ oz. simple syrup
1 egg white

Fill a cocktail shaker ½ full with ice.
Pour in brandy, sloe gin, lemon juice,
simple syrup, and egg white. Give it a
good, vigorous shake, and strain into a
cocktail glass.

La Jolla

2 oz. brandy
½ oz. crème de bananes
¼ oz. lemon juice
¼ oz. orange juice

Fill a cocktail shaker ½ full with ice.
Pour in brandy, crème de bananes,
lemon juice, and orange juice. Give it
a good shake, and strain into a cocktail
glass.

Lady, Be Good

1½ oz. brandy
¾ oz. sweet vermouth
¾ oz. white crème de menthe

Fill a cocktail shaker ½ full with ice.
Pour in brandy, sweet vermouth, and
white crème de menthe. Give it a good
shake, and strain into a cocktail glass.

London Calling

Nolita House chef and co-owner Marc Matyas and his wife lived in London for some time, and this drink is, as Marc puts it, "Memories of London …"

¼ oz. brandy	Pour brandy and grenadine into a
1 dash grenadine	champagne glass. Top with cham-
¾ oz. champagne	pagne, and garnish with lemon twist.
1 lemon twist	

Loudspeaker

1 oz. brandy	Fill a cocktail shaker ½ full with ice.
1 oz. gin	Pour in brandy, gin, triple sec, and
½ oz. triple sec	lemon juice. Give it a good shake,
¼ oz. lemon juice	and strain into a cocktail glass.

Lugger

1 oz. brandy	Fill a cocktail shaker ½ full with ice.
1 oz. apple brandy	Pour in brandy, apple brandy, and
1 oz. apricot brandy	apricot brandy. Give it a good stir, and
1 lemon twist	strain into a cocktail glass. Garnish with lemon twist.

Metropolitan

2 oz. brandy	Fill a cocktail shaker ½ full with ice.
½ oz. sweet vermouth	Pour in brandy, sweet vermouth, and
½ tsp. sugar	sugar, and add bitters. Give it a good
1 dash bitters	shake, and strain into a cocktail glass.

Mikado

2 oz. brandy	Fill a cocktail shaker ½ full with ice.
½ oz. triple sec	Pour in brandy, triple sec, crème de
¼ oz. crème de noyaux	noyaux, and grenadine, and add bit-
½ oz. grenadine	ters. Give it a good shake, and strain
2 dashes bitters	into a cocktail glass.

Montana

1½ oz. brandy	Fill a cocktail shaker ½ full with ice.
½ oz. dry vermouth	Pour in brandy, dry vermouth, and
½ oz. ruby port	ruby port, and add bitters. Give it a
1 dash bitters	good shake, and strain into a cocktail glass.

Nantucket

2 oz. brandy
1 oz. cranberry juice
1 oz. grapefruit juice
1 lime slice

Fill a cocktail shaker ½ full with ice. Pour in brandy, cranberry juice, and grapefruit juice. Give it a good shake, and strain into a highball glass ¾ full of ice. Garnish with lime slice.

Netherland

2 oz. brandy
1 oz. orange curaçao
2 dashes orange bitters

Fill a cocktail shaker ½ full with ice. Pour in brandy and orange curaçao, and add orange bitters. Give it a good shake, and strain into a cocktail glass.

Nicky Finn

1 oz. brandy
1 oz. triple sec
1 tsp. pastis
1 oz. lemon juice

Fill a cocktail shaker ½ full with ice. Pour in brandy, triple sec, pastis, and lemon juice. Give it a good shake, and strain into a cocktail glass.

Olympic

1 oz. brandy
1 oz. orange curaçao
1 oz. orange juice

Fill a cocktail shaker ½ full with ice. Pour in brandy, orange curaçao, and orange juice. Give it a good shake, and strain into a cocktail glass.

On the Square

2 oz. apricot brandy
1 oz. calvados
1 oz. gin

Fill a cocktail shaker ½ full with ice. Pour in brandy, calvados, and gin. Give it a good shake, and strain into a cocktail glass.

Panama Brandy Cocktail

1 oz. brandy
1 oz. white crème de cacao
½ oz. heavy cream

Fill a cocktail shaker ½ full with ice. Pour in brandy, white crème de cacao, and heavy cream. Give it a good shake, and strain into a cocktail glass.

Poop Deck

1 12 oz. blackberry brandy
¾ oz. brandy
¾ oz. ruby port

Fill a cocktail shaker ½ full with ice. Pour in blackberry brandy, brandy, and ruby port. Give it a good stir, and strain into a cocktail glass.

Princess Mary's Pride

2 oz. calvados
½ oz. dry vermouth
½ oz. Dubonnet Rouge

Fill a cocktail shaker ½ full with ice. Pour in calvados, dry vermouth, and Dubonnet Rouge. Give it a good shake, and strain into a cocktail glass.

Saratoga

2 oz. brandy
1 oz. pineapple juice
1 tsp. maraschino liqueur
1 tsp. lemon juice
2 dashes bitters

Fill a cocktail shaker ½ full with ice. Pour in brandy, pineapple juice, maraschino liqueur, and lemon juice, and add bitters. Give it a good shake, and strain into a cocktail glass.

Satin Sheet

2 oz. brandy
1 oz. peach schnapps
1 tsp. grenadine
4 oz. orange juice

Fill a cocktail shaker ½ full with ice. Pour in brandy, peach schnapps, grenadine, and orange juice. Give it a good shake, and strain into a highball glass ¾ full of ice.

Scooter

1 oz. brandy
1 oz. amaretto
1 oz. light cream

Fill a cocktail shaker ½ full with ice. Pour in brandy, amaretto, and light cream. Give it a good shake, and strain into a cocktail glass.

Sidecar

2 oz. brandy
½ oz. triple sec
¼ oz. lemon juice

Fill a cocktail shaker ½ full with ice. Pour in brandy, triple sec, and lemon juice. Give it a good shake, and strain into a cocktail glass.

Cocktail Conversation

Out of rum and can't make a Between the Sheets? That's all right—if you leave it out, you get a Sidecar anyway.

Special Rough

1½ oz. apple brandy
1 oz. brandy
¼ oz. pastis

Fill a cocktail shaker ½ full with ice. Pour in apple brandy, brandy, and pastis. Give it a good stir, and strain into a cocktail glass.

Stinger

2 oz. brandy
¾ oz. white crème de menthe

Fill a cocktail shaker ½ full with ice. Pour in brandy and white crème de menthe. Give it a good shake, and strain into a cocktail glass.

Sun and Shade

1½ oz. brandy
1½ oz. gin

Fill a cocktail shaker ½ full with ice. Pour in brandy and gin. Give it a good shake, and strain into a cocktail glass.

Thunder

2 oz. brandy
1 egg yolk
1 tsp. sugar

Fill a cocktail shaker ½ full with ice. Pour in brandy, egg yolk, and sugar. Give it a good, vigorous shake, and strain into a cocktail glass.

Thunder and Lightning

2 oz. brandy
1 egg yolk
1 tsp. sugar
⅛ tsp. cayenne

Fill a cocktail shaker ½ full with ice. Pour in brandy, egg yolk, sugar, and cayenne. Give it a good, vigorous shake, and strain into a cocktail glass.

Vanderbilt

2 oz. brandy
1 oz. cherry brandy
2 dashes bitters

Fill a cocktail shaker ½ full with ice. Pour in brandy and cherry brandy, and add bitters. Give it a good shake, and strain into a cocktail glass.

Washington

2 oz. brandy
1 oz. dry vermouth
¼ oz. simple syrup
2 dashes bitters

Fill a cocktail shaker ½ full with ice. Pour in brandy, dry vermouth, and simple syrup, and add bitters. Give it a good shake, and strain into a cocktail glass.

Weep No More

1 oz. brandy
1 oz. Dubonnet Rouge
½ oz. lime juice
¼ oz. maraschino liqueur

Fill a cocktail shaker ½ full with ice. Pour in brandy, Dubonnet Rouge, lime juice, and maraschino liqueur. Give it a good shake, and strain into a cocktail glass.

Whip

1½ oz. brandy
½ oz. sweet vermouth
½ oz. dry vermouth
¼ oz. triple sec
1 tsp. pastis

Fill a cocktail shaker ½ full with ice. Pour in brandy, sweet vermouth, dry vermouth, triple sec, and pastis. Give it a good shake, and strain into a cocktail glass.

Widow's Kiss

1½ oz. brandy
¾ oz. Benedictine
¾ oz. yellow Chartreuse
1 dash bitters

Fill a cocktail shaker ½ full with ice. Pour in brandy, Benedictine, and yellow Chartreuse, and add bitters. Give it a good shake, and strain into a cocktail glass.

Zoom

2 oz. brandy
¼ oz. cream
¼ oz. honey

Fill a cocktail shaker ½ full with ice. Pour in brandy, cream, and honey. Give it a good shake, and strain into a cocktail glass.

Chapter  12

Aperitifs and Cordials

Alcohol is the anesthesia by which we endure the operation of life.

—George Bernard Shaw

Absinthe French

1 sugar cube
2½ oz. pastis
1 lemon twist

Fill an old-fashioned glass ½ full with crushed ice. Drop in sugar cube, and slowly pour pastis over sugar until it's almost dissolved. Garnish with lemon twist.

Addison Cocktail

1½ oz. sweet vermouth
1 oz. gin
1 orange twist

Fill a cocktail shaker ½ full with ice. Pour in sweet vermouth and gin. Give it a good stir, and strain into a cocktail glass. Garnish with orange twist.

Alabama Slammer Cocktail

1½ oz. Southern Comfort
1 oz. amaretto
1 oz. sloe gin
2 oz. orange juice
1 TB. lemon juice

Fill a cocktail shaker ½ full with ice. Pour in Southern Comfort, amaretto, sloe gin, orange juice, and lemon juice. Give it a good shake, and strain into a highball glass ½ full of ice.

Allies Cocktail

1 oz. dry vermouth
1 oz. gin
1 tsp. kummel

Fill a cocktail shaker ½ full with ice. Pour in dry vermouth, gin, and kummel. Give it a good stir, and strain into a cocktail glass.

Amaretto Sour

2 oz. amaretto
¾ oz. lemon juice
1 oz. simple syrup
1 maraschino cherry
1 orange slice

Fill a cocktail shaker ½ full with ice. Pour in amaretto, lemon juice, and simple syrup. Give it a good shake, and strain into a sour glass full of ice. Garnish with maraschino cherry and orange slice.

Amer Picon Cocktail

2 oz. *Amer Picon*
¼ oz. grenadine
1 oz. lemon juice

Fill a cocktail shaker ½ full with ice. Pour in Amer Picon, grenadine, and lemon juice. Give it a good shake, and strain into a cocktail glass.

 Liquor Lingo

Amer Picon is a bitter French cordial made of cinchona bark, orange, and gentian created by Gaetan Picon in 1837. It is also referred to as simply Picon.

Amer Picon Cooler

1 tsp. superfine sugar
2 oz. Amer Picon
1 oz. gin
½ oz. lemon juice

Fill a cocktail shaker ½ full with ice. Add superfine sugar and then pour in Amer Picon, gin, and lemon juice. Give it a good shake, and strain into a highball glass ½ full of ice.

Americano

1 oz. sweet vermouth
1 oz. Campari
2 oz. club soda
1 lemon twist

Fill an old-fashioned glass with ice. Pour in sweet vermouth, Campari, and club soda. Give it a good stir, and garnish with lemon twist.

Amour Cocktail

1½ oz. dry vermouth
1½ oz. sherry
1 dash bitters
1 lemon twist

Fill a cocktail shaker ½ full with ice. Pour in dry vermouth and sherry, and add bitters. Give it a good stir, and strain into a cocktail glass. Garnish with lemon twist.

Apocalypse

1 oz. peppermint schnapps
1 oz. Southern Comfort
4 oz. hot chocolate

Pour peppermint schnapps, Southern Comfort, and hot chocolate into an Irish coffee glass. Give it a good stir.

Apple Rouge

2 oz. Dubonnet Blanc
1 oz. applejack brandy
1 lemon twist

Fill a cocktail shaker ½ full with ice. Pour in Dubonnet Blanc and applejack brandy. Give it a good shake, and strain into a cocktail glass. Garnish with lemon twist.

Argentina Cocktail

1½ oz. dry vermouth
1½ oz. gin
¼ oz. Benedictine
¼ oz. triple sec
1 dash orange bitters

Fill a cocktail shaker ½ full with ice. Pour in dry vermouth, gin, Benedictine, and triple sec, and add orange bitters. Give it a good stir, and strain into a cocktail glass.

Artist's Cocktail

1½ oz. sherry
1 oz. bourbon
¼ oz. grenadine
½ oz. lemon juice

Fill a cocktail shaker ½ full with ice. Pour in sherry, bourbon, grenadine, and lemon juice. Give it a good shake, and strain into a cocktail glass.

B-52

1 oz. coffee liqueur
1 oz. Irish cream
1 oz. Grand Marnier

Fill a cocktail shaker ½ full with ice. Pour in coffee liqueur, Irish cream, and Grand Marnier. Give it a good shake, and strain into an old-fashioned glass full of ice.

Bahia Cocktail

1¼ oz. dry vermouth
1¼ oz. sherry
¼ oz. pastis
1 dash bitters
1 lemon twist

Fill a cocktail shaker ½ full with ice. Pour in dry vermouth, sherry, and pastis, and add bitters. Give it a good stir, and strain into a cocktail glass. Garnish with lemon twist.

Banshee

1 oz. crème de bananes
1 oz. white crème de cacao
1 oz. light cream

Fill a cocktail shaker ½ full with ice. Pour in crème de bananes, white crème de cacao, and light cream. Give it a good shake, and strain into a cocktail glass.

Beirut Breeze

This original cocktail comes from the lovely Lebanese eatery Mandaloun in West Hollywood and is a particularly pretty drink.

4 oz. cranberry juice
½ tsp. Pernod bitters
2 oz. *Arak*
1 mint sprig

Fill a Collins glass with ice. Pour in cranberry juice and then Pernod bitters. Top with Arak, and garnish with mint sprig.

Liquor Lingo

Arak is a Lebanese anise-flavored (and very potent) spirit. It's sometimes called "the milk of lions" because it turns from crystal clear to milky white when ice is added. Here it turns a creamy shade of pink when it hits the cranberry juice.

Big Red

1½ oz. sweet vermouth
1 oz. dry vermouth
¾ oz. sloe gin
2 dashes orange bitters
1 orange slice

Fill a cocktail shaker ½ full with ice. Pour in sweet vermouth, dry vermouth, and sloe gin, and add orange bitters. Give it a good shake, and strain into an old-fashioned glass full of ice. Garnish with orange slice.

Bittersweet Cocktail

1½ oz. dry vermouth
1½ oz. sweet vermouth
2 dashes orange bitters
1 dash bitters
1 orange twist

Fill a cocktail shaker ½ full with ice. Pour in dry vermouth, sweet vermouth, and add orange bitters and bitters. Give it a good stir, and strain into a cocktail glass. Garnish with orange twist.

Blackthorn

2 oz. sloe gin
1 oz. sweet vermouth
1 dash orange bitters
1 dash Angostura bitters
1 lemon twist

Fill a cocktail shaker ½ full with ice. Pour in sloe gin and sweet vermouth, and add orange bitters and Angostura bitters. Give it a good stir, and strain into a cocktail glass. Garnish with lemon twist.

Boccie Ball

2 oz. amaretto
3 oz. orange juice
1 oz. club soda

Fill a highball glass ½ full with ice. Pour in amaretto, orange juice, and club soda. Give it a good stir.

Bonsoni Cocktail

2½ oz. sweet vermouth
¾ oz. *Fernet Branca*
1 lemon twist

Fill a cocktail shaker ½ full with ice. Pour in sweet vermouth and Fernet Branca. Give it a good stir, and strain into a cocktail glass. Garnish with lemon twist.

 Liquor Lingo

Fernet Branca is an Italian bitter-sweet digestif.

Boyd of the Loch

2 oz. dry vermouth
1½ oz. Scotch whisky
1 lemon twist

Fill a cocktail shaker ½ full with ice. Pour in dry vermouth and Scotch whisky. Give it a good stir, and strain into a cocktail glass. Garnish with lemon twist.

Bresnan

2 oz. sweet vermouth
1½ oz. dry vermouth
1 TB. crème de cassis
½ oz. lemon juice
1 lemon twist

Fill a cocktail shaker ½ full with ice. Pour in sweet vermouth, dry vermouth, crème de cassis, and lemon juice. Give it a good shake, and strain into a cocktail glass. Garnish with lemon twist.

Burn's Special

2 oz. sweet vermouth
1½ oz. Scotch whisky
1 tsp. Benedictine
1 lemon twist

Fill a cocktail shaker ½ full with ice. Pour in vermouth, Scotch whisky, and Benedictine. Give it a good stir, and strain into a cocktail glass. Garnish with lemon twist.

Charleston

¾ oz. dry vermouth
¾ oz. sweet vermouth
½ oz. gin
½ oz. kirschwasser
¼ oz. orange curaçao
¼ oz. maraschino liqueur
1 maraschino cherry

Fill a cocktail shaker ½ full with ice. Pour in dry vermouth, sweet vermouth, gin, kirschwasser, orange curaçao, and maraschino liqueur. Give it a good stir, and strain into a cocktail glass. Garnish with maraschino cherry.

Chelsea

1½ oz. dry vermouth
1 oz. bourbon
2 tsp. blackberry brandy
1 tsp. triple sec
1 TB. lemon juice
1 lemon twist

Fill a cocktail shaker ½ full with ice. Pour in dry vermouth, bourbon, blackberry brandy, triple sec, and lemon juice. Give it a good shake, and strain into a cocktail glass. Garnish with lemon twist.

Cherry Cocktail

1½ oz. cherry Heering
1 oz. dry vermouth

Fill a cocktail shaker ½ full with ice. Pour in cherry Heering and dry vermouth. Give it a good stir, and strain into a cocktail glass.

Cherry Love Kiss

1 oz. dry vermouth
1 oz. sweet vermouth
½ oz. cherry liqueur
1 maraschino cherry

Fill a cocktail shaker ½ full with ice. Pour in dry vermouth, sweet vermouth, and cherry liqueur. Give it a good stir, and strain into a cocktail glass. Garnish with maraschino cherry.

Chunnel Cocktail

2 oz. Grand Marnier
1 oz. gin
¼ oz. sweet vermouth
2 dashes bitters
1 orange twist

Fill a cocktail shaker ½ full with ice. Pour in Grand Marnier, gin, and sweet vermouth, and add bitters. Give it a good shake, and strain into a cocktail glass. Garnish with orange twist.

Confidential Cocktail

1 oz. dry vermouth
¾ oz. gin
¾ oz. *Strega*
½ oz. cherry Heering

Fill a cocktail shaker ½ full with ice. Pour in dry vermouth, gin, Strega, and cherry Heering. Give it a good shake, and strain into a cocktail glass.

Liquor Lingo

Strega is a sweet, gold-colored Italian liqueur. In Italian, the word literally translates to "witch."

Crème de Menthe Frappé

2½ oz. crème de menthe

Fill a martini glass with crushed ice. Pour in crème de menthe.

Diana

2 oz. white crème de menthe
½ oz. brandy

Pour crème de menthe and brandy into a snifter.

Diplomat

2 oz. dry vermouth
½ oz. sweet vermouth
¼ oz. maraschino liqueur
1 dash bitters
1 maraschino cherry

Fill a cocktail shaker ½ full with ice. Pour in dry vermouth, sweet vermouth, and maraschino liqueur, and add bitters. Give it a good stir, and strain into a cocktail glass. Garnish with maraschino cherry.

Dubonnet Apple Cocktail

1½ oz. Dubonnet Rouge
1½ oz. calvados
1 orange slice

Fill a cocktail shaker ½ full with ice. Pour in Dubonnet Rouge and calvados. Give it a good stir, and strain into a cocktail glass. Garnish with orange slice.

Dubonnet Cocktail

1½ oz. Dubonnet Blonde
1½ oz. gin
1 lemon twist

Fill a cocktail shaker ½ full with ice. Pour in Dubonnet Blonde and gin. Give it a good stir, and strain into a cocktail glass. Garnish with lemon twist.

Dubonnet Fizz

1½ oz. Dubonnet Rouge
¼ oz. cherry brandy
¾ oz. lemon juice
1 oz. simple syrup
2 oz. club soda

Fill a cocktail shaker ½ full with ice. Pour in Dubonnet Rouge, cherry brandy, lemon juice, and simple syrup. Give it a good shake, and strain into a highball glass ½ full of ice. Pour in club soda.

Dubonnet Royal

2 oz. Dubonnet Rouge
1 oz. gin
1 tsp. orange curaçao
1 dash orange bitters
1 maraschino cherry

Fill a cocktail shaker ½ full with ice. Pour in Dubonnet Rouge, gin, and orange curaçao, and add bitters. Give it a good stir, and strain into a cocktail glass. Garnish with maraschino cherry.

Exposition Cocktail

1½ oz. dry vermouth
¾ oz. sloe gin
¾ oz. cherry brandy
1 maraschino cherry

Fill a cocktail shaker ½ full with ice. Pour in dry vermouth, sloe gin, and cherry brandy. Give it a good stir, and strain into a cocktail glass. Garnish with maraschino cherry.

Ferrari

2 oz. dry vermouth
1 oz. amaretto
1 dash bitters
1 orange twist

Fill a cocktail shaker ½ full with ice. Pour in dry vermouth and amaretto, and add bitters. Give it a good stir, and strain into a cocktail glass. Garnish with orange twist.

Fig Leaf

1½ oz. sweet vermouth
1 oz. light rum
¼ oz. lime juice
1 dash bitters

Fill a cocktail shaker ½ full with ice. Pour in sweet vermouth, light rum, and lime juice, and add bitters. Give it a good shake, and strain into a cocktail glass.

French Almond

1½ oz. dry vermouth
¾ oz. amaretto

Fill an old-fashioned glass with ice. Pour in dry vermouth and amaretto. Give it a good stir.

French Cherry

1½ oz. dry vermouth
¾ oz. kirschwasser

Fill an old-fashioned glass with ice. Pour in dry vermouth and kirschwasser. Give it a good stir.

French Orange

1½ oz. dry vermouth
¾ oz. Grand Marnier

Fill an old-fashioned glass with ice. Pour in vermouth and Grand Marnier. Give it a good stir.

French Tri-Color

1½ oz. crème de violette
1½ oz. maraschino liqueur
¼ oz. grenadine

In a pousse-café glass, pour crème de violette, followed by maraschino liqueur, and finally grenadine.

> **Spills**
>
> When making a drink in a pousse-café glass, *always* pour the alcohols or ingredients in order of weight (i.e., heaviest first, and so on). Otherwise, you won't end up with the layered effect desired in a pousse-café–style cordial.

French Wench

2 oz. Dubonnet Rouge
4 oz. ginger ale
1 lime wedge

Fill a highball glass ½ full with ice. Pour in Dubonnet Rouge and ginger ale. Garnish with lime wedge.

Friar Tuck

2 oz. Frangelico
½ oz. crème de cacao
¼ oz. grenadine
¼ oz. lemon juice
1 maraschino cherry

Fill a cocktail shaker ½ full with ice. Pour in Frangelico, crème de cacao, grenadine, and lemon juice. Give it a good shake, and strain into a cocktail glass. Garnish with maraschino cherry.

> **Liquor Lingo**
>
> **Frangelico** is an Italian hazelnut-flavored liqueur.

Golden Cadillac

1½ oz. Galliano
¾ oz. crème de cacao
1 oz. light cream

Fill a cocktail shaker ½ full with ice. Pour in Galliano, crème de cacao, and light cream. Give it a good shake, and strain into a cocktail glass.

Golden Dream

1¼ oz. Galliano
¾ oz. triple sec
1 oz. orange juice
1 oz. light cream

Fill a cocktail shaker ½ full with ice. Pour in Galliano, triple sec, orange juice, and light cream. Give it a good shake, and strain into a cocktail glass.

Golden Slipper

1 oz. green Chartreuse
1 oz. kirschwasser
1 egg yolk

Fill a cocktail shaker ½ full with ice. Pour in green Chartreuse, kirschwasser, and egg yolk. Give it a good, vigorous shake, and strain into a cocktail glass.

Graceland

1 oz. dry vermouth
1 oz. sweet vermouth
1 oz. Scotch whisky
1 dash bitters
1 lemon twist

Fill a cocktail shaker ½ full with ice. Pour in dry vermouth, sweet vermouth, and Scotch whisky, and add bitters. Give it a good stir, and strain into a cocktail glass. Garnish with lemon twist.

Grasshopper

1 oz. green crème de menthe
1 oz. white crème de cacao
1 oz. light cream

Fill a cocktail shaker ½ full with ice. Pour in green crème de menthe, white crème de cacao, and light cream. Give it a good shake, and strain into a cocktail glass.

Green Eyes

2 oz. Lillet
½ oz. crème de menthe
1 dash orange bitters

Fill a cocktail shaker ½ full with ice. Pour in Lillet and crème de menthe, and add orange bitters. Give it a good shake, and strain into a cocktail glass.

Green Gables

1½ oz. sweet vermouth
1 oz. gin
½ oz. green Chartreuse

Fill a cocktail shaker ½ full with ice. Pour in sweet vermouth, gin, and green Chartreuse. Give it a good shake, and strain into a cocktail glass.

Green Lizard

1½ oz. green Chartreuse
1 oz. 151 proof rum

Fill a cocktail shaker ½ full with ice. Pour in green Chartreuse and 151 proof rum. Give it a good shake, and strain into a rocks glass full of ice.

Hilgert

1 oz. dry vermouth
¾ oz. gin
1 tsp. maraschino liqueur
¼ oz. grapefruit juice
1 dash bitters

Fill a cocktail shaker ½ full with ice. Pour in dry vermouth, gin, maraschino liqueur, and grapefruit juice, and add bitters. Give it a good shake, and strain into a cocktail glass.

Irish Flag

1 oz. green crème de menthe
1 oz. Irish cream
1 oz. brandy

In a pousse-café glass, add green crème de menthe, followed by Irish cream, and finally brandy.

Kaytee

1½ oz. dry vermouth
1 oz. dry sherry
1 tsp. pastis
1 lemon twist

Fill a cocktail shaker ½ full with ice. Pour in dry vermouth, dry sherry, and pastis. Give it a good shake, and strain into a cocktail glass. Garnish with lemon twist.

King Alphonse

2 oz. dark crème de cacao
1 oz. heavy cream

Fill an old-fashioned glass with ice. Pour in dark crème de cacao, and top with heavy cream.

King Kenneth

1½ oz. Campari
½ oz. peach brandy
1 oz. orange juice
½ oz. lemon juice
4 oz. tonic water
1 lemon wedge

Fill a cocktail shaker ½ full with ice. Pour in Campari, peach brandy, orange juice, and lemon juice. Give it a good shake, and strain into a Collins glass ½ full of ice. Pour in tonic water. Garnish with lemon wedge.

Lady Evelyn

1½ oz. dry vermouth
1 oz. gin
½ oz. triple sec
1 lemon twist

Fill a cocktail shaker ½ full with ice. Pour in dry vermouth, gin, and triple sec. Give it a good shake, and strain into a cocktail glass. Garnish with lemon twist.

Lady Godiva

1 oz. white crème de cacao
1 oz. anisette
1 oz. light cream

Fill a cocktail shaker ½ full with ice. Pour in white crème de cacao, anisette, and light cream. Give it a good shake, and strain into a cocktail glass.

Lady Hopkins

2 oz. Southern Comfort
½ oz. passion fruit syrup
½ oz. lime juice
1 maraschino cherry
1 orange slice

Fill a cocktail shaker ½ full with ice. Pour in Southern Comfort, passion fruit syrup, and lime juice. Give it a good shake, and strain into a cocktail glass. Garnish with maraschino cherry and orange slice.

Lady Madonna

1½ oz. Lillet
1½ oz. dry vermouth
1 lemon twist

Fill a cocktail shaker ½ full with ice. Pour in Lillet and dry vermouth. Give it a good stir, and strain into a cocktail glass. Garnish with lemon twist.

Leo's Special

1 oz. sweet vermouth
1 oz. brandy
½ oz. Benedictine
¼ oz. lemon juice
1 dash bitters

Fill a cocktail shaker ½ full with ice. Pour in sweet vermouth, brandy, Benedictine, and lemon juice, and add bitters. Give it a good shake, and strain into a cocktail glass.

Lillet Cocktail

2 oz. Lillet
1 oz. gin
1 lemon twist

Fill a cocktail shaker ½ full with ice. Pour in Lillet and gin. Give it a good stir, and strain into a cocktail glass. Garnish with lemon twist.

Mary Jane

1 oz. Dubonnet Rouge
1 oz. gin
½ oz. dry vermouth
½ oz. orange juice

Fill a cocktail shaker ½ full with ice. Pour in Dubonnet Rouge, gin, dry vermouth, and orange juice. Give it a good shake, and strain into a cocktail glass.

Mary's Delight

1½ oz. sweet vermouth
1½ oz. brandy
1 dash orange bitters
1 orange twist

Fill a cocktail shaker ½ full with ice. Pour in sweet vermouth and brandy, and add orange bitters. Give it a good stir, and strain into a cocktail glass. Garnish with orange twist.

Mayflower

1½ oz. sweet vermouth
1 oz. dry vermouth
1 oz. brandy
1 tsp. pastis
1 tsp. triple sec
2 dashes orange bitters
1 lemon twist

Fill a cocktail shaker ½ full with ice. Pour in sweet vermouth, dry vermouth, brandy, pastis, and triple sec, and add orange bitters. Give it a good stir, and strain into a cocktail glass. Garnish with lemon twist.

Memphis Belle

½ peach, pit removed
1 maraschino cherry
2 oz. Southern Comfort
1 oz. club soda

Muddle peach and maraschino cherry in the bottom of an old-fashioned glass. Fill the glass with ice, and pour in Southern Comfort and club soda. Give it a good stir.

Mercenary

2 oz. dry vermouth
½ oz. Armagnac
1 tsp. green crème de menthe

Fill a cocktail shaker ½ full with ice. Pour in dry vermouth, Armagnac, and green crème de menthe. Give it a good shake, and strain into a cocktail glass.

Muddy River

1½ oz. dark crème de cacao
1 oz. coffee liqueur
1 oz. vodka
1 oz. cream

Fill a cocktail shaker ½ full with ice. Pour in dark crème de cacao, coffee liqueur, vodka, and cream. Give it a good shake, and strain into a cocktail glass.

Negroni

1 oz. Campari
1 oz. sweet vermouth
1 oz. gin

Fill a cocktail shaker ½ full with ice. Pour in Campari, sweet vermouth, and gin. Give it a good stir, and strain into a cocktail glass.

Cocktail Conversation

The Negroni comes to us from that beautiful land where the Bellini was born—Italy. The story goes that Count Camillo Negroni asked for gin to be added to his Americano cocktail. From then on, the drink was named after him.

Nice Iced Tea

Erik Johnson, the beverage manager at Sel de La Terre in Boston, created this southern French version of the Long Island Iced Tea, named for the Riviera city, Nice. It's the perfect tipple for summer sipping.

3 oz. lavender-infused Red Lillet (recipe follows)
2 oz. Stoli Ohranj vodka
1 TB. lemon juice
2 oz. ginger ale
1 lemon slice

Pour lavender-infused Red Lillet, Stoli Ohranj vodka, and lemon juice into a Delmonico glass. Top with ginger ale. Give it a good stir, and garnish with lemon slice.

Cocktail Conversation

To make lavender-infused Red Lillet: Add 5 handfuls dried lavender leaf to 1 (750-ml) bottle Red Lillet. Shake to mix and then let it steep on its side for at least 24 hours. Strain liquid, wash out the empty bottle to remove all lavender leaves, and refill with infused Red Lillet. If lavender infusion is too strong, dilute with Lillet to taste.

Paradise

1½ oz. apricot brandy
¾ oz. gin
1 oz. orange juice

Fill a cocktail shaker ½ full with ice. Pour in apricot brandy, gin, and orange juice. Give it a good shake, and strain into a cocktail glass.

Peppermint Patty

1½ oz. white crème de menthe
1½ oz. white crème de cacao

Fill a cocktail shaker ½ full with ice. Pour in white crème de menthe and white crème de cacao. Give it a good shake, and strain into an old-fashioned glass full of ice.

Peppermint Twist

1 oz. peppermint schnapps
1 oz. coffee liqueur
1 oz. dark crème de cacao

Fill a cocktail shaker ½ full with ice. Pour in peppermint schnapps, coffee liqueur, and dark crème de cacao. Give it a good shake, and strain into a cocktail glass.

Phoebe Snow

1½ oz. Dubonnet Rouge
1½ oz. brandy
1 tsp. pastis

Fill a cocktail shaker ½ full with ice. Pour in Dubonnet Rouge, brandy, and pastis. Give it a good shake, and strain into a cocktail glass.

Pimm's Cup

In the French Quarter in sultry, slow-you-down New Orleans is a place called Napolean House. Here you'll get the best Pimm's Cup anywhere, hands down. (And yes, I mean that and stand by it and challenge anyone to find a better example!) It's entirely refreshing—and slightly dangerous in that you can truly throw back a few and not realize it's hitting you at all (all the better that the French Quarter is easier to do on foot). On one of my last visits, I asked my waiter what's in it. He wouldn't reveal exact measurements, but he did give me some basic instructions. After some tinkering, here's a reasonable facsimile:

2½ oz. Pimm's
2 oz. lemonade
1 TB. lemon-lime soda
2 dashes Peychaud bitters
1 cucumber slice

Fill a cocktail shaker ½ full with ice. Pour in Pimm's, lemonade, lemon-lime soda, and bitters. Give it a good stir, and strain into a highball glass ¾ full of ice. Garnish with cucumber slice.

Pink Squirrel

1 oz. crème de cacao
1 oz. crème de noyaux
1 oz. heavy cream

Fill a cocktail shaker ½ full with ice. Pour in crème de cacao, crème de noyaux, and heavy cream. Give it a good shake, and strain into a cocktail glass.

Pousse-Café

1 oz. peach liqueur
1 oz. kirschwasser
1 oz. pastis

In a pousse-café glass, pour peach liqueur, followed by kirschwasser, and finally pastis.

Sloe Comfortable Screw

1 oz. sloe gin
1 oz. Southern Comfort
4 oz. orange juice

Pour sloe gin, Southern Comfort, and orange juice into a highball glass ½ full of ice. Give it a good stir.

Sloe Gin Cocktail

2½ oz. sloe gin
½ oz. dry vermouth
2 dashes orange bitters

Fill a cocktail shaker ½ full with ice. Pour in sloe gin and dry vermouth, and add orange bitters. Give it a good shake, and strain into a cocktail glass.

Sloe Gin Cooler

2 oz. sloe gin
1 oz. gin
2 oz. cranberry juice
½ oz. lemon juice
½ tsp. superfine sugar

Fill a cocktail shaker ½ full with ice. Pour in sloe gin, gin, cranberry juice, and lemon juice, and add superfine sugar. Give it a good shake, and strain into a highball glass ½ full of ice.

Sloe Gin Fizz

2 oz. sloe gin
¾ oz. lemon juice
1 oz. simple syrup
1 oz. club soda

Fill a cocktail shaker ½ full with ice. Pour in sloe gin, lemon juice, and simple syrup. Give it a good shake, and strain into a Delmonico glass. Top with club soda.

Sombrero

2 oz. Kahlùa
1 oz. cream

Fill a cocktail shaker ½ full with ice. Pour in Kahlùa and cream. Give it a good shake, and strain into a cocktail glass.

Southern Coffee

1½ oz. Southern Comfort
½ oz. coffee liqueur
3 oz. hot coffee

Pour Southern Comfort and coffee liqueur into an Irish coffee glass. Add hot coffee, and give it a good stir.

Southern Coffee Deluxe

1½ oz. Southern Comfort
½ oz. crème de cacao
3 oz. hot coffee

Pour Southern Comfort and crème de cacao into an Irish coffee glass. Add hot coffee, and give it a good stir.

Southern Comfort Sour

2 oz. Southern Comfort
¾ oz. lemon juice
1 oz. simple syrup
1 orange slice
1 maraschino cherry

Fill a cocktail shaker ½ full with ice. Pour in Southern Comfort, lemon juice, and simple syrup. Give it a good shake, and strain into a highball glass ¾ full of ice. Garnish with orange slice and maraschino cherry.

Southern Slammer

1½ oz. amaretto
1 oz. Southern Comfort
½ oz. sloe gin
¼ oz. lemon juice

Fill a cocktail shaker ½ full with ice. Pour in amaretto, Southern Comfort, sloe gin, and lemon juice. Give it a good shake, and strain into a cocktail glass.

Sunrise

¼ oz. grenadine
¼ oz. crème de violette
¼ oz. yellow Chartreuse
¼ oz. triple sec

In a pousse-café glass, add grenadine, followed by crème de violette, followed by yellow Chartreuse, and finally triple sec.

Thanksgiving Cocktail

1 oz. dry vermouth
1 oz. gin
1 oz. apricot brandy
1 tsp. lemon juice
1 orange twist

Fill a cocktail shaker ½ full with ice. Pour in dry vermouth, gin, apricot brandy, and lemon juice. Give it a good shake, and strain into a cocktail glass. Garnish with orange twist.

Toasted Almond

2 oz. amaretto
2 oz. coffee liqueur
2 oz. light cream

Fill a cocktail shaker ½ full with ice. Pour in amaretto, coffee liqueur, and cream. Give it a good shake, and strain into a highball glass ½ full of ice.

Triplet

1 oz. Lillet
1 oz. Drambuie
1 oz. Scotch whisky

Fill a cocktail shaker ½ full with ice. Pour in Lillet, Drambuie, and Scotch whisky. Give it a good shake, and strain into a cocktail glass.

Vermouth Cassis

2 oz. dry vermouth
½ oz. crème de cassis
1 lemon twist

Fill a cocktail shaker ½ full with ice. Pour in dry vermouth and crème de cassis. Give it a good stir, and strain into a wine glass. Garnish with lemon twist.

Vermouth Cocktail

1½ oz. sweet vermouth
1½ oz. dry vermouth
2 dashes orange bitters
1 maraschino cherry

Fill a cocktail shaker ½ full with ice. Pour in sweet vermouth and dry vermouth, and add orange bitters. Give it a good stir, and strain into a cocktail glass. Garnish with maraschino cherry.

Vermouth Cooler

2 oz. sweet vermouth
1 oz. vodka
4 oz. lemon-lime soda
1 lemon wedge

Fill a Collins glass ¾ full with ice. Pour in sweet vermouth, vodka, and lemon-lime soda. Give it a good stir, and garnish with lemon wedge.

Vermouth Frappé

2 oz. sweet vermouth
1 dash bitters

Fill a cocktail shaker ½ full with ice. Pour in sweet vermouth, and add bitters. Give it a good stir, and strain into a cocktail glass.

Victor

1½ oz. sweet vermouth
1 oz. brandy
1 oz. gin

Fill a cocktail shaker ½ full with ice. Pour in sweet vermouth, brandy, and gin. Give it a good stir, and strain into a cocktail glass.

Viking

2 oz. Galliano
1 oz. *aquavit*

Fill a cocktail shaker ½ full with ice. Pour in Galliano and aquavit. Give it a good shake, and strain into a rocks glass full of ice.

Liquor Lingo

Aquavit is a caraway-flavored liqueur from Scandinavia.

Wedding Belle

1½ oz. Dubonnet Rouge
¾ oz. gin
¾ oz. cherry Heering
½ oz. orange juice

Fill a cocktail shaker ½ full with ice. Pour in Dubonnet Rouge, gin, cherry Heering, and orange juice. Give it a good shake, and strain into a cocktail glass.

Wild Redhead

2 oz. cherry Heering
1½ oz. lemon juice
1½ oz. simple syrup
1 maraschino cherry

Fill a cocktail shaker ½ full with ice. Pour in cherry Heering, lemon juice, and simple syrup. Give it a good shake, and strain into a Delmonico glass. Garnish with maraschino cherry.

Chapter 13

Wine, Beer, and Sake

Burgundy makes you think of silly things; Bordeaux makes you talk about them, and Champagne makes you do them.

—Anthelme Brillat-Savarin

Wine

Adonis Cocktail

2 oz. sherry
1 oz. sweet vermouth
1 dash orange bitters
1 orange twist

Fill a mixing glass ½ full with ice. Pour in sherry and sweet vermouth, and add orange bitters. Give it a good stir, and strain into a cocktail glass. Garnish with orange twist.

Americana

1 tsp. superfine sugar
1 dash bitters
¼ oz. bourbon
5 oz. champagne
1 brandied peach slice

Fill a cocktail shaker ½ full with ice. Add superfine sugar and bitters and then pour in bourbon. Give it a good stir. Pour in champagne, and garnish with brandied peach slice.

Andalusia

2 oz. dry sherry
½ oz. rum
½ oz. cognac
1 dash bitters

Fill a mixing glass ½ full with ice. Pour in dry sherry, rum, and cognac, and add bitters. Give it a good stir, and strain into a cocktail glass.

Apple Ginger Cocktail

1½ oz. applejack brandy
¾ oz. ginger liqueur
¾ oz. lime juice
1 oz. simple syrup

Fill a mixing glass ½ full with ice. Pour in applejack brandy, ginger liqueur, lime juice, and simple syrup. Give it a good shake, and strain into a cocktail glass.

Apple Ginger Sangaree

½ tsp. superfine sugar
2 oz. *ginger wine*
1 oz. applejack brandy
1 lemon wedge

Fill an old-fashioned glass with ice. Pour in superfine sugar, ginger wine, and applejack brandy. Give it a good stir, and garnish with lemon wedge.

Liquor Lingo

Ginger wine is a British fortified wine flavored with ginger, other spices, and raisins. It contains about 12 percent alcohol.

Bamboo

1½ oz. dry sherry
1½ oz. sweet vermouth
1 TB. lemon juice
1 dash bitters
1 lemon twist

Fill a mixing glass ½ full with ice. Pour in dry sherry, sweet vermouth, and lemon juice, and add bitters. Give it a good stir, and strain into a cocktail glass. Garnish with lemon twist.

Bellini

2 oz. peach nectar
4 oz. *Prosecco*

Pour peach nectar into a champagne flute. Add Prosecco.

Liquor Lingo

Prosecco is a dry, sparkling Italian wine.

Black Pearl

1 oz. cognac
½ oz. coffee liqueur
4 oz. champagne

Pour cognac and coffee liqueur into a champagne flute. Add champagne.

Brandied Madeira

1½ oz. Madeira
1½ oz. brandy
½ oz. dry vermouth
1 lemon twist

Fill a mixing glass ½ full with ice. Pour in Madeira, brandy, and dry vermouth. Give it a good stir, and strain into a cocktail glass. Garnish with lemon twist.

Brandied Port

1½ oz. port
1 oz. brandy
½ oz. maraschino liqueur
¼ oz. lemon juice

Fill a mixing glass ½ full with ice. Pour in port, brandy, maraschino liqueur, and lemon juice. Give it a good shake, and strain into a cocktail glass.

Broken Spur

2 oz. port
1 oz. sweet vermouth
½ oz. orange curaçao

Fill a mixing glass ½ full with ice. Pour in port wine, sweet vermouth, and orange curaçao. Give it a good stir, and strain into a cocktail glass.

Buck's Fizz

2 oz. orange juice
½ oz. triple sec
4 oz. champagne

Pour orange juice and triple sec into a champagne flute. Fill with champagne.

Burgundy Ginger Cocktail

1½ oz. burgundy
¾ oz. gin
¾ oz. orange juice
1 tsp. ginger extract

Fill a mixing glass ½ full with ice. Pour in burgundy, gin, orange juice, and ginger extract. Give it a good shake, and strain into a cocktail glass.

Byculla

1 oz. sherry
1 oz. port
¾ oz. triple sec
¾ oz. ginger brandy

Fill a mixing glass ½ full with ice. Pour in sherry, port, triple sec, and ginger brandy. Give it a good shake, and strain into a cocktail glass.

> **Liquor Lingo**
>
> **Ginger brandy** is—you guessed it—a ginger-flavored brandy liqueur.

Chablis Cooler

1 oz. vodka
¼ oz. grenadine
¼ oz. lemon juice
4 oz. Chablis

Pour vodka, grenadine, and lemon juice into an ice-filled highball glass. Top with Chablis, and give it a good stir.

Champagne Buck

1 oz. gin
¼ oz. cherry brandy
¾ oz. orange juice
2 oz. champagne
1 orange twist

Pour gin, cherry brandy, and orange juice into a highball glass filled with ice. Add in champagne, and garnish with orange twist.

Champagne Cocktail

1 lump sugar
2 dashes bitters
5 oz. champagne
1 lemon twist

Drop sugar lump into a champagne flute, and drip bitters over it. Pour in champagne, and garnish with lemon twist.

Champagne Julep

5 mint leaves
1 tsp. superfine sugar
2 oz. bourbon
4 oz. champagne

Muddle mint leaves with superfine sugar in a few drops water in a high-ball glass. Fill the glass ½ full with ice. Pour in bourbon and champagne.

Champagne Normandy

1 sugar cube or 1 tsp. sugar
1 oz. calvados
2 dashes bitters
3 oz. champagne

Fill a mixing glass ½ full with ice. Add in sugar, and pour in calvados and bitters. Give it a good stir, and strain into a cocktail glass. Pour in champagne.

Champagne Royal

1 oz. raspberry liqueur
1 oz. brandy
4 oz. champagne

Pour raspberry liqueur and brandy into a champagne flute. Top with champagne.

Champagne Velvet

3 oz. stout
3 oz. champagne

Pour stout into a champagne flute, followed by champagne.

Claret Cup

4 oz. *claret*
1 oz. brandy
1 oz. framboise
¼ oz. grenadine
½ oz. lemon juice
3 oz. club soda

Fill a Collins glass ¾ full with ice. Pour in claret, brandy, framboise, grenadine, and lemon juice. Give it a good stir, and top with club soda.

Liquor Lingo

Claret is the British terminology for Bordeaux red.

Czar

1 oz. vodka
1 oz. cherry Heering
1 dash bitters
6 oz. champagne

Fill a mixing glass ½ full with ice. Pour in vodka, cherry Heering, and bitters. Give it a good shake, and strain into a wine glass. Pour in champagne.

Danny's Delight

1 oz. ginger wine
1 oz. Irish whiskey
½ oz. sweet vermouth
1 oz. lemonade
1 dash bitters

Fill a mixing glass ½ full with ice. Pour in ginger wine, Irish whiskey, sweet vermouth, and lemonade, and add bitters. Give it a good shake, and strain into an old-fashioned glass ¾ full of ice.

Double Derby Sour

2 oz. merlot
2 oz. bourbon
¼ oz. grenadine
1 oz. orange juice
½ oz. lime juice
2 oz. iced tea
1 orange slice
1 maraschino cherry

Fill a mixing glass ½ full with ice. Pour in merlot, bourbon, grenadine, orange juice, and lime juice. Give it a good shake, and strain into a Collins glass ¾ full of ice. Pour in iced tea, and give it a good stir. Garnish with orange slice and maraschino cherry.

Gluehwein

4 oz. merlot
1 oz. orange juice
1 tsp. sugar
2 cinnamon sticks
2 orange peels
2 lemon peels
1 whole clove

Pour merlot and orange juice in a small saucepan. Add sugar, cinnamon sticks, orange peels, lemon peels, and whole clove, and give it a good stir. Heat over medium-high flame until simmering. Strain into an Irish coffee glass.

King's Peg

1½ oz. brandy
4 oz. champagne

Pour brandy and then champagne into a champagne flute.

Kir Royale

½ oz. *crème de cassis*
6 oz. champagne

Pour crème de cassis and then champagne into a champagne flute.

Liquor Lingo

Crème de cassis is a black currant–flavored liqueur.

Madeira Cocktail

1½ oz. Madeira
¾ oz. cognac
¾ oz. Strega

Fill a mixing glass ½ full with ice.
Pour in Madeira, cognac, and Strega.
Give it a good stir, and strain into a
cocktail glass.

Mary Rose

1½ oz. port
¾ oz. gin
¾ oz. cherry liqueur

Fill a mixing glass ½ full with ice.
Pour in port, gin, and cherry liqueur.
Give it a good stir, and strain into a
cocktail glass.

Mimosa

½ oz. triple sec
1 oz. orange juice
4 oz. champagne

Pour triple sec and orange juice into
a champagne flute. Top with champagne.

Port Flip

2 oz. port
½ oz. Benedictine
1 egg
1 tsp. sugar
¼ tsp. grated nutmeg

Fill a mixing glass ½ full with ice.
Pour in port, Benedictine, egg, and
sugar. Give it a good, vigorous shake,
and strain into a cocktail glass. Garnish with grated nutmeg.

Port of Comfort

2 oz. tawny port
1½ oz. Southern Comfort
½ oz. dry vermouth
1 orange twist

Fill a mixing glass ½ full with ice.
Pour in tawny port, Southern Comfort, and dry vermouth. Give it a good
shake, and strain into a cocktail glass.
Garnish with orange twist.

Port Wine Cocktail

2½ oz. port
1½ oz. brandy
1 tsp. lemon juice
1 lemon twist

Fill a mixing glass ½ full with ice.
Pour in port, brandy, and lemon juice.
Give it a good stir, and strain into a
cocktail glass. Garnish with lemon
twist.

Queen's Cousin

2 oz. vodka
½ oz. Grand Marnier
1 tsp. triple sec
¼ oz. lime juice
2 dashes orange bitters
4 oz. champagne

Fill a mixing glass ½ full with ice.
Pour in vodka, Grand Marnier, triple
sec, and lime juice, and add orange
bitters. Give it a good shake, and
strain into a wine glass. Top with
champagne.

Red Wine Cooler

4 oz. red wine
½ oz. cherry brandy
½ oz. orange juice
½ oz. simple syrup
1 dash orange bitters
2 oz. club soda
1 orange slice

Fill a highball glass ½ full with ice.
Pour in red wine, cherry brandy,
orange juice, and simple syrup, and
add orange bitters. Give it a good stir,
and top with club soda. Garnish with
orange slice.

Ruby Rosé Punch

3 oz. rosé wine
¾ oz. cherry brandy
¼ oz. grenadine
1 oz. orange juice
½ oz. lemon juice
1 oz. club soda
1 orange slice

Fill a mixing glass ½ full with ice.
Pour in rosé wine, cherry brandy,
grenadine, orange juice, and lemon
juice. Give it a good shake, and strain
into a highball glass ½ full with ice.
Garnish with orange slice.

Sans Souci

2 oz. white port
1 oz. Galliano
½ tsp. kummel
1 dash orange bitters
1 orange twist

Fill a mixing glass ½ full with ice.
Pour in port, Galliano, and kummel,
and add orange bitters. Give it a good,
vigorous shake, and strain into a cocktail glass. Garnish with orange twist.

Spritzer

4 oz. white wine
3 oz. club soda
1 lemon wedge

Fill a highball glass ½ full with ice.
Pour in white wine and club soda.
Garnish with lemon wedge.

Town and Country

While visiting my friend Dave Brown in East Nashville, he took my husband and me to dinner at the fantastic Laundromat-turned-restaurant, The Family Wash. Amiable chef/owner Julia Helton contributed this local favorite, a sort of down-home play on the spritzer.

4 oz. red wine	Fill a highball glass ½ full with ice.
3 oz. cola	Pour in red wine and cola.

White Wine Cooler

4 oz. white wine	Fill a highball glass ½ full with ice.
½ oz. apple brandy	Pour in white wine, apple brandy,
½ oz. lemon juice	lemon juice, and simple syrup, and
¾ oz. simple syrup	add orange bitters. Give it a good stir,
2 dashes orange bitters	and top with club soda. Garnish with
2 oz. club soda	lemon slice.
1 lemon slice	

Beer

Ale Flip

12 oz. dark ale	Fill a mixing glass ½ full with ice.
½ oz. brandy	Pour in dark ale, brandy, sugar, and
2 tsp. sugar	egg. Give it a good, vigorous shake,
1 egg	and strain into a pilsner glass. Garnish
¼ tsp. grated nutmeg	with grated nutmeg.

Atom Tan

6 oz. ale	Fill a mixing glass ½ full with ice.
2 oz. tequila	Pour in ale and tequila. Give it a good
4 oz. lemon-lime soda	shake, and strain into a pilsner glass. Pour in lemon-lime soda.

Beer Buster

2 oz. vodka	Pour vodka, Tabasco sauce, and beer
2 dashes Tabasco sauce	into a pint glass. Give it a good stir.
12 oz. beer	

Black and Tan

6 oz. ale
6 oz. stout

Pour ale into a pilsner glass. Slowly pour stout in on top.

Boilermaker

12 oz. beer
1½ oz. bourbon

Pour beer into a pint glass. Pour bourbon into a shot glass, and drop the shot glass in the pint glass full of beer.

Bomber

12 oz. beer
1½ oz. tequila

Pour beer into a pint glass. Pour tequila into a shot glass, and drop the shot glass in the pint glass full of beer.

Dog's Nose

1½ oz. gin
12 oz. ale

Pour gin into a pint glass and then fill with ale.

Dr. Pepper

1½ oz. amaretto
6 oz. cola
6 oz. ale

Pour amaretto, cola, and ale into a pilsner glass.

La Michelada

Manhattan's Rosa Mexicano serves this traditional popular Mexican drink.

1 lime wedge
1 tsp. salt
2 dashes Tabasco sauce
2 dashes Worcestershire sauce
1 oz. fresh lime juice
1 Mexican beer (traditionally Tecate)

Gently rub the rim of an old-fashioned glass with lime wedge. Sprinkle salt in a small dish, and place the glass upside down in the dish so the rim is coated with salt. Fill the glass ⅔ full with ice, and add Tabasco sauce, Worcestershire sauce, and lime juice. Pour in beer until the glass is ¾ full. Garnish with lime wedge.

Cocktail Conversation _____

Traditionally in Mexico, Maggi—which has a sweet, dry, earthy mushroom flavor—is used instead of Worcestershire sauce.

Lager and Lime

1 oz. Rose's lime juice
12 oz. beer
1 lime wedge

Pour Rose's lime juice into a beer stein. Pour in beer. Garnish with lime wedge.

Panache

10 oz. beer
4 oz. lemonade

Pour beer and lemonade into a pilsner glass.

Pink Panache

10 oz. beer
4 oz. pink lemonade

Pour beer and pink lemonade into a pilsner glass.

Red Eye

12 oz. beer
2 oz. tomato juice

Pour beer and tomato juice into a pilsner glass.

Root Beer

1½ oz. vodka
1½ oz. Galliano
6 oz. ale
4 oz. cola

Pour vodka, Galliano, ale, and cola into a pint glass. Give it a good stir.

Shandy

10 oz. ale
4 oz. lemon-lime soda

Pour ale and lemon-lime soda into a pilsner glass.

Stout Sangaree

1 tsp. superfine sugar
2 tsp. lemon juice
12 oz. stout
1 oz. brandy

Dissolve superfine sugar with lemon juice in a pilsner glass. Pour in stout, and drip brandy on top.

Sake

Asian Blush

Whether you're at the original in La Jolla, or the newer outpost in Palm Springs, Roppingi's desire to marry exotic Far Eastern and classic European flavors and techniques makes it a prime example of the exciting culinary adventures to be found on Southern California's restaurant scene. And it doesn't just stop on the plate, as you can see here with one of their signature cocktails.

1 oz. sake
1 oz. Skyy vodka
½ oz. peach schnapps
¾ oz. pineapple juice
¾ oz. cranberry juice
1 maraschino cherry

Fill a cocktail shaker ½ full with ice. Pour in sake, Skyy vodka, peach schnapps, pineapple juice, and cranberry juice. Give it a good shake, and strain into a chilled martini glass. Garnish with maraschino cherry.

(Adapted from SushiSamba.)

BBG's Sakura Matsuri Saketini

In spring 2005, Kenneth McClure, food and beverages director at The World Bar in The Trump World Tower, specially created a springtime saketine to celebrate the Sakura Matsuri, a.k.a. the Annual Cherry Blossom Festival—and, of course, the arrival of spring. Here, he graciously shares it with us.

3 oz. Sakura sake
½ oz. Cointreau
½ oz. maraschino liqueur
½ oz. lemon juice
½ oz. maraschino cherry juice
1 maraschino cherry
1 cherry blossom flower (season permitting)

Fill a cocktail shaker ½ full with ice. Pour in sake, Cointreau, maraschino liqueur, lemon juice, and maraschino cherry juice. Give it a good shake, and strain into a chilled martini glass. Garnish with maraschino cherry and cherry blossom flower.

Bo Hai

Created at Riingo in New York City, the Bo Hai is the restaurant's tribute to the classic "prohibition-era" martini, when bathtub gin was cut with roughly equal parts of vermouth. The beauty of this drink is the light fruitiness of the plum sake, which perfectly balances the particular herbal qualities of gin.

5 oz. Tanqueray No. Ten gin
3 oz. hakusan plum sake
1 ume boshi (pickled plum)

Fill a cocktail shaker ½ full with ice. Pour in Tanqueray No. Ten gin and hakusan plum sake. Give it a good shake, and strain into a cocktail glass. Garnish with ume boshi.

KiraKira

From the sake-savvy mixologists at SushiSamba Rio in Chicago comes this cutting-edge sake cocktail.

2 oz. shochu
2 oz. plum sake
1 TB. *sparkling sake*
1 crystallized star fruit

Fill a cocktail shaker ½ full with ice. Pour in the shochu and plum sake. Give it a good shake, and strain into a cocktail glass. Pour in sparkling sake, and garnish with crystallized star fruit.

Liquor Lingo

Kirakira is the Japanese word for "sparkling." Similar to champagne, **sparkling sake** undergoes a secondary fermentation in the bottle. The product is a sweet, slightly cloudy, effervescent sake.

Rising Sun

2 oz. Masumi sake
5 oz. orange juice
¼ tsp. grenadine

Fill a cocktail shaker ½ full with ice. Pour in Masumi sake, orange juice, and grenadine. Give it a good shake, and strain into a highball glass ½ full of ice.

Sake Cooler

Whether cooking with it or mixing up some new drinkable delight, Riingo is known for its love of sake. This simple Sake Cooler is as refreshing as it is easy to make.

1 lime slice
2 tsp. superfine bar salt
1 cucumber slice
2½ oz. Fukunishiki sake

Gently rub the rim of an old-fashioned glass with lime. Sprinkle superfine bar salt in a small dish, and place the glass upside down in the dish so the rim is coated with salt. Muddle cucumber and lime in a cocktail shaker. Pour in sake. Give it a good shake, and pour into an old-fashioned glass.

Sake Passion Fruit Caipirinha

For years, Tocqueville has been blazing the way on the dining scene in New York (a very tough town in which to be a pioneer), incorporating sake into its regular list of spirits years before the "saketini" became hot. The Sake Passion Fruit Caipirinha is its signature drink.

1 lime wedge
2 tsp. sugar
3 oz. sake
1 oz. Alizé
1 oz. passion fruit juice

Muddle lime and sugar in a 6-ounce glass. Add sake, Alizé, and passion fruit juice, and fill the glass with ice. Give it a good stir.

Sake to Me

1 oz. sake
3 oz. Grey Goose vodka
½ oz. white crème de cacao
2 coffee beans

Fill a cocktail shaker ½ full with ice. Pour in sake, Grey Goose vodka, and white crème de cacao. Give it a good shake, and strain into a cocktail glass. Garnish with coffee beans.

Cocktail Conversation

The Sake to Me and Rising Sun were created by the Broadway Lounge bartenders at Katan, the Time Square sushi bar in the Marriott Marquis.

Chapter 14

Punches and Pitchers

I have taken more good from alcohol than alcohol has taken from me.

—Winston Churchill

After-Party Punch

1 cup sugar
2½ cups vodka
4 cups pineapple juice
4 cups cranberry juice
64 oz. ginger ale

Add sugar to a punch bowl and then pour in vodka, pineapple juice, cranberry juice, and ginger ale. Fill punch bowl with ice.

Ambassador's Punch

1 qt. Eggnog (nonalcoholic; recipe in Chapter 17)
½ cup brandy
½ cup rum
¼ cup crème de cacao
1 TB. grated nutmeg

Pour Eggnog into a punch bowl. Whisk in brandy, rum, and crème de cacao. Fill punch bowl with ice, and top with grated nutmeg.

American Punch

25 oz. Southern Comfort (1 fifth)
1 oz. maraschino liqueur
2 qt. cola
16 oz. club soda
1 orange, cut into thin, round slices
1 lemon, cut into thin, round slices
1 lime, cut into thin, round slices
8 to 10 maraschino cherries

Pour Southern Comfort and maraschino liqueur into a punch bowl. Add cola and club soda. Stir with a wooden spoon, and fill punch bowl with ice. Garnish with orange, lemon, and lime slices and maraschino cherries.

Apricot Punch

1 qt. apricot brandy
1 qt. orange juice
1 (750-ml) bottle champagne
64 oz. lemon-lime soda

Pour apricot brandy and orange juice into a punch bowl. Add champagne and lemon-lime soda. Stir with a wooden spoon, and fill punch bowl with ice.

Artillery Punch

1 qt. bourbon
1 qt. red wine
2 cups dark rum
1 cup brandy
1 qt. iced orange pekoe tea
2 cups orange juice
1 cup lemon juice
1 cup simple syrup
1 lemon, cut into thin, round slices

Pour bourbon, red wine, dark rum, brandy, iced orange pekoe tea, orange juice, lemon juice, and simple syrup into a punch bowl. Stir with a wooden spoon, and fill punch bowl with ice. Garnish with lemon slices.

Aztec Punch

½ cup sugar
1 (10-oz.) can frozen lemonade
1 qt. tequila
64 oz. ginger ale
1 cup lime juice

Add sugar and frozen lemonade to a punch bowl. Pour in tequila, ginger ale, and lime juice. Stir with a wooden spoon, and fill punch bowl with ice.

Banana Rum Punch

1 (10-oz.) can frozen orange juice
1 qt. rum
1 cup crème de bananes
32 oz. ginger ale

Add frozen orange juice to a punch bowl. Pour in rum, crème de bananes, and ginger ale. Stir with a wooden spoon, and fill punch bowl with ice.

Bombay Punch

2 cups sweet sherry
2 cups brandy
⅓ cup triple sec
⅓ cup maraschino liqueur
1 (750-ml) bottle champagne
1 qt. soda water
1 cup lemon juice
1 cup simple syrup

Pour sweet sherry, brandy, triple sec, maraschino liqueur, champagne, soda water, lemon juice, and simple syrup into a punch bowl. Stir with a wooden spoon, and fill punch bowl with ice.

Brandy Punch

2 cups brandy
1 cup rum
4 cups pineapple juice
1 cup lemon juice
1 cup simple syrup
1 qt. ginger ale

Pour brandy, rum, pineapple juice, lemon juice, and simple syrup into a punch bowl. Pour in ginger ale last. Stir with a wooden spoon, and fill punch bowl with ice.

Brown Betty

⅔ cup brown sugar
2 cups water
32 oz. ale
8 oz. brandy
2 TB. lemon juice
3 whole cloves
1 tsp. cinnamon

Pour brown sugar and water into a large pot. Heat over low heat until sugar is dissolved. Add ale, brandy, lemon juice, cloves, and cinnamon. Simmer for 15 minutes. Serve in heat-proof cups, mugs, or Irish coffee glasses.

Canadian Rum Punch

4 cups water
2 cups sugar
2 cups Canadian whisky
2 cups rum
2 cups lemon juice

In a medium saucepan, heat water and sugar until sugar dissolves. Allow to cool. Pour Canadian whisky, rum, and lemon juice into a punch bowl. Add in water and sugar mix. Stir with a wooden spoon, and fill punch bowl with ice.

Champagne Pineapple Punch

1 (750-ml) bottle champagne
1 cup triple sec
½ cup brandy
4 cups pineapple juice
1 qt. club soda

Pour champagne, triple sec, brandy, pineapple juice, and club soda into a punch bowl. Stir with a wooden spoon, and fill punch bowl with ice.

Champagne Punch

1 (750-ml) bottle champagne
½ cup triple sec
½ cup brandy
1 qt. club soda

Pour champagne, triple sec, brandy, and club soda into a punch bowl. Stir with a wooden spoon, and fill punch bowl with ice.

Charlie's Coquito

My gentle-giant brother-in-law, Charlie "Carlos" Gueits, may have left his tiny town of Ponce, Puerto Rico, to live in New York, but he brought his family's coquito recipe with him, thank goodness. Making this rich, delicious, addictive punch may seem like an arduous process to endure, but it's well worth it.

12 coconuts, split
8 egg yolks
1 TB. vanilla extract
1 (14-oz.) can condensed milk
2 (14-oz.) cans evaporated milk
1 (16-oz.) can coconut milk
2 tsp. cinnamon
1 pt. brandy
1 pt. whisky
1 (1.5-l) bottle Barcardi white rum
2 (15-oz.) cans Coco López

Scrape out coconut meat and set aside. Beat egg yolks with vanilla extract until pale. Beat in condensed milk, evaporated milk, coconut milk, and cinnamon until smooth. Pour in brandy, whisky, Barcardi white rum, and Coco López and reserved coconut meat. Using a funnel, pour mixture into several empty 750-milliliter bottles with screwable tops. Shake and chill. Pour into a pitcher when ready to serve.

Cider Punch

1½ qt. hard cider
4 oz. Scotch whisky
4 oz. dry sherry
2 oz. lemon juice
4 oz. simple syrup
16 oz. apple juice
32 oz. club soda

Pour hard cider, Scotch whisky, dry sherry, lemon juice, simple syrup, apple juice, and club soda into a punch bowl. Stir with a wooden spoon, and fill punch bowl with ice.

Cranberry Punch

1 (750-ml) bottle vodka
2 qt. cranberry juice cocktail
1 cup lemon juice
1 cup simple syrup
1 qt. ginger ale

Pour vodka, cranberry juice cocktail, lemon juice, and simple syrup into a punch bowl. Pour in ginger ale last. Stir with a wooden spoon, and fill punch bowl with ice.

Donkey Punch

2 cups rum
1 cup grenadine
2 cups pineapple juice
48 oz. orange juice
32 oz. ginger ale
6 to 8 orange slices

Pour rum, grenadine, pineapple juice, and orange juice into a punch bowl. Pour in ginger ale last. Stir with a wooden spoon, and fill punch bowl with ice. Garnish with orange slices.

Down Home Punch

2 cups Jack Daniel's Tennessee whiskey
2 cups peach schnapps
¼ cup grenadine
¾ cup lemon juice
4 cups orange juice
1 cup simple syrup
16 oz. lemon-lime soda

Pour Jack Daniel's, peach schnapps, grenadine, lemon juice, orange juice, and simple syrup into a punch bowl. Pour in lemon-lime soda last. Stir with a wooden spoon, and fill punch bowl with ice.

Eggnog

12 eggs, separated
1 cup bourbon
1 cup cognac
3 pt. heavy cream
2 cups milk
2 tsp. vanilla extract
1 cup sugar
½ tsp. salt
3 tsp. grated nutmeg

Beat egg yolks until pale yellow and then mix in bourbon, cognac, heavy cream, milk, vanilla extract, and ½ cup sugar. In a separate bowl, whip egg whites with remaining ½ cup sugar and salt until they form stiff peaks. Fold egg whites into yolk-liqueur-cream mixture and chill. When ready to serve, garnish with grated nutmeg.

Fish House Punch

The Fish House is another name for the oldest men's club in the United States, The State in Schuylkill in Schuylkill County, Pennsylvania. The recipe for Fish House Punch comes from this old institution.

2 cups sugar
2 cups water
16 oz. lemon juice
16 oz. lime juice
50 oz. dark rum (2 fifths)
25 oz. cognac (1 fifth)
3 oz. peach brandy

Dissolve sugar with water, lemon juice, and lime juice in a punch bowl. Pour in dark rum, cognac, and peach brandy. Stir with a wooden spoon, and fill punch bowl with ice.

Florida Punch

1 (750-ml) bottle dark rum
1 qt. pineapple juice
2 cups orange juice
1 l club soda
1 orange, cut into thin round slices

Pour dark rum, pineapple juice, and orange juice into a punch bowl. Add club soda. Stir with a wooden spoon, and fill punch bowl with ice. Garnish with orange slices.

Fruit Basket Punch

4 oz. blackberry brandy
4 oz. triple sec
12 oz. crème de bananes
8 oz. coconut rum
12 oz. orange juice
8 oz. pineapple juice
12 oz. club soda

Pour blackberry brandy, triple sec, crème de bananes, coconut rum, orange juice, and pineapple juice into a punch bowl. Pour in club soda last. Stir with a wooden spoon, and fill punch bowl with ice.

Gin Bucket Punch

1 l gin
16 oz. lemonade
16 oz. fruit punch
32 oz. lemon-lime soda
6 orange slices
6 lemon slices
6 maraschino cherries

Pour gin, lemonade, and fruit punch into a punch bowl. Pour in lemon-lime soda last. Stir with a wooden spoon, and fill punch bowl with ice. Garnish with orange and lemon slices and maraschino cherries.

Glogg

1 (750-ml) bottle red wine
25 oz. brandy (1 fifth)
1½ cups sugar
1 cup raisins
1 cup blanched almonds
6 cardamom pods, crushed
3 cinnamon sticks
3 whole cloves
1 whole orange peel

Combine red wine, brandy, sugar, raisins, blanched almonds, crushed cardamom pods, cinnamon sticks, whole cloves, and orange peel in a heavy enamel or stainless-steel pot. Heat over medium heat until sugar is dissolved and liquid is simmering. Simmer 10 minutes and then remove from heat and serve warm.

Holiday Cheer

1 (10-oz.) can frozen cranberry juice cocktail
1 (750-ml) bottle champagne
½ cup Rose's lime juice
1 lime, cut into thin, round slices

Add frozen cranberry juice cocktail to a punch bowl. Pour in champagne and Rose's lime juice. Stir with a wooden spoon, and fill punch bowl with ice. Garnish with lime slices.

Holiday Rum Punch

1 (750-ml) bottle light rum
2 cups orange juice
½ cup lemon juice
¾ cup simple syrup
2 cups brewed and chilled orange pekoe tea
1 orange, cut into thin, round slices

Pour light rum, orange juice, lemon juice, simple syrup, and orange pekoe tea into a punch bowl. Stir with a wooden spoon, and fill punch bowl with ice. Garnish with orange slices.

Jamaican Punch

8 oz. dark rum
8 oz. coconut rum
4 oz. 151 proof rum
2 cups pineapple juice
2 cups orange juice
½ cup lime juice
¼ cup grenadine
1 lime, cut into thin, round slices

Pour dark rum, coconut rum, 151 proof rum, pineapple juice, orange juice, lime juice, and grenadine into a pitcher. Stir with a wooden spoon, and fill pitcher with ice. Garnish with lime slices.

Jungle Boogie Punch

25 oz. dark rum (1 fifth)
25 oz. light rum (1 fifth)
1 qt. pineapple juice
1 qt. orange juice
½ cup lime juice
16 oz. mango juice
16 oz. club soda
½ cup pineapple chunks
½ cup orange chunks
½ cup mango chunks

Pour dark rum, light rum, pineapple juice, orange juice, lime juice, and mango juice into a punch bowl. Pour in club soda last. Stir with a wooden spoon, and fill punch bowl with ice. Garnish with pineapple, orange, and mango chunks.

Mountain Red Punch

3 (750-ml) bottles red wine
½ cup amaretto
½ cup brandy
½ cup cherry liqueur
16 oz. ginger ale
¼ cup julienned almonds

Pour red wine, amaretto, brandy, and cherry liqueur into a punch bowl. Pour in ginger ale. Stir with a wooden spoon, and fill punch bowl with ice. Garnish with julienned almonds.

Nashville Eggnog

6 oz. bourbon
3 oz. brandy
3 oz. dark rum
1 qt. Eggnog (recipe in Chapter 17)
3 tsp. nutmeg

Pour bourbon, brandy, dark rum, and Eggnog into a punch bowl. Chill. Stir with a wooden spoon, and garnish with nutmeg.

Pineapple Punch

1 (750-ml) bottle champagne
16 oz. brandy
1 qt. pineapple juice
1 cup lemon juice
1 cup simple syrup
16 oz. club soda
1 cup pineapple chunks

Pour champagne, brandy, pineapple juice, lemon juice, and simple syrup into a punch bowl. Pour in club soda. Stir with a wooden spoon, and fill punch bowl with ice. Garnish with pineapple chunks.

Red Sangria "Cuba"

This great sangria recipe comes from Cuba restaurant in New York City.

1 apple, diced
1 orange, diced
2 TB. sugar
2 oz. Bacardi rum
1½ oz. triple sec
1 (750-ml) bottle pinot noir
¼ cup club soda

Fill a 32-ounce pitcher with ice. Add diced apple, diced orange, sugar, Bacardi rum, and triple sec. Stir with a wooden spoon, add pinot noir, and chill. Top with splash of club soda before serving.

Red Wine Punch

¼ cup superfine sugar
1 (750-ml) bottle red wine
1 cup orange juice
1 l club soda
6 orange slices

Add superfine sugar to a pitcher. Pour in red wine, orange juice, and club soda. Stir with a wooden spoon, and fill pitcher with ice. Garnish with orange slices.

Cocktail Conversation

For the Red Wine Punch or Red Sangria, use a less tannic red wine such as a pinot noir or a beaujolais.

Sauternes House Punch

½ cup sugar
1½ bottles Sauternes
1 oz. Grand Marnier
1 oz. orange curaçao
1 oz. maraschino liqueur

Add sugar to a pitcher. Pour in Sauternes, and stir with a wooden spoon until sugar dissolves. Pour in Grand Marnier, orange curaçao, and maraschino liqueur. Stir, fill pitcher with ice, and serve.

Liquor Lingo

Sauternes is a blend of sauvignon blanc and Semillon grapes. It is an elegant, fruity, sweet white wine mostly known as a dessert beverage. Sauternes can be expensive, so shop around and price-compare before purchasing.

Sparkling Sherbet Punch

2 (750-ml) bottles champagne

1 qt. cranberry juice

1 qt. orange sherbet

Pour champagne and cranberry juice into a punch bowl. Fill with ice, and add orange sherbet.

Sylva's Sangria Vida

Vida restaurant is my home away from home for many reasons. First and most important, the food is fantastic—deceptively simple but packed with well-thought-out and well-executed flavors. It's the same with owner Sylva Popaz's sangria. It looks innocent enough, sitting there in a glass jar on the pretty copper bar, but the flavors? Wow. It's a fruit explosion. This particular recipe makes about a gallon of sangria. Do—please do—try this at home.

½ cup sugar

3 bay leaves

3 cloves

2 star anise

4 (750-ml) bottles red Rioja wine

2 cups orange liqueur

2 cups brandy

2 cups peach juice

2 cups mango juice

In a punch bowl, add sugar, bay leaves, cloves, and star anise. Pour in Rioja wine, orange liqueur, brandy, peach juice, and mango juice. Fill with ice. Allow to sit overnight (or at least about 8 hours) in the refrigerator before serving.

Tocqueville Toddy

The genius of New York's Tocqueville in Union Square is that you have no idea how much work, planning, and genius goes into making it the local favorite it is. When you sit in the golden-walled serene dining room sipping a Tocqueville Toddy, the only thing on your mind is, *Ooo, I feel warm and happy.* Can't get there? Re-create the mood at home.

1 qt. apple cider

1 cup calvados

5 star anise

15 coriander seeds

5 whole cloves

5 cardamom pods

5 allspice berries

2 cinnamon sticks

1 vanilla bean, cut lengthwise, seeds scraped (use both for stronger flavor)

Zest of 1 lemon

Zest of 1 orange

In a medium to large pot, pour in apple cider and calvados. Add in star anise, coriander seeds, cloves, cardamom pods, allspice berries, cinnamon sticks, and vanilla bean. Simmer over low heat for 1 hour. Strain out star anise, coriander seeds, cloves, cardamom pods, allspice berries, cinnamon sticks, and vanilla bean. Add lemon zest and orange zest. Serve warm.

Vin d'Orange

Next to home, New Orleans may well be my favorite city—and certainly one that knows a few secrets about how to mix a proper cocktail (and has originated a few as well). On a recent visit, I dined at lovely Peristyle on Dumaine Street in the French Quarter, just up from Jackson Square. I noticed a corked glass jar the size and shape of a very, very large pumpkin on the bar with a gorgeous, golden-hued beverage with pieces of orange floating inside. The luscious, quenching concoction was Vin d'Orange, and Peristyle was kind enough to share it with me.

1 (750-ml) bottle dry white wine
½ cup 80 proof brandy, grappa, or vodka
4 oranges, quartered
1 lemon, quartered
½ vanilla bean, split lengthwise
½ cup simple syrup, or to taste
6 to 10 orange twists

Combine dry white wine, brandy, orange quarters, lemon quarters, and vanilla bean in an airtight container. Refrigerate for a maceration period of 3 to 4 weeks. Strain mixture through a cheesecloth into a pitcher or punch bowl to remove pulp, et al. Keep chilled until ready to serve. Add simple syrup just before serving. Garnish with orange twists.

A Yard of Flannel

32 oz. ale
4 oz. gold rum
4 eggs
¼ cup sugar
1 tsp. cinnamon
1 tsp. grated nutmeg

In a saucepan, heat ale over low heat. In a bowl, beat together gold rum, eggs, sugar, cinnamon, and grated nutmeg. Pour into a pitcher, and add in warm ale. Stir with a wooden spoon.

Spills

When serving warm drinks, be sure your glassware—whether it be a pitcher or individual glasses—is heat resistant!

Chapter 15

Frozen Drinks

Candy is dandy, but liquor is quicker.

—Ogden Nash

Anna's Banana

½ banana
1 TB. honey
3 oz. vodka
1 oz. lime juice

Fill a blender ¼ full with ice. Add banana and honey. Pour in vodka and lime juice. Blend on medium speed for 15 to 20 seconds. Pour into a goblet.

Apple Daiquiri

1½ oz. light rum
1 oz. applejack brandy
1 oz. lime juice
2 tsp. sugar
1 green apple slice

Fill a blender ¼ full with ice. Pour in light rum, applejack brandy, and lime juice, and add sugar. Blend on medium speed for 15 to 20 seconds. Pour into a goblet, and garnish with apple slice.

Banana Daiquiri

½ banana
1 tsp. sugar
2 oz. dark rum
1 oz. crème de bananes
1 tsp. grenadine
1 oz. lime juice

Fill a blender ¼ full with ice. Add banana and sugar. Pour in dark rum, crème de bananes, grenadine, and lime juice. Blend on medium speed for 15 to 20 seconds. Pour into a goblet.

Barbados Punch

2 oz. spiced rum
¼ oz. triple sec
2 oz. pineapple juice
1 oz. lime juice
1 tsp. sugar

Fill a blender ¼ full with ice. Pour in spiced rum, triple sec, pineapple juice, lime juice, and sugar. Blend on medium speed for 15 to 20 seconds. Pour into a goblet.

Batida Guava

2½ oz. *cachaca*
3 oz. guava nectar
½ oz. simple syrup

Fill a blender ¼ full with ice. Pour in cachaca, guava nectar, and simple syrup. Blend on medium speed for 15 to 20 seconds. Pour into a goblet.

Batida Mango

2½ oz. cachaca
3 oz. mango nectar
½ oz. simple syrup

Fill a blender ¼ full with ice. Pour in cachaca, mango nectar, and simple syrup. Blend on medium speed for 15 to 20 seconds. Pour into a goblet.

Batida Pineapple

½ cup pineapple chunks
2½ oz. cachaca
½ oz. simple syrup

Fill a blender ¼ full with ice. Add pineapple chunks. Pour in cachaca and simple syrup. Blend on medium speed for 15 to 20 seconds. Pour into a goblet.

Batida Strawberry

6 strawberries
2½ oz. cachaca
½ oz. simple syrup

Fill a blender ¼ full with ice. Add strawberries. Pour in cachaca and simple syrup. Blend on medium speed for 15 to 20 seconds. Pour into a goblet.

Berkeley

2 oz. light rum
½ oz. brandy
½ oz. passion fruit syrup
½ oz. lime juice
1 tsp. sugar

Fill a blender ¼ full with ice. Pour in light rum, brandy, passion fruit syrup, and lime juice, and add sugar. Blend on medium speed for 15 to 20 seconds. Pour into a goblet.

Blue Breeze

1½ oz. light rum
½ oz. blue curaçao
1 oz. cream of coconut
2 oz. pineapple juice

Fill a blender ¼ full with ice. Pour in light rum, blue curaçao, cream of coconut, and pineapple juice. Blend on medium speed for 15 to 20 seconds. Pour into a goblet.

Blue Hawaiian

2 oz. light rum
1 oz. blue curaçao
2 oz. pineapple juice
1 oz. cream of coconut
1 pineapple slice
1 maraschino cherry

Fill a blender ¼ full with ice. Pour in light rum, blue curaçao, pineapple juice, and cream of coconut. Blend on medium speed for 15 to 20 seconds. Pour into a goblet, and garnish with pineapple slice and maraschino cherry.

Cantaloupe Cup

3 oz. diced cantaloupe
1 tsp. sugar
2 oz. light rum
1 oz. orange juice
½ oz. lime juice

Fill a blender ¼ full with ice. Add cantaloupe and sugar. Pour in light rum, orange juice, and lime juice. Blend on medium speed for 15 to 20 seconds. Pour into a goblet.

Chi-Chi

2 oz. vodka
2 oz. cream of coconut
2 oz. pineapple juice
1 pineapple slice
1 maraschino cherry

Fill a blender ¼ full with ice. Pour in vodka, cream of coconut, and pineapple juice. Blend on medium speed for 15 to 20 seconds. Pour into a goblet, and garnish with pineapple slice and maraschino cherry.

Chilly Green Eyes

2 oz. light rum
1 oz. melon liqueur
½ oz. Rose's lime juice
½ oz. cream of coconut
2 oz. pineapple juice

Fill a blender ¼ full with ice. Pour in light rum, melon liqueur, Rose's lime juice, cream of coconut, and pineapple juice. Blend on medium speed for 15 to 20 seconds. Pour into a goblet.

Chocolate White Russian

1½ oz. vodka
½ oz. Kahlúa
1 oz. dark crème de cacao
2 oz. milk

Fill a blender ¼ full with ice. Pour in vodka, Kahlúa, and dark crème de cacao. Add milk. Blend on medium speed for 15 to 20 seconds. Pour into a goblet.

Variation: Really want to be decadent and throw calorie-caution to the wind? Add a scoop of vanilla ice cream to the Chocolate White Russian.

Coconut Toastie

2 oz. light rum
½ oz. coconut rum
2 scoops vanilla ice cream
¼ oz. cream
1 TB. toasted, shredded coconut

Pour light rum, coconut rum, vanilla ice cream, and cream into a blender. Blend on medium speed for 15 to 20 seconds. Pour into a goblet, and garnish with toasted coconut.

 Cocktail Conversation

To toast coconut, spread shredded coconut on a baking sheet and bake in a 350°F oven for 10 minutes or until light brown.

Cold Coffee Break

1½ oz. vodka
1½ oz. coffee liqueur
2 oz. cold espresso coffee
1 oz. cream

Fill a blender ¼ full with ice. Pour in vodka, coffee liqueur, cold espresso coffee, and cream. Blend on medium speed for 15 to 20 seconds. Pour into a goblet.

Devil's Tale

1½ oz. gold rum
1 oz. vodka
2 tsp. grenadine
¼ cup. lime juice
½ tsp. sugar
1 tsp. apricot liqueur

Fill a blender ¼ full with ice. Pour in gold rum, vodka, grenadine, lime juice, and sugar. Blend on medium speed for 15 to 20 seconds. Pour into a goblet. Drip apricot liqueur into center of cocktail.

Frozen Grasshopper

1½ oz. green crème de menthe
1½ oz. white crème de cacao
2 oz. light cream
1 mint sprig

Fill a blender ¼ full with ice. Pour in green crème de menthe, white crème de cacao, and light cream. Blend on medium speed for 15 to 20 seconds. Pour into a goblet, and garnish with mint sprig.

Frozen Mango Margarita

2 oz. tequila
1 oz. triple sec
1 oz. mango nectar
2 oz. lime juice
1 lime slice

Fill a blender ¼ full with ice. Pour in tequila, triple sec, mango nectar, and lime juice. Blend on medium speed for 15 to 20 seconds. Pour into a goblet, and garnish with lime slice.

Frozen Margarita

2 oz. tequila
1 oz. triple sec
2 oz. lime juice
1 lime slice

Fill a blender ¼ full with ice. Pour in tequila, triple sec, and lime juice. Blend on medium speed for 15 to 20 seconds. Pour into a goblet, and garnish with lime slice.

Cocktail Conversation

If you'd like salt with your margarita, rub the rim of the goblet with a lime wedge, and dip it into a saucer of bar salt, gently twisting the glass to coat the rim.

Frozen Matador

2 oz. tequila
2 oz. pineapple juice
½ oz. lime juice
1 TB. grenadine
1 lime wedge

Fill a blender ¼ full with ice. Pour in tequila, pineapple juice, lime juice, and grenadine. Blend on medium speed for 15 to 20 seconds. Pour into a goblet, and garnish with lime wedge.

Frozen Mud Slide

2 oz. vodka
2 oz. Kahlúa
2 oz. Irish cream
3 or 4 scoops vanilla ice cream

Pour vodka, Kahlúa, and Irish cream into a blender. Add in ice cream. Blend on medium speed for 15 to 20 seconds. Pour into a goblet.

Frozen Tidal Wave

1 oz. dark rum
1 oz. light rum
½ oz. tequila
½ oz. gin
½ oz. vodka
3 oz. pineapple juice
¼ oz. grenadine
1 pineapple slice

Fill a blender ¼ full with ice. Pour in dark rum, light rum, tequila, gin, vodka, pineapple juice, and grenadine. Blend on medium speed for 15 to 20 seconds. Pour into a goblet, and garnish with pineapple slice.

Gauguin

2½ oz. light rum
½ oz. passion fruit syrup
½ oz. lime juice
½ oz. lemon juice
1 tsp. sugar

Fill a blender ¼ full with ice. Pour in light rum, passion fruit syrup, lime juice, and lemon juice, and add sugar. Blend on medium speed for 15 to 20 seconds. Pour into a goblet.

Georgia Peach

2 oz. Southern Comfort
1 oz. peach schnapps
4 oz. orange juice
1 peach slice

Fill a blender ¼ full with ice. Pour in Southern Comfort, peach schnapps, and orange juice. Blend on medium speed for 15 to 20 seconds. Pour into a goblet, and garnish with peach slice.

Hawaiian Eye

2 oz. dark rum
1 oz. light rum
2 oz. pineapple juice
1 oz. guava nectar
1 tsp. rock candy syrup
1 pineapple slice

Fill a blender ¼ full with ice. Pour in dark rum, light rum, pineapple juice, guava nectar, and rock candy syrup. Blend on medium speed for 15 to 20 seconds. Pour into a goblet, and garnish with pineapple slice.

Jamaican Banana Colada

½ banana
2 oz. dark rum
1 oz. light crème de cacao
2 oz. Coco López
1 oz. pineapple juice
1 apple slice

Fill a blender ¼ full with ice. Add in banana. Pour in dark rum, light crème de cacao, Coco López, and pineapple juice. Blend on medium speed for 15 to 20 seconds. Pour into a goblet, and garnish with apple slice.

Kentucky Blizzard

2½ oz. bourbon
1 tsp. grenadine
1 oz. cranberry juice
½ oz. lime juice
¼ oz. simple syrup

Fill a blender ¼ full with ice. Pour in bourbon, grenadine, cranberry juice, lime juice, and simple syrup. Blend on medium speed for 15 to 20 seconds. Pour into a goblet.

Mango Daiquiri

2 oz. light rum
2 oz. mango nectar
1 oz. lime juice
2 tsp. sugar

Fill a blender ¼ full with ice. Pour in light rum, mango nectar, and lime juice, and add sugar. Blend on medium speed for 15 to 20 seconds. Pour into a goblet.

Mint Daiquiri

2 oz. light rum
½ oz. peppermint schnapps
1 oz. lime juice
2 tsp. sugar
8 mint leaves
1 mint sprig

Fill a blender ¼ full with ice. Pour in light rum, peppermint schnapps, and lime juice, and add sugar and mint leaves. Blend on medium speed for 15 to 20 seconds. Pour into a goblet, and garnish with mint sprig.

Peach Daiquiri

2 oz. light rum
2 oz. peach nectar
1 oz. lime juice
2 tsp. sugar

Fill a blender ¼ full with ice. Pour in light rum, peach nectar, and lime juice, and add sugar. Blend on medium speed for 15 to 20 seconds. Pour into a goblet.

Pensacola

2 oz. light rum
1 oz. guava nectar
½ oz. orange juice
½ oz. lemon juice

Fill a blender ¼ full with ice. Pour in rum, guava nectar, orange juice, and lemon juice. Blend on medium speed for 15 to 20 seconds. Pour into a goblet.

Piña Colada

1½ oz. light rum
1½ oz. dark rum
2 oz. Coco López
3 oz. pineapple juice
½ oz. heavy cream
1 pineapple slice
1 maraschino cherry

Fill a blender ¼ full with ice. Pour in light rum, dark rum, Coco López, pineapple juice, and heavy cream. Blend on medium speed for 15 to 20 seconds. Pour into a goblet, and garnish with pineapple slice and maraschino cherry.

Pineapple Daiquiri

1 cup pineapple chunks
2 oz. light rum
1 oz. lime juice
2 tsp. sugar

Fill a blender ¼ full with ice. Add in pineapple chunks, pour in light rum and lime juice, and add sugar. Blend on medium speed for 15 to 20 seconds. Pour into a goblet.

Strawberry Daiquiri

8 strawberries
2 oz. light rum
1 oz. lime juice
2 tsp. sugar

Fill a blender ¼ full with ice. Add in strawberries, pour in light rum and lime juice, and add sugar. Blend on medium speed for 15 to 20 seconds. Pour into a goblet.

Swimming Pool

2 oz. vodka
½ oz. blue curaçao
2 oz. cream of coconut
2 oz. pineapple juice

Fill a blender ¼ full with ice. Pour in vodka, blue curaçao, cream of coconut, and pineapple juice. Blend on medium speed for 15 to 20 seconds. Pour into a goblet.

Tidbit

2 oz. gin
1 TB. dry sherry
2 scoops vanilla ice cream

Pour gin and sherry into a blender. Add ice cream. Blend on medium speed for 10 to 15 seconds. Pour into a goblet.

Chapter 16

Shots

Man, being reasonable, must get drunk; the best of life is but intoxication.

—Lord Byron

 Cocktail Conversation

Note: The recipes in this chapter make approximately 2 shots per recipe, so adjust the measurements according to how many drinks you need to make.

A.B.C.

1 oz. amaretto
1 oz. Bailey's Irish cream
1 oz. cognac

In 2 shot glasses, gently layer ½ ounce amaretto, ½ ounce Bailey's Irish cream, and ½ ounce cognac.

After Eight

1 oz. coffee liqueur
1 oz. crème de menthe
1 oz. Irish cream

In 2 shot glasses, gently layer ½ ounce coffee liqueur, ½ ounce crème de menthe, and ½ ounce Irish cream.

After Five

1 oz. coffee liqueur
1 oz. peppermint schnapps
1 oz. Irish cream

In 2 shot glasses, gently layer ½ ounce coffee liqueur, ½ ounce peppermint schnapps, and ½ ounce Irish cream.

Alabama Slammer

1 oz. Southern Comfort
½ oz. amaretto
½ oz. sloe gin
1 oz. orange juice
1 TB. lemon juice

Fill a cocktail shaker ½ full with ice. Pour in Southern Comfort, amaretto, sloe gin, orange juice, and lemon juice. Give it a good shake, and strain into 2 shot glasses.

Almond Joy

1 oz. crème de cacao
1 oz. amaretto
1 oz. coconut rum

Fill a cocktail shaker ½ full with ice. Pour in crème de cacao, amaretto, and coconut rum. Give it a good shake, and strain into 2 shot glasses.

Baby Guinness

2½ oz. coffee liqueur
1 oz. Irish cream

In 2 shot glasses, gently layer 1¼ ounce coffee liqueur, followed by ½ ounce Irish cream.

Bad Habit

1½ oz. vodka
1½ oz. peach schnapps

In 2 shot glasses, gently layer ¾ ounce vodka, followed by ¾ ounce peach schnapps.

Banana Cream Pie

1 oz. crème de bananes
1 oz. vodka
1 oz. light cream

Fill a cocktail shaker ½ full with ice. Pour in crème de bananes, vodka, and light cream. Give it a good shake, and strain into 2 shot glasses.

Banana Split

1 oz. crème de bananes
1 oz. light crème de cacao
1 oz. vodka

Fill a cocktail shaker ½ full with ice. Pour in crème de bananes, crème de cacao, and vodka. Give it a good shake, and strain into 2 shot glasses.

Beam Me Up, Scotty

1 oz. coffee liqueur
1 oz. crème de bananes
1 oz. Irish cream

In 2 shot glasses, gently layer ½ ounce coffee liqueur, ½ ounce crème de bananes, and ½ ounce Irish cream.

Bite of the Iguana

1 oz. tequila
½ oz. triple sec
1 oz. orange juice
½ oz. lemon-lime soda

Fill a cocktail shaker ½ full with ice. Pour in tequila, triple sec, orange juice, and lemon-lime soda. Give it a good shake, and strain into 2 shot glasses.

Black Cactus

1 oz. tequila
1 oz. blackberry brandy
1 oz. club soda

Fill a cocktail shaker ½ full with ice. Pour in tequila, blackberry brandy, and club soda. Give it a good shake, and strain into 2 shot glasses.

Black Cat

1½ oz. black Sambuca
1½ oz. amaretto

Fill a cocktail shaker ½ full with ice. Pour in black Sambuca and amaretto. Give it a good shake, and strain into 2 shot glasses.

Black Sabbath

1 oz. bourbon
1 oz. dark rum
1 oz. *Jagermeister*

Fill a cocktail shaker ½ full with ice. Pour in bourbon, rum, and Jagermeister. Give it a good shake, and strain into 2 shot glasses.

Liquor Lingo

Jagermeister is a German liqueur made from a blend of 50 herbs, spices, and fruits.

Blue Banana

1 oz. crème de bananes
1 oz. blue curaçao
1 oz. vodka

Fill a cocktail shaker ½ full with ice. Pour in crème de bananes, blue curaçao, and vodka. Give it a good shake, and strain into 2 shot glasses.

Boomer

½ oz. tequila
½ oz. crème de bananes
½ oz. triple sec
½ oz. orange juice
½ oz. lemon juice
½ oz. simple syrup

Fill a cocktail shaker ½ full with ice. Pour in tequila, crème de bananes, triple sec, orange juice, lemon juice, and simple syrup. Give it a good shake, and strain into 2 shot glasses.

Breath Freshener

1½ oz. vodka
1½ oz. white crème de menthe

Fill a cocktail shaker ½ full with ice. Pour in vodka and white crème de menthe. Give it a good shake, and strain into 2 shot glasses.

Bubble Gum

¾ oz. vodka
¾ oz. crème de bananes
¾ oz. peach schnapps
¾ oz. orange juice

Fill a cocktail shaker ½ full with ice. Pour in vodka, crème de bananes, peach schnapps, and orange juice. Give it a good shake, and strain into 2 shot glasses.

Buffalo Sweat

2½ oz. bourbon
½ oz. orange juice
2 dashes Tabasco sauce

Fill a cocktail shaker ½ full with ice. Pour in bourbon and orange juice. Give it a good shake, and strain into 2 shot glasses. Add 1 dash Tabasco sauce to each shot.

Buttery Nipple

1½ oz. butterscotch schnapps
1½ oz. Irish cream

In 2 shot glasses, gently layer ¾ ounce butterscotch schnapps, followed by ¾ ounce Irish cream.

Caramel Apple

1½ oz. *butterscotch schnapps*
1½ oz. apple schnapps

Fill a cocktail shaker ½ full with ice. Pour in butterscotch schnapps and apple schnapps. Give it a good shake, and strain into 2 shot glasses.

Liquor Lingo

Butterscotch schnapps is a butterscotch-flavored liqueur with a base of brown sugar, vanilla, and butter.

Chocolate-Covered Cherry

1 oz. white crème de cacao
1 oz. amaretto
1 oz. coffee liqueur
1 tsp. grenadine

Fill a cocktail shaker ½ full with ice. Pour in white crème de cacao, amaretto, and coffee liqueur. Give it a good shake, and strain into 2 shot glasses. Add ½ teaspoon grenadine to each glass.

Dakota

1½ oz. bourbon
1½ oz. tequila

Fill a cocktail shaker ½ full with ice. Pour in bourbon and tequila. Give it a good shake, and strain into 2 shot glasses.

Fireball

3 oz. cinnamon schnapps
2 dashes Tabasco sauce

Pour 1½ ounce cinnamon schnapps into 2 shot glasses. Add 1 dash Tabasco sauce to each.

Flat Tire

2 oz. tequila
1 oz. black Sambuca

Fill a cocktail shaker ½ full with ice. Pour in tequila and black Sambuca. Give it a good shake, and strain into 2 shot glasses.

Freight Train

1½ oz. Jack Daniel's Tennessee
  whiskey
1½ oz. tequila

Fill a cocktail shaker ½ full with ice. Pour in Jack Daniel's and tequila. Give it a good shake, and strain into 2 shot glasses.

French Toast

1 oz. Irish cream
1 oz. cinnamon schnapps
1 oz. butterscotch schnapps

In 2 shot glasses, gently layer ½ ounce Irish cream, ½ ounce cinnamon schnapps, and ½ ounce butterscotch schnapps.

Fruit Bomb

1 oz. Southern Comfort
1 oz. triple sec
1 oz. pineapple juice

Fill a cocktail shaker with ice. Pour in Southern Comfort, triple sec, and pineapple juice. Give it a good shake, and strain into 2 shot glasses.

Grape Crush

1 oz. vodka
1 oz. raspberry liqueur
½ oz. lemon juice
½ oz. simple syrup

Fill a cocktail shaker ½ full with ice. Pour in vodka, raspberry liqueur, lemon juice, and simple syrup. Give it a good shake, and strain into 2 shot glasses.

Green Geisha Shot

1½ oz. melon liqueur
1 oz. Canadian whisky
½ oz. pineapple juice

Fill a cocktail shaker ½ full with ice. Pour in melon liqueur, Canadian whisky, and pineapple juice. Give it a good shake, and strain into 2 shot glasses.

Green Sneaker

1 oz. vodka
½ oz. melon liqueur
½ oz. triple sec
½ oz. orange juice
½ oz. light cream

Fill a cocktail shaker ½ full with ice. Pour in vodka, melon liqueur, triple sec, orange juice, and light cream. Give it a good shake, and strain into 2 shot glasses.

Hot Shot

1½ oz. vodka
1½ oz. cinnamon schnapps
2 dashes Tabasco sauce

Fill a cocktail shaker ½ full with ice. Pour in vodka and cinnamon schnapps. Give it a good shake, and strain into 2 shot glasses. Add 1 dash Tabasco sauce to each shot.

Indian Summer

1 oz. vodka
1 oz. amaretto
1 oz. coffee liqueur

Fill a cocktail shaker ½ full with ice. Pour in vodka, amaretto, and coffee liqueur. Give it a good shake, and strain into 2 shot glasses.

Jell-O Shots

1 box cherry (or favorite flavor) flavored gelatin
1 cup vodka
1 cup boiling water

Dissolve gelatin in vodka and boiling water. Pour into an 8×8 glass or Pyrex baking dish and chill. When gelatin has set, cut into 1-inch squares and serve in paper candy cups. Makes about 16 "shots."

Kamikaze

2 oz. vodka
1 oz. triple sec
½ oz. Rose's lime juice

Fill a cocktail shaker with ice. Pour in vodka, triple sec, and Rose's lime juice. Give it a good shake, and strain into 2 shot glasses.

Keremiki

1 oz. 151 proof rum
1 oz. *Goldschlager*
1 oz. peppermint schnapps

Fill a cocktail shaker with ice. Pour in 151 proof rum, Goldschlager, and peppermint schnapps. Give it a good shake, and strain into 2 shot glasses.

Liquor Lingo

Goldschlager is a Swiss-made cinnamon schnapps, better known for the 24-carat flecks of gold that float in the liqueur.

Lemon Drop

2 lemon wedges
1 TB. sugar
2½ oz. vodka
½ oz. lemon juice

Coat lemon wedges in sugar, and set aside. Fill a cocktail shaker with ice. Pour in vodka and lemon juice. Give it a good shake, and strain into 2 shot glasses. Suck on sugared lemon wedges after shooting drink.

Little Leprechaun

1 oz. Irish whiskey
1 oz. Goldschlager
1 oz. green crème de menthe

Fill a cocktail shaker with ice. Pour in Irish whiskey, Goldschlager, and green crème de menthe. Give it a good shake, and strain into 2 shot glasses.

Love Hotel

1½ oz. sake
1½ oz. cranberry juice
½ tsp. grenadine

Fill a cocktail shaker with ice. Pour in sake and cranberry juice. Give it a good shake, and strain into 2 shot glasses. Float ¼ teaspoon grenadine on top of each shot.

Lube Job

1½ oz. Irish cream
1½ oz. vodka

In 2 shot glasses, gently layer ¾ ounce Irish cream, followed by ¾ ounce vodka.

Mother's Milk

1 oz. butterscotch schnapps
1 oz. Goldschlager
1 oz. light cream

Fill a cocktail shaker with ice. Pour in butterscotch schnapps, Goldschlager, and light cream. Give it a good shake, and strain into 2 shot glasses.

Mussolini

1 oz. Sambuca
1 oz. Goldschlager
1 oz. Jagermeister

Fill a cocktail shaker with ice. Pour in Sambuca, Goldschlager, and Jagermeister. Give it a good shake, and strain into 2 shot glasses.

New York Marriage

1½ oz. Irish whiskey
1½ oz. *Frangelico*

Fill a cocktail shaker with ice. Pour in Irish whiskey and Frangelico. Give it a good shake, and strain into 2 shot glasses.

Peanut Butter and Jelly

1½ oz. raspberry liqueur
1½ oz. Frangelico

Fill a cocktail shaker with ice. Pour in raspberry liqueur and Frangelico. Give it a good shake, and strain into 2 shot glasses.

Penalty Shot

1 oz. melon liqueur
1 oz. triple sec
1 oz. blue curaçao

Fill a cocktail shaker with ice. Pour in melon liqueur, triple sec, and blue curaçao. Give it a good shake, and strain into 2 shot glasses.

Pumpkin Pie

1½ oz. Irish cream
1½ oz. cinnamon schnapps

In 2 shot glasses, gently layer ¾ ounce Irish cream, followed by ¾ ounce cinnamon schnapps.

Purple Haze

1½ oz. Sambuca
1½ oz. raspberry liqueur

In 2 shot glasses, gently layer ¾ ounce Sambuca, followed by ¾ ounce raspberry liqueur.

Raging Bull

1 oz. coffee liqueur
1 oz. Sambuca
1 oz. tequila

In 2 shot glasses, gently layer ½ ounce coffee liqueur, followed by ½ ounce Sambuca, and finally ½ ounce tequila.

Red Devil

2 oz. vodka
1 oz. *Clamato juice*
2 drops Tabasco sauce

Fill a cocktail shaker ½ full with ice. Pour in vodka and Clamato juice. Give it a good shake, and strain into 2 shot glasses. Add 1 dash Tabasco sauce to each shot.

Liquor Lingo

Clamato juice is a blend of tomato and clam juices.

Ruby Slipper

2 oz. rye whisky
¼ oz. grenadine
½ oz. lemon juice

Fill a cocktail shaker ½ full with ice. Pour in rye whisky, grenadine, and lemon juice. Give it a good shake, and strain into 2 shot glasses.

Sangrita

Manhattan's Rosa Mexicano likes to keep things real, and the Sangrita is the perfect example. It originated in Chapala, Jalisco, Mexico, nearly 60 years ago in the home of Edmundo Sánchez and his wife. Because tequila was handmade, it was very strong. To temper it, Mrs. Sánchez put slices of fresh oranges, salt, and powdered red chili on the table for her husband and their guests. This mixture of ingredients was such a success that Edmundo asked his wife to squeeze the oranges in a jar instead of putting them in a bowl, and to add the salt and the red-hot chili to the mixture. It gave the drink an alluring reddish hue that later on was the basis of the name given to it, "Sangrita."

4 ancho chilies, lightly toasted and
  soaked in cold water for 30 min.
1 qt. orange juice
3 TB. chopped onion
4 TB. grenadine
Juice of 3 limes
Salt

Combine ancho chilies, orange juice, onion, grenadine, lime juice, and salt in a blender or food processor until very smooth. Use cheesecloth to strain, bottle remaining liquid, and refrigerate. Serve in shot glasses.

Variation: Use lime and salt if serving silver tequilas.

Cocktail Conversation

It is customary to serve Sangrita with silver "blanco," reposado, or añejo tequilas.

Slippery Nipple

1½ oz. Sambuca
1½ oz. Irish cream
½ tsp. grenadine

In 2 shot glasses, gently layer ¾ ounce Sambuca, followed by ¾ ounce Irish cream. Float ¼ teaspoon grenadine on top of each shot.

Snowshoe

1½ oz. peppermint schnapps
1½ oz. bourbon

In 2 shot glasses, gently layer ¾ ounce peppermint schnapps, followed by ¾ ounce bourbon.

Spice Cake

1 oz. Irish cream
1 oz. amaretto
1 oz. cinnamon schnapps

Fill a cocktail shaker with ice. Pour in Irish cream, amaretto, and cinnamon schnapps. Give it a good shake, and strain into 2 shot glasses.

Surfer on Acid

1 oz. Jagermeister
1 oz. coconut rum
1 oz. pineapple juice

Fill a cocktail shaker with ice. Pour in Jagermeister, coconut rum, and pineapple juice. Give it a good shake, and strain into 2 shot glasses.

Sweetheart

1 oz. coconut rum
1 oz. peach schnapps
1 oz. triple sec

Fill a cocktail shaker with ice. Pour in coconut rum, peach schnapps, and triple sec. Give it a good shake, and strain into 2 shot glasses.

T.K.O.

1 oz. tequila
1 oz. Kahlúa
1 oz. *ouzo*

In 2 shot glasses, gently layer ½ ounce tequila, ½ ounce Kahlúa, and ½ ounce ouzo.

Liquor Lingo

Ouzo is a strong Greek liqueur made from grapes and herbs with prominent licorice and anise flavors.

Teddy Bear

1 oz. root beer schnapps
1 oz. vodka
1 oz. coffee liqueur

Fill a cocktail shaker with ice. Pour in root beer schnapps, vodka, and coffee liqueur. Give it a good shake, and strain into 2 shot glasses.

Tequila Pop

2 oz. tequila
1 oz. lemon-lime soda

In 2 shot glasses, pour 1 ounce tequila and ½ ounce lemon-lime soda. Cover the shot glass with a coaster, lift the glass, bang it down on a hard surface (like … a bar!), remove the coaster, and drink immediately.

Three Wise Men

1 oz. Johnnie Walker Scotch whisky
1 oz. Jim Beam bourbon
1 oz. Jack Daniel's Tennessee whiskey

Fill a cocktail shaker with ice. Pour in Johnnie Walker Scotch whisky, Jim Beam bourbon, and Jack Daniel's Tennessee whiskey. Give it a good shake, and strain into 2 shot glasses.

Tiger Tail

1 oz. coffee liqueur
1 oz. Grand Marnier
1 oz. peppermint schnapps

In 2 shot glasses, gently layer ½ ounce coffee liqueur, ½ ounce Grand Marnier, and ½ ounce peppermint schnapps.

Washington Apple

1½ oz. Canadian whisky
1½ oz. apple schnapps
½ oz. lemon-lime soda

Fill a cocktail shaker with ice. Pour in Canadian whisky, apple schnapps, and lemon-lime soda. Give it a good shake, and strain into 2 shot glasses.

Whistling Gypsy

1 oz. Tia Maria coffee liqueur
1 oz. Irish cream
1 oz. vanilla vodka

In 2 shot glasses, gently layer ½ ounce Tia Maria coffee liqueur, ½ ounce Irish cream, and ½ ounce vanilla vodka.

Woo Woo

2 oz. vodka
½ oz. peach schnapps
½ oz. cranberry juice

Fill a cocktail shaker with ice. Pour in vodka, peach schnapps, and cranberry juice. Give it a good shake, and strain into 2 shot glasses.

Wookie

1 oz. amaretto
1 oz. peach schnapps
1 oz. heavy cream

Fill a cocktail shaker with ice. Pour in amaretto and peach schnapps. Give it a good shake, and strain into 2 shot glasses. Float ½ ounce heavy cream on top of each.

Chapter 17

Nonalcoholic Drinks

Though in silence, with blighted affection, I pine,
Yet the lips that touch liquor must never touch mine!
—G. W. Young, "The Lips That Touch Liquor"

Afterglow

4 oz. orange juice
4 oz. pineapple juice
½ oz. grenadine

Fill a Collins glass with ice. Pour in orange juice, pineapple juice, and grenadine. Give it a good stir.

Alice Cocktail

2 oz. orange juice
2 oz. pineapple juice
1 oz. light cream
½ oz. grenadine
1 orange twist

Fill a cocktail shaker ½ full with ice. Pour in orange juice, pineapple juice, light cream, and grenadine. Give it a good shake, and strain into a cocktail glass. Garnish with orange twist.

Apple Spritzer

3 oz. apple juice
4 oz. club soda
1 lemon wedge

Fill a Collins glass with ice. Pour in apple juice and club soda. Give it a good stir, and garnish with lemon wedge.

Babylove

4 oz. pineapple juice
1 oz. banana syrup
2 oz. coconut milk
1 oz. heavy cream

Fill a cocktail shaker ½ full with ice. Pour in pineapple juice, banana syrup, coconut milk, and heavy cream. Give it a good shake, and strain into a Collins glass full of ice.

Blackberry Collins

1 oz. blackberry syrup
1 oz. lemon juice
1 oz. simple syrup
3 oz. club soda
1 maraschino cherry
1 orange slice

Fill a cocktail shaker ½ full with ice. Pour in blackberry syrup, lemon juice, and simple syrup. Give it a good shake, and strain into a Collins glass ¾ full of ice. Pour in club soda, and garnish with maraschino cherry and orange slice.

Bora Bora

4 oz. pineapple juice
2 oz. passion fruit juice
1 oz. lemon juice
½ oz. grenadine
1 pineapple slice

Fill a cocktail shaker ½ full with ice. Pour in pineapple juice, passion fruit juice, lemon juice, and grenadine. Give it a good shake, and strain into a highball glass ½ full of ice. Garnish with pineapple slice.

Brown Pelican

5 oz. apple juice
3 oz. ginger beer

Fill a cocktail shaker ½ full with ice. Pour in apple juice and ginger beer. Give it a good stir, and strain into a highball glass ½ full of ice.

Café Mocha

1 tsp. sugar
2 TB. chocolate syrup
1 oz. heavy cream
4 oz. hot coffee

Pour sugar, chocolate syrup, and heavy cream into an Irish coffee mug. Pour in coffee and stir.

Café Viennese

1 TB. semisweet powdered cocoa
1 tsp. cinnamon
1 tsp. sugar
4 oz. hot coffee
¼ cup whipped cream

Pour semisweet powdered cocoa, ½ teaspoon cinnamon, and sugar into an Irish coffee mug. Pour in coffee and stir. Top with whipped cream, and garnish with remaining ½ teaspoon cinnamon.

Canadian Pride

4 oz. grapefruit juice
3 oz. ginger ale
½ oz. maple syrup
1 lemon wedge

Fill a cocktail shaker ½ full with ice. Pour in grapefruit juice, ginger ale, and maple syrup. Give it a good shake, and strain into a highball glass ½ full of ice. Garnish with lemon wedge.

Cinderella

2 oz. orange juice
2 oz. pineapple juice
1 oz. cranberry juice
¾ oz. lemon juice
1 oz. simple syrup
2 oz. club soda

Fill a cocktail shaker ½ full with ice. Pour in orange juice, pineapple juice, cranberry juice, lemon juice, and simple syrup. Give it a good shake, and strain into a highball glass ½ full of ice. Top with club soda.

Citrus Collins

2 oz. orange juice
1 oz. lemon juice
1 oz. simple syrup
3 oz. club soda
1 maraschino cherry
1 orange slice

Fill a cocktail shaker ½ full with ice. Pour in orange juice, lemon juice, and simple syrup. Give it a good shake, and strain into a Collins glass ¾ full of ice. Pour in club soda, and garnish with maraschino cherry and orange slice.

Citrus Cream

2 oz. orange juice
2 oz. grapefruit juice
1 oz. grenadine
1 oz. light cream
1 orange twist

Fill a cocktail shaker ½ full with ice. Pour in orange juice, grapefruit juice, and grenadine. Give it a good shake, and strain into a Collins glass ¾ full of ice. Pour in light cream, and garnish with orange twist.

Coconut Kiss

3 oz. pineapple juice
1 oz. coconut cream
1 oz. light cream
1 tsp. grenadine
1 maraschino cherry

Fill a cocktail shaker ½ full with ice. Pour in pineapple juice, coconut cream, light cream, and grenadine. Give it a good shake, and strain into a cocktail glass. Garnish with maraschino cherry.

Cranberry Cooler

4 oz. cranberry juice
1 oz. white grape juice
3 oz. lemon-lime soda
1 lime wedge

Fill a Collins glass ¾ full with ice. Pour in cranberry juice, white grape juice, and lemon-lime soda. Give it a good stir, and garnish with lime wedge.

Cranberry Flip

2 oz. cranberry juice
1 oz. light cream
1 egg
1 tsp. superfine sugar
½ tsp. grated nutmeg

Fill a cocktail shaker ½ full with ice. Pour in cranberry juice, light cream, egg, and superfine sugar. Give it a good, vigorous shake, and strain into a Delmonico glass. Garnish with grated nutmeg.

Cranberry Mint Bomb

6 mint leaves
1 oz. simple syrup
4 oz. cranberry juice
1 oz. orange juice
2 oz. lemon juice
1 oz. club soda

Muddle mint leaves with a little simple syrup in a Collins glass. Fill the glass ½ full with ice. Fill a cocktail shaker ½ full with ice. Pour in cranberry juice, orange juice, lemon juice, and remaining simple syrup. Give it a good shake, and strain into the Collins glass. Pour in club soda.

Creamy Pineapple Frosty

½ cup pineapple chunks
2 tsp. sugar
3 oz. pineapple juice
1 oz. light cream
1 pineapple slice

Fill a blender ¼ full with ice. Add pineapple chunks and sugar. Pour in pineapple juice and light cream. Blend on medium speed for 15 to 20 seconds. Pour into a goblet, and garnish with pineapple slice.

Dream

6 oz. orange juice
1 oz. grenadine
1 egg

Fill a cocktail shaker ½ full with ice. Pour in orange juice, grenadine, and egg. Give it a good, vigorous shake, and strain into a Collins glass ¾ full of ice.

Egg Cream

Some claim you shouldn't mix syrup and milk if you're using chocolate for aesthetic reasons, but that just seems silly to me. After all, it's really about flavor.

2 TB. chocolate or vanilla syrup	Using a pint or Collins glass, pour in syrup and milk. Quickly pour in seltzer water, and give it a good stir.
6 oz. whole milk	
6 oz. seltzer water	

Eggnog

4 oz. light cream	Fill a cocktail shaker ½ full with ice. Pour in light cream, milk, egg, vanilla extract, and sugar. Give it a good, vigorous shake, and strain into an old-fashioned glass. Garnish with grated nutmeg.
2 oz. milk	
1 egg	
1 tsp. vanilla extract	
2 tsp. sugar	
½ tsp. grated nutmeg	

Flying Fairbrother

2 oz. grapefruit juice	Fill a cocktail shaker ½ full with ice. Pour in grapefruit juice, orange juice, cranberry juice, lemon juice, and honey. Give it a good shake, and strain into a highball glass ½ full of ice. Top with ginger ale.
1 oz. orange juice	
1 oz. cranberry juice	
1 TB. lemon juice	
1 TB. honey	
3 oz. ginger ale	

Fruit Juice Cooler

3 oz. peach nectar	Fill a cocktail shaker ½ full with ice. Pour in peach nectar, pineapple juice, orange juice, and grapefruit juice. Give it a good shake, and strain into a highball glass ½ full of ice. Top with club soda.
1 oz. pineapple juice	
1 oz. orange juice	
1 oz. grapefruit juice	
2 oz. club soda	

Fruit Loop Fizz

2 oz. pineapple juice	Fill a cocktail shaker ½ full with ice. Pour in pineapple juice, orange juice, lemon juice, lime juice, and grenadine. Give it a good shake, and strain into a Collins glass ½ full of ice. Top with club soda, and garnish with pineapple and orange slices.
2 oz. orange juice	
1 oz. lemon juice	
1 oz. lime juice	
1 oz. grenadine	
2 oz. club soda	
1 pineapple slice	
1 orange slice	

Fuzzy Lemon Fizz

3 oz. peach nectar
¾ oz. lemon juice
1 oz. simple syrup
1 oz. club soda
1 lemon twist

Fill a cocktail shaker ½ full with ice. Pour in peach nectar, lemon juice, and simple syrup. Give it a good shake, and strain into a cocktail glass. Top with club soda, and garnish with lemon twist.

Golden Grapefruit

4 oz. grapefruit juice
1 oz. orange juice
½ oz. grenadine
1 oz. club soda
1 maraschino cherry

Fill a cocktail shaker ½ full with ice. Pour in grapefruit juice, orange juice, and grenadine. Give it a good shake, and strain into an old-fashioned glass ½ full of ice. Top with club soda, and garnish with maraschino cherry.

Grape Flip

2 oz. white grape juice
1 oz. light cream
1 egg
1 tsp. superfine sugar
½ tsp. grated nutmeg

Fill a cocktail shaker ½ full with ice. Pour in white grape juice, light cream, egg, and superfine sugar. Give it a good, vigorous shake, and strain into a Delmonico glass. Garnish with grated nutmeg.

Grape Juice Rickey

2 oz. white grape juice
½ oz. lime juice
1 oz. simple syrup
4 oz. club soda
1 lime wedge

Fill a cocktail shaker ½ full with ice. Pour in white grape juice, lime juice, and simple syrup. Give it a good shake, and strain into a highball glass full of ice. Pour in club soda, and garnish with lime wedge.

Grenadine Cocktail

2 oz. pineapple juice
2 oz. orange juice
½ oz. grenadine
1 maraschino cherry

Fill a cocktail shaker ½ full with ice. Pour in pineapple juice, orange juice, and grenadine. Give it a good shake, and strain into a cocktail glass. Garnish with maraschino cherry.

Honey Bunny

3 oz. carrot juice
1½ oz. orange juice
1 tsp. grenadine

Fill a cocktail shaker ½ full with ice. Pour in carrot juice, orange juice, and grenadine. Give it a good shake, and strain into a cocktail glass.

Horchata

2 cups whole milk
1 qt. water
2 cinnamon sticks
½ cup sugar
⅛ cup white uncooked rice, puréed in a blender or food processor
2 tsp. vanilla extract
½ tsp. grated nutmeg
½ tsp. cinnamon

Bring milk to a boil (but don't scald!) in a saucepan over medium-high heat, and simmer for 20 minutes. Pour in water and add cinnamon sticks. Simmer for 10 to 15 minutes and then remove from heat and discard cinnamon sticks. In a separate bowl, combine sugar, puréed rice, and vanilla extract, and add warm milk mixture. Give it good stir, and refrigerate overnight. Strain mixture through a cheesecloth, and garnish with grated nutmeg and cinnamon.

Liquor Lingo

Horchata is a rice-, nut-, or chufa (root)-based drink flavored with sugar and cinnamon. It's popular in Spain and Mexico.

Hot Chocolate

6 oz. milk
1 tsp. vanilla extract
1 TB. cocoa powder
2 TB. whipped cream
1 tsp. shaved semisweet chocolate

Warm milk, vanilla extract, and cocoa powder in a saucepan over medium heat. Pour into an Irish coffee glass, and top with whipped cream. Garnish with shaved semisweet chocolate.

Hot Cider

6 oz. apple cider
2 whole cloves
2 cinnamon sticks

Heat apple cider, cloves, and 1 cinnamon stick over medium heat for 15 minutes. Strain into an Irish coffee glass. Garnish with remaining cinnamon stick.

Hot Vanilla

6 oz. milk
2 tsp. vanilla extract
2 TB. whipped cream
½ tsp. cinnamon

Warm milk and vanilla extract in a saucepan over medium heat. Pour into an Irish coffee glass, and top with whipped cream. Garnish with cinnamon.

Lemon Flip

2 oz. lemon juice
1 oz. light cream
1 egg
2 tsp. superfine sugar
½ tsp. grated nutmeg

Fill a cocktail shaker ½ full with ice. Pour in lemon juice, light cream, egg, and superfine sugar. Give it a good, vigorous shake, and strain into a Delmonico glass. Garnish with grated nutmeg.

Lemonade Fizz

1½ oz. lemon juice
1½ oz. simple syrup
1 oz. club soda
1 lemon twist

Fill a cocktail shaker ½ full with ice. Pour in lemon juice and simple syrup. Give it a good shake, and strain into a cocktail glass. Top with club soda, and garnish with lemon twist.

Lime and Tonic

1 oz. Rose's lime juice
1 dash bitters
4 oz. tonic water
1 lime twist

Fill a cocktail shaker ½ full with ice. Pour in Rose's lime juice, and add bitters. Give it a good shake, and strain into a highball glass ½ full of ice. Top with tonic water, and garnish with lime twist.

Lime Cooler

2 oz. lime juice
2 oz. simple syrup
2 dashes bitters
4 oz. tonic water
1 lime twist

Fill a cocktail shaker ½ full with ice. Pour in lime juice and simple syrup, and add bitters. Give it a good shake, and strain into a highball glass ½ full of ice. Top with tonic water, and garnish with lime twist.

Lime Rickey

¾ oz. lime juice
1 oz. simple syrup
4 oz. club soda
1 lime wedge

Fill a cocktail shaker ½ full with ice. Pour in lime juice and simple syrup. Give it a good shake, and strain into a highball glass full of ice. Pour in club soda, and garnish with lime wedge.

Limeade Fizz

1½ oz. lime juice
1½ oz. simple syrup
1 oz. club soda
1 lime twist

Fill a cocktail shaker ½ full with ice.
Pour in lime juice and simple syrup.
Give it a good shake, and strain into a
cocktail glass. Top with club soda, and
garnish with lime twist.

Mango Lassi

2 cups plain yogurt
4 oz. mango purée
2 TB. sugar
¼ cup cold water

Pour plain yogurt, mango purée,
sugar, and water into a blender. Blend
on low speed for 10 seconds.

Mexican Hot Chocolate

10 oz. milk
2 oz. semisweet chocolate
1 egg yolk
½ tsp. cinnamon
1 pinch cayenne

Heat milk and chocolate in a saucepan
over medium-low heat until chocolate
melts. Beat egg yolk until pale, and
add to chocolate-milk mixture along
with cinnamon and cayenne. Heat
until mixture thickens, and pour into a
large mug.

Mock Mai Tai

½ oz. orange juice
½ oz. orgeat syrup
½ oz. lime juice
¼ oz. simple syrup
1 lime wedge
1 mint sprig

Fill a cocktail shaker with crushed ice.
Pour in orange juice, orgeat syrup,
lime juice, and simple syrup. Give it a
good shake, and strain into an old-
fashioned glass ¾ full of ice. Garnish
with lime wedge and mint sprig.

Mock Manhattan

1½ oz. cranberry juice
1½ oz. orange juice
¼ tsp. grenadine
3 dashes bitters
1 maraschino cherry

Fill a cocktail shaker with crushed ice.
Pour in cranberry juice, orange juice,
and grenadine, and add bitters. Give it
a good shake, and strain into a cocktail
glass. Garnish with maraschino cherry.

Mock Mint Julep

6 fresh mint leaves, stems removed
1 tsp. superfine sugar
2 tsp. water
¾ oz. lime juice
4 oz. ginger ale
1 mint sprig

In a Collins glass, muddle mint leaves with superfine sugar and water. Fill the glass with crushed ice, and pour in lime juice and ginger ale. Give it a good stir, and garnish with mint sprig.

Mock Mudslide

3 oz. cold espresso coffee
1 light cream
1 TB. orgeat syrup
1 tsp. vanilla extract
1 tsp. sugar

Fill a cocktail shaker with ice. Pour in cold espresso coffee, light cream, orgeat syrup, vanilla extract, and sugar. Give it a good shake, and strain into an old-fashioned glass ¾ full of ice.

Mock Pink

1½ oz. cranberry juice
½ oz. orange juice
1 tsp. lemon juice
1 tsp. sugar
3 oz. club soda

Pour cranberry juice, orange juice, lemon juice, and sugar into a champagne flute. Top with club soda.

Orange Eggnog

4 oz. light cream
2 oz. milk
1 egg
1 tsp. vanilla extract
1 tsp. orange extract
2 tsp. sugar
½ tsp. grated nutmeg

Fill a cocktail shaker ½ full with ice. Pour in light cream, milk, egg, vanilla extract, orange extract, and sugar. Give it a good, vigorous shake, and strain into an old-fashioned glass. Garnish with grated nutmeg.

Orange Flip

2 oz. orange juice
1 oz. light cream
1 egg
1 tsp. superfine sugar
½ tsp. grated nutmeg

Fill a cocktail shaker ½ full with ice. Pour in orange juice, light cream, egg, and superfine sugar. Give it a good, vigorous shake, and strain into a Delmonico glass. Garnish with grated nutmeg.

Orange Frosty

4 oz. orange juice
2 oz. light cream
1 tsp. sugar
1 orange slice

Fill a blender ¼ full with ice. Pour in orange juice, light cream, and sugar. Blend on medium speed for 15 to 20 seconds. Pour into a goblet, and garnish with orange slice.

Orange Sunshine

3 oz. orange juice
1 tsp. lemon juice
2 tsp. grenadine
1 egg
1 orange twist

Fill a cocktail shaker ½ full with ice. Pour in orange juice, lemon juice, grenadine, and egg. Give it a good, vigorous shake, and strain into a Delmonico glass. Garnish with orange twist.

Orange Velvet

3 oz. orange juice
1 oz. pineapple juice
1 oz. light cream
1 orange twist

Fill a cocktail shaker ½ full with ice. Pour in orange juice, pineapple juice, and light cream. Give it a good shake, and strain into a cocktail glass. Garnish with orange twist.

Orangeade

2 oz. orange juice
½ oz. lemon juice
¾ oz. simple syrup
1 oz. club soda
1 lemon twist

Fill a cocktail shaker ½ full with ice. Pour in orange juice, lemon juice, and simple syrup. Give it a good shake, and strain into a cocktail glass. Top with club soda, and garnish with lemon twist.

Passionate Colada

2 oz. passion fruit juice
2 oz. pineapple juice
1 oz. orange juice
1 oz. Coco López
1 maraschino cherry

Fill a blender ¼ full with ice. Pour in passion fruit juice, pineapple juice, orange juice, and Coco López. Blend on medium speed for 15 to 20 seconds. Pour into a goblet, and garnish with maraschino cherry.

Peach Flip

2 oz. peach nectar
1 oz. light cream
1 egg
1 tsp. superfine sugar
½ tsp. grated nutmeg

Fill a cocktail shaker ½ full with ice. Pour in peach nectar, light cream, egg, and superfine sugar. Give it a good, vigorous shake, and strain into a Delmonico glass. Garnish with grated nutmeg.

Pineapple Flip

2 oz. pineapple juice
1 oz. light cream
1 egg
1 tsp. superfine sugar
½ tsp. grated nutmeg

Fill a cocktail shaker ½ full with ice. Pour in pineapple juice, light cream, egg, and superfine sugar. Give it a good, vigorous shake, and strain into a Delmonico glass. Garnish with grated nutmeg.

Pomegranate Soda

2 oz. pomegranate syrup
6 oz. club soda
1 mint sprig

Fill a highball glass ½ full with ice. Pour in pomegranate syrup and club soda. Give it a good stir, and garnish with mint sprig.

Pretty Baby (a.k.a. Virgin Mary)

I've named this after the Columns Inn in New Orleans. That's where *Pretty Baby* was filmed and where, more important, you can get one of the best Bloody Marys, with or without alcohol, in all the land. In honor of the southern location, I substitute pickled okra for the usual-suspect garnish.

4 oz. tomato juice
½ oz. lemon juice
¼ tsp. Worcestershire sauce
½ tsp. Tabasco sauce
½ tsp. horseradish
⅛ tsp. salt
⅛ tsp. black pepper
1 pickled okra

Fill a cocktail shaker with ice. Pour in tomato juice, lemon juice, Worcestershire sauce, Tabasco sauce, horseradish, salt, and black pepper. Give it a good shake. Strain into a highball glass ¾ full of ice, and garnish with pickled okra.

Rail Splitter

¾ oz. lemon juice
1 oz. simple syrup
6 oz. ginger beer
1 lemon slice

Fill a highball glass ½ full with ice.
Pour in lemon juice, simple syrup,
and ginger beer. Give it a good stir.
Garnish with lemon slice.

Roy Rodgers

½ oz. lemon juice
½ oz. lime juice
1 oz. simple syrup
1 tsp. grenadine
4 oz. ginger ale
1 maraschino cherry

Fill a highball glass ¾ full with ice.
Pour in lemon juice, lime juice, simple
syrup, grenadine, and ginger ale. Give
it a good stir, and garnish with maraschino cherry.

Safe Sex on the Beach

2 oz. peach nectar
2 oz. orange juice
2 oz. cranberry juice
1 maraschino cherry

Fill a highball glass ¾ full with ice.
Pour in peach nectar, orange juice, and
cranberry juice. Give it a good stir,
and garnish with maraschino cherry.

Saint Clemence

4 oz. orange juice
4 oz. *Limonata*

Fill a highball glass ¾ full with ice.
Pour in orange juice and Limonata.
Give it a good stir.

Liquor Lingo

Limonata is a carbonated Italian lemon soda with a bittersweet
taste. It's made by San Pellegrino.

Shirley Temple

2 tsp. grenadine
4 oz. ginger ale
2 oz. lemon-lime soda
1 maraschino cherry

Fill a highball glass ¾ full with ice.
Pour in grenadine, ginger ale, and
lemon-lime soda. Give it a good stir,
and garnish with maraschino cherry.

Sophia Rose

Who's Sophia Rose? She's the very adorable daughter of my dear friends Tamar Smith and Mike Golub. She was just starting to get really interested in different flavors when I was writing this book, so I thought a drink of her own would be a good way to whet her appetite for this big, wide world of eating and drinking. Cheers, Sophster.

4 oz. pineapple juice
½ oz. Rose's lime juice
2 tsp. grenadine
½ oz. light cream
1 pineapple wedge

Fill a cocktail shaker ½ full with ice. Pour in pineapple juice, Rose's lime juice, grenadine, and light cream. Give it a good shake, and strain into a cocktail glass. Garnish with pineapple wedge.

Sour Apple Frosty

3 oz. apple juice
¾ oz. lime juice
1 oz. simple syrup
½ tsp. freshly grated ginger
1 green apple slice

Fill a blender ¼ full with ice. Pour in apple juice, lime juice, and simple syrup, and add grated ginger. Blend on medium speed for 15 to 20 seconds. Pour into a goblet, and garnish with green apple slice.

Southampton

½ oz. lime juice
2 dashes bitters
6 oz. tonic water
1 lime slice

Fill a highball glass ¾ full with ice. Pour in lime juice, and add in bitters. Pour in tonic water, and give it a good stir. Garnish with lime slice.

Spiky Hedgehog

1 oz. cranberry juice
1 oz. grenadine
1 tsp. lime juice
6 oz. club soda
1 lime wedge

Fill a highball glass ¾ full with ice. Pour in cranberry juice, grenadine, and lime juice. Pour in club soda, and give it a good stir. Garnish with lime wedge.

Strawberry Dream

8 strawberries
2 tsp. powered sugar
2 oz. strawberry-pineapple-orange juice
2 oz. light cream

Fill a blender ¼ full with ice. Add in 7 strawberries and powdered sugar. Pour in strawberry-pineapple-orange juice and light cream. Blend on medium speed for 15 to 20 seconds. Pour into a goblet, and garnish with remaining strawberry.

Summer Cooler

6 mint leaves
1 tsp. superfine sugar
1 tsp. lemon juice
1 oz. orange juice
6 oz. lemon-lime soda
1 lemon slice
1 lime slice

Muddle mint leaves with superfine sugar and lemon juice in a highball glass. Fill the glass ¾ full with ice, and pour in orange juice and lemon-lime soda. Give it a good stir, and garnish with lemon and lime slices.

Summer Rain

2 oz. pineapple juice
2 oz. grapefruit juice
¾ oz. lemon juice
1 tsp. raspberry syrup
1 scoop orange sherbet
1 tsp. superfine sugar
1 pineapple slice

Fill a blender ¼ full with ice. Pour in pineapple juice, grapefruit juice, lemon juice, and raspberry syrup, and add in orange sherbet and superfine sugar. Blend on medium speed for 15 to 20 seconds. Pour into a goblet, and garnish with pineapple slice.

Tame Black and Tan

3 oz. milk
4 oz. cola

Fill a highball glass ½ full with ice. Pour in milk and then cola.

Tequilaless Sunrise

6 oz. orange juice
1 TB. lemon juice
1 TB. grenadine

Pour orange juice and lemon juice into a highball glass ¾ full of ice. Give it a good stir, and drip grenadine into center of cocktail.

Thai Tea

1 tsp. sugar
2 TB. sweetened, condensed milk
6 oz. chai tea, chilled

Fill a highball glass ¾ full with ice. Add sugar and condensed milk, and pour in chilled chai tea. Give it a good stir until condensed milk is blended in.

Tropical Banana

½ banana
2 oz. pineapple juice
1 oz. Coco López
1 oz. banana syrup

Fill a blender ¼ full with ice. Add in banana. Pour in pineapple juice, Coco López, and banana syrup. Blend on medium speed for 15 to 20 seconds. Pour into a goblet.

Tropical Milkshake

½ banana
½ cup pineapple chunks
2 oz. pineapple juice
1 oz. orange juice
1 oz. Coco López
1 TB. shredded coconut

Fill a blender ¼ full with ice. Add in banana and pineapple chunks. Pour in pineapple juice, orange juice, and Coco López. Blend on medium speed for 15 to 20 seconds. Pour into a goblet, and garnish with shredded coconut.

Unfuzzy Navel

6 oz. orange juice
2 oz. peach nectar

Fill a cocktail shaker ½ full with ice. Pour in orange juice and peach nectar. Give it a good shake, and strain into a highball glass ½ full of ice.

Virgin Colada

6 oz. pineapple juice
2 oz. Coco López
1 pineapple wedge
1 maraschino cherry

Fill a blender ¼ full with ice. Pour in pineapple juice and Coco López. Blend on medium speed for 15 to 20 seconds. Pour into a goblet, and garnish with pineapple wedge and maraschino cherry.

Virgin Daiquiri

1 oz. lime juice
2 oz. simple syrup
8 strawberries

Fill a blender ¼ full with ice. Pour in lime juice and add in simple syrup and 7 strawberries. Blend on medium speed for 15 to 20 seconds. Pour into a goblet, and garnish with remaining strawberry.

Appendix A

Glossary

151 proof rum A highly alcoholic rum used in specialty drinks, like a Zombie, or flamed drinks.

aguardiente de caña The general name for rum in South America.

Amer Picon A bitter French cordial made of cinchona bark, orange, and gentian created by Gaetan Picon in 1837. Also referred to as Picon.

añejo Superpremium blue agave tequila wood aged for at least a year.

anisette A clear, Italian, licorice-flavored liqueur made from anise seeds.

aperitif A low-alcohol drink usually consumed prior to dinner.

apple brandy The aged, distilled product of fermented apple cider. Popular examples are applejack brandy (from the United States) and Calvados (from France).

aquavit A caraway-flavored liqueur from Scandinavia.

Benedictine Created in the sixteenth century by French monks, Benedictine is an herbal cognac-based liqueur that can be consumed alone or in mixed drinks.

bitters The result of distilling aromatic herbs, flowers, seeds, bark, roots, and other plant products. Used to flavor cocktails or as a *digestif*. There are several kinds, among the most well known: Peychaud, Abbott's, Bonnecamp, Angostura, and orange.

black Sambuca An anise-flavored liqueur. Slightly more robust than its mellower sibling, white Sambuca.

blue agave The plant from which tequila is made.

bourbon American whiskey made from a minimum of 51 percent corn mash.

brandewijn The Dutch word from which brandy is derived. It literally means "burned wine."

butterscotch schnapps A butterscotch-flavored liqueur with a base of brown sugar, vanilla, and butter.

cachaca rum A Brazilian liqueur made by distilling sugarcane juice.

Campari Also known as Campari bitters, this herbal, slightly bitter Italian aperitif contains 24 percent alcohol and is often used as an ingredient in various classic cocktails such as the Negroni or the Americano.

Canadian whisky Similar to Scotch, but must always be designated as a blended whisky by law.

Chablis A white wine made predominantly from the chardonnay grape in the Burgundy, France, region of Chablis. It is crisp and dry in style, because Chablis are not, as a rule, aged in oak, and therefore will have a much different flavor profile than, say, a California-style chardonnay.

Chambord A brandy-based raspberry-flavored liqueur made from black raspberries, honey, and herbs.

cherry Heering Danish brandy-based dark cherry liqueur.

clamato juice A blend of tomato and clam juices.

claret The British terminology for Bordeaux red.

Coco López A nonalcoholic cream of coconut mixer.

cognac Aged, burnt wine made only in the Cognac region of France. *See* V.S.; V.S.O.P.; and X.O. for aging distinctions on a bottle.

Cointreau A refined, brandy-based orange liqueur.

cordial A liqueur made from one main spirit base and fermented fruit.

crème de bananes A banana-flavored liqueur.

crème de cacao A chocolate-flavored liqueur that comes in both dark and white (clear) varieties.

crème de cassis A black currant–flavored liqueur.

crème de noyaux A brandy-based almond-flavored liqueur.

crème de violette Also known as liqeur de violet, this violet-flavored liqueur can be difficult to find. Parfait amour can sometimes be used as a substitute.

curaçao   A sweet liqueur made from dried bitter orange peel. The island Curaçao in the Caribbean, as one might guess, produces much of what's on the market. Curaçao, or orange curaçao, is the general, run-of-the-mill kind, but you can also find it colored blue, green, or just plain clear for hued cocktail purposes.

Delmonico glass   A 5- or 6-ounce glass used for fizzes or Rickeys. Was named after the near-ancient restaurant responsible for many coiffing and edible originals: the once-glorious Delmonico's in New York City.

Drambuie   A Scotch whisky blended with honey, herbs, and spices.

Dubonnet   Dubonnet is a *quinquina* (a sweetened aperitif wine), that comes in rouge (or red), which is the sweetest, and blond, which is semi-sweet.

eau-de-vie   A clear, fruit-based French brandy. Examples include kirschwasser and frambois. The direct translation is "water of life."

Fernet Branca   An Italian bitter-sweet digestif.

Forbidden Fruit liqueur   A brandy-based honey-flavored liqueur with citrus notes. Sadly, it's no longer made. Try using parfait amour as a substitute.

fortified wine   Wines that have been fortified with another spirit such as brandy. The best examples are sherry, Madeira, and Port.

Frangelico   An Italian hazelnut-flavored liqueur.

Galliano   A sweet, herbaceous Italian liqueur made from anise, licorice, vanilla, flowers, spices, and herbs. It is yellow in color.

gin   A clear liquor made when juniper berries are distilled with a grain mash usually made up of some or all of the following—corn, barley, rye, and wheat—as well as other flavors, such as cassis, coriander, fennel, ginger, lemon peel, and a host of other botanical flavorings.

ginger brandy   A ginger-flavored brandy liqueur.

ginger wine   A British fortified wine flavored with ginger, other spices, and raisins. It contains about 12 percent alcohol.

Goldschlager   A Swiss-made cinnamon schnapps, better known for the 24-carat flecks of gold that float in the liqueur.

grenadine   A bright red, super-sweet syrup flavored, most often, with artificial pomegranate, used in mixing both alcoholic and nonalcoholic cocktails.

horchata   A rice-, nut-, or chufa (root)-based drink flavored with sugar and cinnamon. It's popular in Spain and Mexico.

Irish Mist   An Irish whiskey–based liqueur made with honey and herbs.

Jagermeister   A German liqueur made from a blend of 50 herbs, spices, and fruits.

julab   An Arabic word for "rosewater," which eventually morphed into *julap*, and *julep*, that minty, refreshing concoction we know and adore.

kirschwasser   An unaged cherry brandy usually made in Germany, France, and Switzerland. Some are also produced in the United States.

kummel   A sweet, caraway-flavored liqueur.

Lillet   A *quinquina* (a sweetened aperitif wine), which comes in rouge (or red), which is the sweetest, and blanc, which is semi-sweet.

Limonata   A carbonated Italian lemon soda with a bittersweet taste made by San Pellegrino.

Limoncello   An Italian lemon liqueur.

Madeira   A fortified wine that comes from the eponymous island in Portugal.

maraschino liqueur   A neutral-spirit–based liqueur that gets its flavor from marasca cherries.

mash   The ground or crushed grains used as a base for whisky, beer, or other spirits.

mezcal   A clear, strong spirit made from the juice of the maguey plant.

mixto   Your average, run-of-the-mill tequila. Mixto must contain a minimum of 51 percent blue agave; the rest of the mix can come from other sources.

neat   A drink served straight up—no ice, no nuthin'.

orgeat syrup   A nonalcoholic almond-flavored syrup with hints of orange flower water used to flavor drinks.

ouzo   A strong Greek liqueur made from grapes and herbs with prominent licorice and anise flavors.

parfait amour   A vanilla-flavored liqueur with hints of marshmallow and citrus. Can be used as a substitute for liqueur de violette or crème de violette, which can be difficult to find.

pastis   A generic French term for their slightly sweet version of anise-flavored liqueur.

proof   The amount of alcohol in a spirit. In the United States, we distinguish proof as a measurement that translates into twice the percentage of alcohol, e.g., 100 proof bourbon contains 50 percent alcohol.

Prosecco   A dry, sparkling Italian wine.

reposada   100 percent blue agave tequila that must be wood-aged 60 days to a year. Caramel may be added for coloring and taste as well. Literally means "rested."

Ricard   A French anise-flavored liqueur with notes of citrus and a touch of sweetness.

rocks   Ice; or a way to serve a spirit (e.g., over ice).

Rose's lime juice   Nonalcoholic, sweetened lime juice that's really more like a syrup. It's the easiest to find and usually carried by just about every supermarket in the nation. Whatever you do, when a recipe calls for it specifically, *do not* substitute Rose's lime juice for fresh lime juice, and vice versa.

rum   A spirit made from sugarcane.

rye   Whisky made from rye grain.

sloe gin   A sloeberry-flavored liqueur that has nothing to do with half its namesake, gin.

sour mash   In whisky-making, the result when new sweet mash is combined with some of the residue from the previous batch's fermentation.

Southern Comfort   A peach-flavored, bourbon-based liqueur that has citrus hints. Many people frequently mistake SoCo (as it is sometimes referred) for bourbon, but technically it falls in the liqueur category.

Strega   A sweet, gold-colored Italian liqueur. In Italian, the word literally translates to "witch."

Swedish punsch   A Scandinavian liqueur made from Batavia Arak rum, tea, lemon, spices, and sugar, and even sometimes wine.

sweet mash   Mash for whisky that's made from scratch with fresh yeast.

Tennessee whiskey   Straight whiskey made from a mash of (usually) 51 percent corn and aged in oak barrels. It is similar to a bourbon, but it isn't one. In fact, it has its own classification by law.

tequila   A spirit made from the juice of the blue agave plant in Jalisco, Mexico.

triple sec   A strong orange-flavored liqueur made from the peel of curaçao oranges and most often used for mixing.

uisge beatha   The Gaelic term meaning "water of life," from which the word *whisky* is derived.

vermouth   Fortified wine that can be either sweet (usually brownish-red) or dry (clear).

voda   The Russian word meaning "water," from which the word *vodka* is derived.

vodka   A clear spirit usually made from grains or potatoes and filtered through coal filters after distilling.

V.S.   Very Special: minimum aging of 2½ years.

V.S.O.P.   Very Special Old Pale: minimum aging of 4½ years.

X.O.   Extra Old: aged 5 years and longer.

Appendix B

Where to Get It

Can't find those cute little umbrellas to go in your daiquiri? Not so sure where to get Peychaud bitters? Wish you knew where you could find a good bourbon festival? Curious as to if there's an entire museum devoted to the history of the cocktail? Me, too. That's why I've put together this helpful compilation of resources of where to get various bar paraphernalia and where to go if your thirst for bartender knowledge just can't be quenched in the glass.

Merchandise

Sometimes you can't find a particular gadget or sundry in your regular stops. If that's the case, here are a few great resources for barware, mixers, and garnishes to get your bar in super-stocked shape.

www.mixologys.com
From brass rails to books, this site has everything you need and so much more you had no idea you were missing.

www.crateandbarrel.com
Good source for glass and barware.

www.cooking.com
Decent source for basic, although slightly pricey, barware.

www.candyfavorites.com
Can't find Pop Rocks? Here's your online resource so you can make Le Pop Rocks Martini from Chapter 9.

www.tradervics.com
Great source for syrups, mixers, and spices.

www.barsupplywarehouse.com
For gear like the pros use, this site has a ton of barware, mixers, et al.

www.sableandrosenfeld.com
Fantastic online source for basic and not-so-basic cocktail garnishes.

www.sazerac.com
Source for the sometimes-hard-to-find Peychaud bitters.

www.pickledveggies.com
Forest Floor Foods in Wisconsin has all your pickled garnish needs covered—from olives to onions to beans, it's here. Also, a great selection of specialty stuffed olives (think anchovy, habañero, and garlic!), and special olive juice just for dirty martinis.

www.lehmannfarms.com
What is it about Wisconsin and garnishes? Here, there are olives, olives, and more olives, plus other specialty items and mixes.

www.swankmartini.com
If you like a little twist to your glassware as well as your garnishes, Swank has an eclectic selection of fun cocktail glasses with names such as the Flirtini, the Diva, the Swinger, and the Paparazzi, as well as a small selection of olives, bar gear, and party extras.

www.vintagemartini.com
If you sped right past the minimum and medium bar stocking lists in Chapter 4 and went straight to maximum-bar level, you might be a candidate for the collectible antique shakers and such on this site. Because they're dealing with very limited quantities, if you're willing to plunk down the cash and see something you want (like, at the time of this writing, there was an awesome 1940s glass shaker with red dancing pigs all over it for $98), sooner is better than later.

www.gourmetfoodmall.com
Click on the Bar & Wine Accessories link on the left, and then go to KegWorks for a super bar accessories one-stop shopping resource (seriously—it really is a mall). You'll find everything from Jell-O shot containers to campy swizzle sticks to those tiny paper umbrellas to a ton of other bar gear for the serious home bartender.

Tours

Sometimes sipping just isn't enough. When you're feeling thirsty and itchin' to explore, why not engage in a little liquor exploration? Here are a few great resources for travel.

Tequila

Julio Bermejo
www.tommystequila.com

Bourbon

Buffalo Trace
1001 Wilkinson Boulevard
Franklin County, KY
502-696-5926

Four Roses
1224 Bonds Mill Road
Lawrenceburg, KY
502-839-3436

Heaven Hill
1064 Loretto Road
Bardstown, KY
502-348-3921

Jim Beam
149 Happy Hollow Road
Clarmont, KY
502-543-9877

Maker's Mark
3350 Burk Springs Road
Loretto, KY
502-865-2099

Wild Turkey
U.S. Highway 62 East
Lawrenceburg, KY
502-839-4544

Gin

Junipero
Anchor Steam Brewery
1705 Mariposa Street
San Francisco, CA
415-863-8350

Vodka

Charbay Distillery
St. Helena, CA
1-800-634-7845

Museums

The Museum of the American Cocktail
514 Chartres Street
New Orleans, LA

Oscar Getz Museum of Whiskey History
114 North Fifth Street
Bardstown, KY
502-348-2999

Index of Drinks

General Index

S

X–Y–Z